Public-Private Partnerships and Constitutional Law

This book aims to explore the systems which are set within the Economic Constitution for holding the executive to account when it uses public money in Public-Private Partnerships (PPPs) in the UK and the USA. The specific point of focus in the exploration of these systems is the criteria of accountability.

In the UK, a clear and well-established constitutional principle requiring the enactment of legislation for implementing systems and criteria of accountability for PPPs does not seem to exist. The predominant system of accountability for PPPs is the default system designed for all financial matters. We propose that the UK Economic Constitution for PPPs should recognise the need for legislation for every PPP sector, and that there exists the need for affirmative resolution procedure for every new PPP project.

In the USA, legislation is generally recognised as constitutionally necessary for the authorisation of the government to use PPPs and for the setting of criteria and accountability arrangements for them. There is, however, no general system of accountability for all PPPs. Instead, accountability is based on the many criteria that the many laws provide. We propose that the Economic Constitution for PPPs should recognise that there is a positive governmental duty to systematise these criteria.

The underlying framework of the analysis is one of seeking an appropriate balance between effectiveness and accountability for PPPs in the Economic Constitution.

Dr Nikiforos Meletiadis, BA, CDT, LL.M., M.St. (Oxon), PhD (Cam), is a member of the Doing Business team of the World Bank and works on the design of the Contracting with the Government indicator.

Public-Private Partnerships and Constitutional Law

Accountability in the United Kingdom and the United States of America

Dr Nikiforos Meletiadis

Routledge
Taylor & Francis Group

LONDON AND NEW YORK

First published 2019
by Routledge
2 Park Square, Milton Park, Abingdon, Oxon OX14 4RN

and by Routledge
52 Vanderbilt Avenue, New York, NY 10017

First issued in paperback 2020

Routledge is an imprint of the Taylor & Francis Group, an informa business

British Library Cataloguing-in-Publication Data
A catalogue record for this book is available from the British Library

Library of Congress Cataloging-in-Publication Data
Names: Meletiadis, Nikiforos, author.
Title: Public private partnerships and constitutional law : accountability in the United Kingdom and the United States of America / by Nikiforos Meletiadis.
Description: Abingdon, Oxon : New York, NY : Routledge, 2019. | Includes bibliographical references and index.
Identifiers: LCCN 2018035708 | ISBN 9781138332621 (hbk) | ISBN 9780429821813 (adobe) | ISBN 9780429821806 (epub) | ISBN 9780429821790 (mobipocket)
Subjects: LCSH: Public-private sector cooperation—Law and legislation—United States. | Public-private sector cooperation—Law and legislation—Great Britain.
Classification: LCC K1367 .M45 2019 | DDC 346.41/0668—dc23
LC record available at https://lccn.loc.gov/2018035708

ISBN 13: 978-0-367-58261-6 (pbk)
ISBN 13: 978-1-138-33262-1 (hbk)

Typeset in Galliard
by Apex CoVantage, LLC

Contents

Conclusions

Tables of cases

Tables of legislation

Legislation United Kingdom

Legislation United States of America

Acknowledgements

This book's focus is on Public-Private Partnerships (PPPs), or – as they are usually known in the UK – Private Finance Initiative projects (PFI). Under either name, these are transactions between the public and the private sector in which the latter undertakes important responsibilities with respect to the provision of public service. Typically, they are fully enforceable, binding contracts, and they are extensively used by governments worldwide in areas as diverse as transport, health and defence. This book is based on my research, undertaken primarily at Cambridge, but also at Oxford and Harvard Universities, as well as my practice as an international development lawyer, and focuses on PPPs, discussing the systems which are in place for holding the executive to account when it uses PPPs.

Public Accountability for PPPs and the PFI is a topic which has always attracted a great deal of interest and attention, both in academia and from the general public. Simply put, civil society seems eager to explore how government is held accountable when the delivery of public service is assigned to a private consortium of companies, instead of a public authority. When a public authority is the basic point of reference in the delivery of a public service, as in the case of traditional public procurement, the lines of accountability are usually – but not always – relatively clear, running from the public servant all the way through to the competent minister. However, when the private sector takes the place of a public authority, this line often appears to be distorted or broken. The intensity of the demands of civil society for better accountability and transparency in PPPs has grown due to the fact that PPPs usually involve a significant amount of public money, and because of their use in sectors which are sensitive from the perspective of human rights.

In other words, PPPs and their use are a contested and complicated subject. In finding my way through the challenges that research into this subject has involved, the help and input of numerous people has been invaluable.

I would like to begin with offering my thanks to my PhD supervisor, Professor John Bell, who has been a vital and invaluable source of support and inspiration. With his comments and throughout our many discussions, he guided me towards shaping a logical and consistent structure for the main argument and helped me to avoid significant methodological pitfalls. At the same time, he has been keen to help me distinguish valid and promising ways to proceed, to understand the material with greater clarity and to select the best sources to consult. In that same respect, the assistance of three academics who are – like Professor Bell – authorities on the subject, Professors David Feldman, Tony Prosser and Dr Yseult Marique, has been invaluable. Their comments and our discussions on the main argument supported by the book, helped me profoundly as I sought to sharpen it and to define its parameters. Their input has also been instrumental in pinpointing avenues for the further development of my ideas in this area, and in inspiring me towards better outreach and dissemination of my research findings.

Acknowledgement must also to be made to the financial supporters of this project. The generous financial assistance received by the Onassis Foundation, Hughes Hall College, Cambridge, and the Santander Bank, provided me with the means to proceed with my research across the project. Furthermore, it also served as an important reminder – and a bolster – that their involvement was a token of trust that this research would be led to a fruitful completion.

It is also imperative to recognise here, and to thank for their invaluable contribution, the many academics who acted as an additional source of support and consultation for developing my understanding of PPPs. Among them, the input of Professors Ramu De Bellescize, Paul Craig, Mark Freedland, Costas Grammenos, Howell Jackson, Duncan Kennedy, Jeff King, Stephen Presser. At various stages of my research project, each one has, in his own way, offered me their academic insight, generously sharing precious research experience, and contributing advice and knowledge in order to aid my progress. Thanks is also due to others too numerous to mention for smaller but significant support, and I hope that those will recognise that this omission is only due to the inherent limitations in human attention, rather than an inappropriate limitation in human gratefulness.

I would like to extend my sincere gratefulness to the Doing Business Unit of the World Bank Group in Washington DC for allowing me to contribute my expertise to the development of its new and promising indicator on Contracting with the Government. Special thanks in this context is due to Mr. Santiago Croci Downes, Mrs. Valentina Saltane, Mrs. Erica Bosio and Mr. Albert Nogués i Comas for helping me expand my experience in the field of public procurement and for orienting its application towards the appropriate direction. Of course, the opinions expressed in this book are solely my own, they were shaped before my work within Doing Business, and they do not necessarily represent the views of the unit, its affiliates and associated organizations, or their employees.

I would also especially like to thank Prof David Howarth (University of Cambridge), as well as the many practitioners, from both private and public sectors, who have been generous in spending time answering my questions during my PhD investigations and helping me to clarify my understanding of technical matters pertaining to PPPs. The book represents neither individual's nor their institutions' views or opinions, and any mistakes are my own.

In addition, I would also like to express my gratefulness to Dr Kirsty Byrne, who supported the book as a proofreader, demonstrating an analytical rigour which is genuinely admirable. Her work has been instrumental in preparing the book and, at times, her input has been vital in the presentation of its main ideas.

Finally, I think it is more than essential to thank my friends, who come from such a variety of avenues in life. Many of these friends shared my time at colleges in Oxford and Cambridge. Kellogg College in Oxford and Hughes Hall College in Cambridge have been a tremendously helpful source of support, providing an intellectually fruitful environment for me to discuss and to develop my ideas. Mr Selçuk Bedük, Dr Jason Cole, Dr Maja Djundeva, Mrs Ruth Equipaje, Mr Alessandro Rodolfo Guazzi, Mr John Magyar, Mr Tasos Papastylianou, Mr Ioannis Petrou, Dr Maciej Piróg, Mrs Natalia Quiñones, Mrs Amanda Shriwise, Dr Barry Sol, Mrs Martina Tevceva, Mrs Bindu Vinodhan and Mr Dominik Wanner have been great friends, and their support has been invaluable in the successful completion of this project. Each one, originating from different disciplines, ranging from sociology and education to physics and engineering, provided me with an opportunity to see in practice the benefits and opportunities offered by intellectual cross-fertilisation of ideas and approaches. This is both lesson and legacy for which I will be grateful to them forever.

The material of this book solely represents the views of the writer, and not of the people mentioned herein. Neither does it represent those of any of the institutions involved, including the institutions and organisations in which the writer was, or is, currently employed. All mistakes are my own. Finally, for brevity and consistency in presentation, I have used the pronoun 'he' throughout, intending it to be understood in a generic sense.

Abbreviations

Accounting Standards Board	ASB
Comptroller and Auditor General	C&AG
General Accountability Office	GAO
National Audit Office	NAO
Net Present Value	NPV
New Public Management	NPM
Non-Departmental Public Bodies	NDPB
Private Finance Initiative	PFI
Private Finance Initiative 2	PFI2
Public Accounts Committee	PAC
Public Sector Comparator	PSC
Public-Private Partnerships	PPPs
Value for Money	VfM

Introduction

It would be an accurate observation to make that recent years have witnessed important changes in the ways that public services are delivered. Many governments worldwide have been proactive in assigning important roles to private contractors in the provision of public services. Since the early 1990s, the UK government has pioneered this trend, and many important government sectors, such as education, health, and transport – to name but a few – have been outsourced to private parties. This outsourcing of public service delivery has been carried out using a variety of arrangements and legal instruments. One of the most important, frequently-used and – at the same time – one of the most controversial arrangements, are a type of contracts which are known as 'public-private partnerships' or PPPs.

In the first instance, a good way to describe PPPs is that they are legal arrangements under the form of a fully enforceable and binding contract. Under a PPP contract, a private contractor undertakes important obligations with respect to the provision of a public service. He typically undertakes to finance the construction of a facility, to design it, build it, and often, to operate and manage it, too. The government, for its part in the contract, undertakes to provide payments to private contractors for these services, with these payments being offered at regular intervals, and extending over the duration of the contract. This duration of the contract covers decades, normally extending to 30 years. However, some can extend for much longer periods of time, in some cases, as long as 99 years.

The decision to use PPPs by the government is therefore an important decision. It is a decision which binds the resources of the public purse for decades, and it involves acceptance that the private sector will be responsible for important aspects of the provision of public services. These aspects, which extend from the financing to the operation and management of a facility, have an enormous effect upon considerable periods of the contract throughout delivery of the service to the citizen. Furthermore, the payment to the contractor over the provision of these services originates from tax-payers' money, or other public sources of finance which, collectively, comprise the government's money.

The importance of these aspects of PPPs have driven governments in Europe and overseas to create new mechanisms (or shape existing ones accordingly) through which the government can be held accountable over the use of public money in PPPs. These mechanisms or systems of public accountability operate based on a number of criteria and follow a number of constitutional principles, which are responsible for their setting into place and operation. The purpose of the present paper is to explore these criteria and constitutional principles in two countries which have been pivotal for the promotion of PPPs: the UK and the USA. Both of these two jurisdictions, UK first and then the USA, are global leaders in the PPP market, investing substantial amounts of public capital in PPPs and awarding important powers to private contractors. Further to that, each one of these two systems has struck a particular and distinct balance between the promotion of economic effectiveness and constitutional accountability. The comparison between the balance which was achieved by each one of these two systems is interesting from the perspective of Constitutional Law, in part, because the roots for its ideas are often found among systems in institutional design.

The most appropriate framework of Constitutional Law for our inquiry is that of the Economic Constitution. According to Tony Prosser, one of the perspectives of the Economic Constitution is that it focuses upon 'the key constitutional principles and institutional arrangements which may be relevant to the management of the economy'.[1] This perspective of the Economic Constitution is very important for our examination, because PPPs, with the important public capital that they involve, constitute a way through which the government invests, intervenes in and manages the economy. Our book will focus on the Economic Constitution of PPPs in the UK and the USA, using the prism of this perspective provided by Prosser. We will explore the criteria of public accountability which have been developed for the systems of accountability for PPPs, and the principles of the Economic Constitution which direct and shape their operation in the respective systems. Further to that, we will explore ways in which the respective systems of accountability for PPPs can be improved to better reflect the principles of the Economic Constitution which are applicable to them.

Before outlining the framework for our research, it will be useful to reiterate the original research question: our purpose in this book is to explore the systems of accountability which have been developed for holding to account two governments for their use of public money in the promotion of PPPs in the UK and the USA. This exploration will specifically focus on the criteria of accountability which are used in these systems and the constitutional principles which direct the shaping and operation of these criteria in the respective systems of public accountability.

1.   The notion of PPPs – initial approaches

A good place to begin our introductory account of the components of our research question is with the notion of PPPs. It is important to highlight in

---

1 Tony Prosser, *The Economic Constitution* (Oxford University Press 2014) 8.

advance that the nature and scope of PPPs is different in the UK and the USA, and a significant proportion of each chapter will thus be specifically targeted to providing the particular characteristics of PPPs in each country. However, the aim of this section is to provide the basic general narrative of the rationale of PPPs as a system of provision of public services with the involvement of public money.

One of the first characteristics of PPPs which we need to consider is that they are arrangements between the public and private sectors which appear under the legal form of contracts.[2] They are binding contracts, which create specific responsibilities, and are extremely finely-tuned for the public and private sectors. The contractual, binding character of PPPs makes them enforceable in the courts, and the rules of contract law apply to them. In this way, PPPs create legal responsibilities for the parties, and these are very precisely and extensively defined in the respective contracts.

The responsibilities of the private sector which derive from a PPP contract generally extend in four directions: the financing of a facility, its design, construction, and its operation.[3] When the contractor undertakes to finance a facility, he undertakes to seek and solicit sources of financial contribution to the project. These sources can come from the private sector, and can include bank loans and equity, which – in the UK – amount to a contribution of 90 per cent and 10 per cent respectively.[4] Apart from loans and equity, under the 2012 reform of the Private Finance Initiative (PFI), which is the typical model of PPPs in the UK, it was declared that finance can also be sought from pension funds and institutional investors.[5] The responsibility for finance, as well as the responsibilities of design, construction, and the operation of the facility, have to be exercised to achieve the outputs defined in the PPP contract. In this way, the government will allow considerable freedom to the private contractor around how the facility can be designed, constructed and operated, as long as the specific outputs are achieved. To illustrate this point, a PPP contract for the construction of a motorway, for example, will provide the output which the government seeks to achieve, such as, for instance, the ability for this motorway to serve a certain number of cars per hour. However, the responsibility to envision an appropriate design, to construct the motorway in an appropriate way in order to achieve this goal, and to operate it, will largely rest on the shoulders of the private contractor. The PPP contracts are thus contracts which define

2 Paul Craig, *Administrative Law* (7th edn, Sweet & Maxwell 2012) 121.
3 Graham Allen, *The Private Finance Initiative (PFI)* (House of Commons Research Paper 03/79, 2003) 9; E. R. Yescombe, *Public-Private Partnerships: Principles of Policy and Finance* (Elsevier 2007) 2–3.
4 HM Treasury (Treasury), *Reform of the Private Finance Initiative* (HMSO 2011) 17; Treasury, *PFI: Meeting the Investment Challenge* (HMSO 2003) 37; Yescombe 1–14.
5 Treasury, *A New Approach to Public-Private Partnerships* (2012) 30.

outputs, and not contracts which direct specific detailed choices on how these outputs are to be achieved.

This array of responsibilities which are undertaken by the private contractor by means of a PPP, are paid for by the public sector partner, in the form of a stream of payments known as a 'unitary charge'.[6] The unitary charge is the periodic payment that the public sector agrees to pay for the provision of services by the PFI contractor.[7] It normally includes three different elements: the service element to run the projects (including services offered by the private contractor such as cleaning, catering, maintenance and security), and repayment of the capital asset built, plus interest on this capital.[8] Deductions are then made from this unitary charge to penalise, for instance, poor performance by the private sector or a lack of availability.[9] For example, if an operating theatre in a PFI hospital became unavailable there would be deduction from the unitary charge, up until the time when the theatre became available again. If pipes in a school burst, flooding and causing damage to its fabric, the private sector would be responsible for fixing the pipes and returning the school to its proper working condition, and in the meantime it would not be paid unitary charges for the parts which were not operational. In a PFI project, as a result of the mechanism of unitary charges, the costs are spread throughout the years of the duration of the contract.[10] Increases in the unitary charge should theoretically occur to reflect inflation and for contract variations (in other words, when the authority requested changes in the specifications) throughout the lifetime of the contract.[11]

This basis of reward based on incentives and outputs is fairly absent from a conventional project, procured using non-PPP methods. In such a project, the government, not the private contractor, maintains control of all the important decisions related to the facility. The government decides how the facility will be designed, constructed, and operated. It alone has to contract and pay an architect, in order for him to design the hospital of our example. In a similar way, it contracts and pays a company to construct it, according to designs that the government has approved. After the hospital is ready, the government will provide it with civil servants, whose task is to manage and operate it. However, as was the

---

6 Ibid 18; Treasury, *PFI: Meeting the Investment Challenge* 23, 33–34; National Audit Office (NAO), *Savings from Operational PFI Contracts* (2013) 10; Treasury, *Reform of the Private Finance Initiative* 17.

7 NAO, *A Framework for Evaluating the Implementation of Private Finance Initiative Projects: Volume 2* (2006) 63.

8 Treasury, *A New Approach to Public-Private Partnerships* 23; NAO, *Savings from Operational PFI Contracts* 10; Treasury, *Whole of Government Accounts: Year ended 31 March 2010* (HC 1601, 2011) 88.

9 Treasury, *PFI: Meeting the Investment Challenge* 33.

10 NAO, *Review of the VFM Assessment Process for PFI* (2013) 5.

11 NAO, *A Framework for Evaluating the Implementation of Private Finance Initiative Projects: Volume 1* (May 2006) 15.

case with the theoretical PPP-procured hospital, in a government hospital, any of these decisions has the potential to have an undesirable outcome. It is equally as likely that the hospital could be constructed following a design which is not optimal, and the resulting construction exposed to inefficiencies. Similarly, it could be the case that the material used in the actual construction is inadequate and the hospital, as a consequence, suffers from problematic fluctuations in temperature, getting colder in the winters, and oppressively warm in the summers, or that the personnel therein do not perform as they should. All these cases of poor outcomes, which are technically referred to as 'project risks', are borne by the government, and it will be its exclusive responsibility to resolve them – if it chooses – and, consequently, to bear all the associated costs.

With a PPP contract, many of these potential problems, which are termed the 'risks of the project', are transferred to the private contractor. The private contractor will be the one to suffer damages if the project is inoperative or if it has been constructed with inefficiencies. In these cases, he will suffer deductions from the unitary charge that he is to receive from the government. In this way, the private contractor has every incentive to make sure that the facility is designed, constructed and that it operates in the most effective, optimal and least potentially problematic manner. The unitary charge is at the heart of a PPP contract for precisely this reason, and it is the incentive for which the contractor decides to participate in a PPP, and the vehicle through which certain risks of the project are transferred between the public and the private sector.

PPP contracts, as we have described, involve both financial expenses provided from the government's purse[12] and the award of serious responsibilities to the private contractor. The private contractor designs the actual facility, constructs it, manages and operates it, and all of these factors are crucial for the actual delivery of the public service to the citizen. The PPP facility looks and operates differently to one designed, constructed, managed and operated by the public sector, because there would be different choices which would have been made at all these stages. In this way, a PPP project not only signifies an important governmental financial commitment, but also an important change to the ways that the actual service is delivered to the citizen. For the proponents of PPPs, this change – of bringing private efficiency to the public sector – is understood as a key advantage of the model, while detractors find this overvalued, claiming that PPPs is merely a way for the private sector to gain money from the public purse without any real risk transfer or improvement of services.[13]

The funds in both the UK and the USA which are invested in PPPs are substantial. We will enlarge on this in their respective chapters, but we can

---

12 Committee of Public Accounts (PAC), *Lessons from PFI and other Projects* (HC 2010–12, 1201) Ev 14, Q 128.

13 For a list of the advantages and disadvantages of the PFI, see NAO, *Lessons from PFI and other Projects* (HC 2010–12, 920) 13.

briefly say here that, as per 31 March 2014, there were 728 PFI projects in the UK, out of which 671 were operational, with a capital value of £56.6 billion (bn).[14] In the USA during the period 1985–2011, 495 PPPs were undertaken with a value of about US$ 213 bn.[15] In both cases, PPPs have been agreed in a variety of sectors, such as health, education, transportation, detention, defence, water provision and waste treatment and facilities, amongst others.

These sums, payable through the unitary payments, are public money, originating from the public purse. This is in accordance with a very comprehensive definition of public money provided by Lord Sharman in his classic report of 2001, entitled 'Managing Public Money':

> Classic thinking on what constitutes public money concentrates on how revenue is raised and on Parliamentary authorisation of expenditure. On the first of these bases, public money will consist of tax revenues and government borrowings, as well as income generated by public bodies from fees and charges. On the second, public money would consist largely of money voted in estimates, but would also cover cases where money was raised under statutory powers (for example, through levies on particular industries).[16]

He proceeds by elaborating that modern definitions of public money focus more on the subjective element, on the sense of the public nature of the money depending on the public nature of the organ spending it. Among these organs are government departments (including agencies and trading funds), non-departmental public bodies (NDPBs), public corporations, devolved administrations, local authorities, Parliamentary bodies (such as the National Audit Office, NAO), bodies connected to the Monarchy, and local public spending bodies, as well as the contractors of PFI contracts themselves.

As we may observe, the unitary charges payable by the government in PPPs fit comfortably with the definition provided by Lord Sharman, which even refers directly to the PFI. The money used for the payment of unitary charges originate from taxation, is appropriated by the Parliament, and, ultimately, is spent by departments, agencies or other bodies which are public.

In this way, PPPs signify an important expenditure by the government, because they are taken from public money and involve regular payments extending over the lengthy periods of time built into individual PPP contracts. These periods can be as long as 30 years, as is typical in the UK, but they can extend to much lengthier timeframes, even, in the USA, occasionally as much as a

---

14 Treasury, *Private Finance Initiative Projects: 2014 Summary Data* (2014) 3.
15 Etienne B. Yehoue, 'Financial and Sovereign Debt Crises and PPP Market Structure' in Piet De Vries and Etienne B. Yehoue (eds), *The Routledge Companion to Public–Private Partnerships* (Routledge 2013) 354.
16 Lord Sharman of Redlynch, *Holding to Account: The Review of Audit and Accountability of Central Government* (2001) 9.

century. Most significantly, these payments are made by virtue of contracts, which, as we mentioned earlier, are fully binding and legally enforceable. This signifies that the government cannot simply decide to leave a contract if it changes its mind; the PPP contract will need to continue to run up until its expiry, and, should the government prefer to leave any particular contractual arrangement, it will have to do so following either the provisions of the contract itself or the rules of the general contract law, paying corresponding damages. It could be accurately asserted, therefore, that, in this sense, PPPs bind future generations, since government makes a fixed commitment for the future. It would also, perhaps, be accurate to say that PPPs curtail – on a pragmatic level – the freedom of the Parliament to approve expenses incurred by the government; although at the level of constitutional theory, the Parliament certainly remains fully able, at any time, to disapprove the expenses which are involved in the unitary charges payable in PPPs at any given year. Of course, this freedom is curtailed, to some degree, through the political consequences that a potential disapproval would involve. These political consequences would be negative because they would signify the government's inability to perform an obligation which it has already undertaken, and this would be likely to affect the credit rating of the government, with all the accompanying negative consequences involved for the future possibilities of government lending.

This brings us naturally to the conclusion that it is worthwhile examining how the government is held accountable over its use of public money in PPPs, which is the broader subject of this book.

2. The notion of the Economic Constitution

In the previous section we provided a number of central characteristics of PPPs, highlighting the contractual nature of these arrangements and their property to bind important public funds for long periods of time for the provision of infrastructure and public services. These characteristics of PPPs orient the examination of their accountability arrangements to the features which are collectively identified with the Economic Constitution. In this section, we will provide an introductory account of the reasons for which the Economic Constitution constitutes an appropriate framework for our research, which focuses on these accountability arrangements.

The Economic Constitution, as noted by Prosser in his book on the subject, is a framework which has barely been used and developed in the UK. In his work, he used this framework in order to examine the mechanisms through which the government manages the economy, and thereby to assess their legitimacy and accountability.[17] A first perspective of the Economic Constitution, according to Prosser, is descriptive and focuses upon 'the key constitutional

17 Prosser 2.

principles and institutional arrangements which may be relevant to the management of the economy'.[18] A further perspective which he distinguishes focuses on its function as promoting 'a particular value or set of social values in the process of economic management'.[19] An additional perspective is that of the form of 'new constitutionalism', which sees the Economic Constitution as a system designed for the protection of private capital, placing constraints on collective democratic choice.[20]

As we can observe, the first perspective of this account stresses the focus of the Economic Constitution to the mechanisms through which the government manages the economy and on the relevant constitutional principles. Throughout the present paper we will predominantly be using this first perspective; the reason for this is that PPPs possess a number of characteristics which make them an important mechanism for the management of economic life in both the UK and the USA.

The first of these characteristics is that PPPs are generally linked with the creation of public infrastructure, which – by its very nature – is likely to affect the economy on macroeconomic terms. Schools, hospitals, and motorways, which are frequent projects undertaken through PPPs, constitute economic infrastructure, having the ability to affect and determine the development of the productivity of the economy. When the government invests public money in these projects, the government estimates their usefulness and suitability for private provision, as well as the ways they can benefit the economic life in particular geographical areas and communities.

The second characteristic of PPPs which renders them a means through which the government manages the economic life of the country derives from the size of the respective investments. As we have seen, the PPP activity of the government entails significant transfer of funds by the government to the private sector, and, in this way, constitutes injection of capital into the market. Through the unitary charges that the government will pay to the private contractor, the contractor will pay the employees working in the project, make its profit and channel it to other projects which belong to its circle of activities. In this way, public money which originates from the government is injected into the market, and flows into and across the sectors in which the contractors' consortia operate. The economic consequences of the provision of government money to the market is a subject which is central in macroeconomic theory, and it is an important determinant in the development of the economy.

Through the government's use of PPPs, it determines, through the creation of infrastructure and via the channelling of significant capital into the market, the development prospects and properties of the economic life of the country,

18 Ibid 8.
19 Ibid 10.
20 Ibid 10–11.

establishing an economic relationship between public and private sectors. This function of PPPs as instruments shaping and determining important aspects of national economic life, is an element which makes them well suited to exploration from the perspective of the Economic Constitution. Furthermore, an additional reason for which the framework of the Economic Constitution has been selected for our analysis derives from the economic nature of PPPs themselves. The framework of the Economic Constitution – as is particularly stressed in its first perspective – is designed to discuss economic arrangements and relationships. Such economic arrangement is similarly employed in a PPP. A PPP is a contract in which there is exchange between money – which the public sector provides to the contractor – and services, which the private contractor provides to the public sector and/or the citizens. The nature of the relationship is economic; this fact makes PPPs a subject which finds its native points of reference in a framework of Constitutional Law analysis which is oriented towards the analysis of economic relationships, such as that of the Economic Constitution. In this way, the Economic Constitution constitutes a suitable framework which can be employed to discuss both the dynamics of the economic relationship of PPPs and the constitutional principles, such as those related to public accountability, which affect the operation of this economic relationship towards the public.

This linkage of PPPs to the framework of the Economic Constitution can be explored thematically in numerous ways, and these are reflected in the broader theory of Economic Constitutional Law, as developed by Prosser. The first of these links which we aim to introduce and to probe relates to the theme of plurality. Prosser highlights this theme from the perspective of institutions which are involved in the operation of the Economic Constitution. The same theme of plurality, from the perspective of the criteria of accountability for PPPs, can be observed, and we will see that this applies to the USA's systems for PPPs. A second example is one of limited Parliamentary input which Prosser identifies as a theme of governmental policy in the broader context of government intervention in the economy. This theme, as we will see in the UK chapter, is also relevant with respect to the government's use of PPPs, with the government feeling less obliged to involve Parliament either in the enactment of legislation for PPPs or in the design of their accountability arrangements.

Our approach and purpose in examining the subject of accountability from the perspective of the Economic Constitution will – to some extent – be descriptive, but will also include aspects of the normative. In doing so, we will focus on how the criteria of accountability operate in the respective systems and institutional arrangements through the descriptive part of our inquiry. At a more normative level, we will also discuss to what extent, and under which adaptations, the existing systems which operate by reference to the relevant criteria of accountability can be adapted so that they better serve their purpose.

It needs to be noted that, given that the Economic Constitution refers to the management of the economy by the government, it follows that the integration of PPPs in the broader framework of the Economic Constitution differs between jurisdictions. The reason behind this is that different jurisdictions – such as those of the UK and the USA – use and promote PPPs in different ways. For this reason, the integration of PPPs to the Economic Constitution will be examined in their respective chapters. We will examine the nature and scope of PPPs and the ways in which the government has responded to their account-ability challenges. Bearing in mind that our discussion around these account-ability challenges is to some extent descriptive and to some extent normative, the descriptive dimension of our work will include description of how each government has responded to the accountability challenges of PPPs by designing relevant management mechanisms intended to answer this need. In the norma-tive dimension of our work, we will discuss how these mechanisms can be improved so that they better serve their purpose of holding a government to account over its use of public money in PPPs.

3.   The notion of public accountability

In this introductory chapter to our book, we have already provided a very brief and rudimentary overview of PPPs and of their basic points of reference to the theory of the Economic Constitution. This theory, acting as the framework for our analysis in this book, refers to constitutional principles, among which is that of public accountability, which will be our subject. The concept of accountability, however, has, historically, been surrounded by controversy. The context is therefore very complex and so, for this reason, it is necessary that we select the basic characteristics of the concept of accountability which we will be using throughout the book.

3.1.   Different perspectives of accountability

This book will be employing a narrow perspective of accountability, which dif-ferentiates accountability from other values, such as transparency or public participation. In order to substantiate and qualify this decision, it will be useful to refer to the corpus of writers which has established the theoretical framework, different perspectives on, and concepts of, accountability.

A useful starting point in explaining the reasons and qualifications of this decision are the theories on accountability developed by Marc Bovens. Accord-ing to him, public accountability can be defined through a broad or narrow perspective. The broad perspective perceives accountability as embracing conceptually-different notions such as transparency, equity, democracy, efficiency, responsiveness, responsibility and integrity.[21] In a narrow interpretation, account-ability is defined as 'a relationship between an actor and a forum, in which the

---

21 Mark Bovens, 'Analysing and Assessing Accountability: A Conceptual Framework' (2007) 13 European Law Journal 447, 449.

actor has an obligation to explain and to justify his conduct, the forum can pose questions and pass judgement, and the actor may face consequences'.[22] From the perspective of the forum to which the actor is accountable, public accountability takes a number of forms: political, legal, administrative, professional and social. One of the perspectives of political accountability is that of the constitutional; the function of the constitutional perspective of accountability is to prevent the abuse of power by absolute leaders, elected leaders or by a decentralised or privatised public bureaucracy.[23] Through this constitutional perspective, public accountability aims to limit and control the tendency of the executive to concentrate more and more power.

Bovens has distinguished the narrow perspective of accountability and provided its basic characteristics and form. The broad perspective of accountability has also been extensively discussed by Richard Mulgan. For Mulgan, the notion of accountability has expanded significantly in the recent past, and this can – in some cases – weaken the importance of external scrutiny.[24] Mulgan recognises the original understanding of accountability to which there is general consent by researchers. It includes the 'process of being called 'to account' to some authority for one's actions'.[25] The expansion of the notion of accountability can be demonstrated through five separate features: the first aspect is one of accountability as responsibility. Here, accountability is perceived as carrying characteristics or as being equated with responsibility. In a sense, this mirrors the inner responsibility of the individual to his conscience. An additional dimension to this form of responsibility relates to the Westminster perception of Parliamentary responsibility, and the understanding of accountability under this notion. A further feature embraced by this expansion of accountability could be defined by many different names, such as 'professional', 'personal', 'inward', and 'subjective'. This understanding of accountability is based on the idea that the members of professional bodies will comply with the standards which these bodies uphold. The third feature of expansion relies upon accountability being perceived not only as a mechanism of control but upon it being identified as control itself. For Mulgan, the notion of control not only includes accountability but also other mechanisms, such as constitutional constraints or legal regulations which restrict the freedom of action of governments by requiring them to follow specific procedures or pursue specific outcomes. The fourth feature of expansion equates accountability with responsiveness, which refers to the aim of making governments accord with the preferences of the people. As in the case of control, accountability is a means of promoting

---

22 Ibid 450.
23 Mark Bovens, Thomas Schillemans and Paul T Hart, 'Does Public Accountability Work? An Assessment Tool' (2008) 86 Public Administration 225.
24 Richard Mulgan, '"Accountability": An Ever-Expanding Concept?' (2000) 78 Public Administration 555.
25 Ibid.

responsiveness, but responsiveness has additional mechanisms, such as motives that compel the officials to correspond to the wishes of their superiors, who, in turn, represent the people. The fifth area of expansion of accountability relates to the use of the term 'accountability' as signifying the public dialogue as a component of democracy. Although, according to Mulgan, accountability involves public explanation and justification – such as occurs in public dialogue – the two kinds of dialogue are different. The dialogue in an accountability relationship is a dialogue between public officials in a relationship between superior and subordinate. The public dialogue is between the citizens, discussing as equals.

In addition to Mulgan and Bovens, other commentators discuss the contents of accountability, similarly distinguishing it into categories. Examples of these include Antonio Bar Cendón,[26] for whom accountability can be distinguished in political,[27] administrative,[28] professional,[29] and democratic accountability.[30] For Neil McGarvey,[31] accountability can be analysed in terms of the traditional hierarchical perspective,[32] the democratic perspective,[33] the professional perspective,[34] the managerialist perspective,[35] the governance perspective,[36] the

26 Antonio Bar Cendón, 'Accountability and Public Administration: Concepts, Dimensions, Developments' (Openness and Transparency in Governance: Challenges and Opportunities, Maastricht, October 1999).
27 Ibid 28–29: political accountability in its vertical dimension is the relationship which links the higher members of administrative structures and in its horizontal dimension is the relationship between the Government and the Parliament.
28 Ibid 34: administrative accountability in its vertical dimension is a relationship that links inferior administrative positions with superior positions. In its horizontal dimension it links the public administration with the citizen and other external organs.
29 Ibid 39: professional accountability is a species of administrative accountability and is based on norms and practices which bind members of a specific profession.
30 Ibid 42: democratic accountability focuses on the relationship between the citizens and officials.
31 Neil McGarvey, 'Accountability in Public Administration: A Multi-Perspective Framework of Analysis' (2001) 16 Public Policy and Administration 17.
32 Ibid 18: the traditional perspective of accountability is based on a chain of accountability from official to official, from official to minister, from minister to Parliament and from Parliament to the people.
33 Ibid 19: the democratic perspective is closely linked to the traditional perspective, but it highlights representative and participatory forms of democracy as channels for holding public administration to account.
34 Ibid 19–20: the professional perspective emphasises the role of the apolitical professional bodies in enforcing their standards of public administration.
35 Ibid 20: from a managerial perspective accountability emphasises the requirement for direct accountability between the administrators and the users of public services.
36 Ibid 22: the governance perspective focuses on the importance of networks and other governance bodies in accountability.

regulatory perspective,[37] and the rational choice perspective.[38] A distinction which could be made between the contributions of these writers and Mulgan's theory relates to the point of focus in their analyses: Mulgan discusses the different conceptualisations of accountability in terms of the values upheld by them, while Bar Cendón and McGarvey approach the subject from the perspective of techniques and methods which can be employed in securing accountability.

As we can readily observe, the writers to whom we referred provide us with a very rich and diverse palette of colours which we can use in drawing the picture of accountability we will be employing in the next chapters. It is clear that the first question we need to ask with respect to the notion of public accountability we will be using refers to the selection between broader and narrower understandings of the concept. As Mulgan and Bovens elaborated, accountability can be understood as a broader concept, which includes many different notions, such as transparency and responsiveness; it can also be understood from a narrower perspective, as a concept which focuses on the provision of explanations by an actor standing before a forum, accounting for his choices and conduct. After consideration of these two perspectives, the one which seems more suitable for our research is arguably the latter perspective, which employs a narrower, more restrictive, understanding of public accountability.

The first reason for which a narrow perspective has been selected refers to the complexity of the mechanisms of accountability which exist for PPPs. These mechanisms, consistent to the observations of Prosser, involve many organs which employ accountability in numerous different ways. Consequently, the nature of our inquiry involves delving into this complexity. A broader understanding of accountability involving all the other concepts which Mulgan and Bovens and the other writers distinguish, such as transparency and responsiveness, to name a few, would further complicate an already complicated subject, at the expense of clarity. Furthermore, the notions on which a broad understanding of accountability is based are themselves subject to inquiry and debate and it is uncertain how they are related to each other. So, if we would approach accountability from a broad perspective, we would also have to address the relationship between all these different notions, expanding the subject of this book significantly, and beyond its appropriate parameters. In addition to the previous two reasons – and as both Bovens and Mulgan seem rightfully to suggest – the expansion of the notion of accountability is a tendency which weakens its usefulness as a system of analysis. For all these reasons, a narrow

---

37 Ibid 23: the regulatory perspective focuses on the regulation, rather than management relations, as instruments of accountability.

38 Ibid 24–25: the rational choice perspective highlights that only by focusing on the individual political strategies of the political actors can a true picture of accountability emerge.

perspective of accountability seems to be preferable for the purposes of this book. This perspective is captured in a very comprehensive way by Bovens, who defines accountability as 'a relationship between an actor and a forum, in which the actor has an obligation to explain and to justify his or her conduct, the forum can pose questions and pass judgement, and the actor may face consequences'.[39]

If we now 'filter' our research question through Bovens' framework, we can view it with a greater degree of accuracy. In this way, this book aims at exploring the systems of accountability, or the systems through which the government, as 'an actor', is required to explain and justify its conduct over the use of public money in PPPs. As we observe, however, Bovens' framework does not just contain actors and conducts; it also expounds the concept of the forum, towards which the actor has to explain its conduct. This readily further opens up the subject which we need to discuss, and which relates to the forum which will be our primary point of reference in our inquiry into systems of accountability. This forum exists as the legislature in our current examination. This is because of the importance of the legislature's status and function in the constitutional systems of the UK and the USA over financial matters. In both of these systems, the Constitution has invested the legislature with important powers with respect to holding the government to account over its use of public money. The government, in other words, does not generally, by virtue of the constitutional principle, enjoy a 'free ride' with respect to using public capital. In each one of these constitutional models, there are mechanisms which will make the government provide account of its use of public money. Given that PPPs involve a significant expenditure of public money, the issue which arises, and on which we will focus our inquiry here, relates to how well these mechanisms of public accountability serve their purpose.

Given our focus on the accountability of the government towards the legislature, an important point of departure for our examination will be the enactment of legislation in the two systems. The reason why we choose to begin with the legislation, is that legislation represents one of the most important instruments of accountability: the executive, as an actor, will have to explain to the legislature the reasons why it intends to proceed with PPPs and thus justify its need to commit public money to them. If it does not argue sufficiently convincingly, then the legislature might not agree to enact the legislation desired by the executive. Of course, this scenario refers to the enactment of legislation as a mechanism of accountability in its own right, but legislation is also important because it is a means by which criteria of accountability for PPPs can be set.

This latter point brings us naturally to the next part of our introductory account on the concept of accountability, which focuses on our decision to

---

39 Bovens, 'Analysing and Assessing Accountability: A Conceptual Framework' 450.

research public accountability from the perspective of the relevant criteria. We will now turn our attention to this aspect.

3.2. *The importance of the criteria of accountability and the use of legislation*

The mechanisms of constitutional accountability towards the legislature over the use of PPPs operate on the basis of a number of criteria, which are the concepts which will be crucial in the accountability process.

To illustrate this, when legislation provides that the Comptroller and Auditor General (C&AG), as auditor of Parliament, will examine whether the government has acted according to the criterion of Value for Money (VfM) in public expenditure, this legislation provides a criterion upon which the accountability process is to be based, that of VfM. The government will need to persuade the forum in the accountability process that its disposal of public money in PPPs has been done in a way which satisfies the criterion of VfM. Similarly, when a piece of legislation provides that a PPP contract has to be made when it is 'in the public interest', this piece of legislation once again provides a criterion of accountability, that of the 'public interest'. This is a criterion of accountability because the government, in making a specific PPP contract, will have to explain to the legislature why this contract is in the 'public interest'. The criteria of accountability are thus very important features of the accountability systems, because they are the basic concepts that the accountability process in these systems aims to establish. In its role as an 'actor', the government if it does not establish that it has achieved these criteria in its expenditure of public money in PPPs, is likely to face consequences, such as political exposure, loss of political capital or – in more serious cases – consequences which include the non-approval of funds by the legislature for the repayment of these contracts. This latter possibility, which is more theoretical in the UK, but which is more likely to happen in the USA, is one of the negative consequences that the government can face if it does not satisfy the legislature that it has achieved the standards provided by the relevant criteria of accountability.

A further reason for which the criteria of accountability are important for the systems of public accountability is that they permit the establishment of accepted practices in these systems. The bodies which will use the criteria develop their own interpretation and then, by applying the resulting traditions in practice, they have a substantial ability to direct government practice in PPPs. In this way, an elaboration of the criterion of 'VfM' by the Public Accounts Committee (PAC), which is the committee of the legislature which holds the government accountable for expenditure in the UK, does not exhaust its value solely in terms of the accountability process. Furthermore, it develops its own normative dynamics which serve to direct future decisions of the government in this context. The reason that the criteria of accountability have this property is rooted in the negative consequences that the government – as an 'actor' – may face in the accountability process. If it does not take into account past elaborations of the forums which use these criteria, then it risks receiving negative feedback from these forums in the accountability process, and facing the consequent negative political fall-out. For this additional reason, the criteria of accountability are important; they can develop their own dynamics inside the relevant systems, and thereby significantly impact upon the government's future practice.

A third reason for which the criteria of accountability are important to the systems of public accountability is that, to a large extent, the overall effectiveness of the accountability mechanisms is dependent upon them. Clear, well-defined and accurate criteria mean that all the participants in the accountability process have clarity of understanding over precisely which concepts the accountability process seek to establish. The government will therefore know from previous experience that it will be held accountable over a specific notion, with a specific interpretation, and, as long as it manages to provide a persuasive, specifically-targeted justification around its satisfactory performance, then it should be reasonably protected from having to face the negative consequences of the accountability process. The forum of accountability, from its unique position, will be able to judge with a good level of accuracy exactly through which concept, and over which interpretation of this concept, the government is to be held accountable. This will help the forum to ask questions which are targeted and focused to the specific dimension of government conduct which is interesting for the purposes of constitutional accountability, and which, according to Bovens, aims to prevent the abuse of power by the executive.[40] In this way, the third reason for which the criteria of accountability are so important for the performance of the systems of accountability is that, dependent on their quality, they have the propensity meaningfully to affect both the quality and the effectiveness of the systems of accountability themselves.

For all these reasons, the particular perspective of the systems of accountability on which we will focus is that of the criteria of accountability. We will see how these criteria operate in the respective systems, which constitutional principles forge, and how these criteria affect the respective systems of public accountability in which they operate.

4.   The reasons for comparing the UK and the USA

Up until this point we have introduced a skeletal discussion around the basic properties of our research question. The concern which needs to be discussed at this point relates to the reasons why a comparison between the UK and the USA is meaningful in terms of the research question which we set to explore.

---

40 Bovens, Schillemans and Hart, 'Does Public Accountability Work? An Assessment Tool' 233.

The first point which needs to be highlighted in the context of establishing why the comparison between the UK and the USA is meaningful relates to the use of PPPs by these two jurisdictions. As we have already seen, both the UK and the USA are countries with extensive exposure to PPPs with billions worth of PPPs. In this way, when examining the UK and the USA, we know we are examining systems which have rich experience in PPPs and which have committed significant amounts to their use and promotion.

The second point which needs to be highlighted relates to the broader constitutional principle of accountable government expenditure. Both the UK and the USA respect the principle that the executive will have to explain its conduct with respect to the expenditure it incurs to the legislature, and they have both developed their own mechanisms in order to achieve this constitutional outcome. The legislature in both systems has the power to ask questions of the government over how it has used – and over how it intends to use – public money, and the government has to explain its conduct in terms of accountability relationships. As a result, when examining the UK and the USA governments' accountability when committing public money to PPPs, we are examining two systems which are both based on the principle of accountable governance in expenditure.

What differs, however, and what makes this comparison particularly interesting, is that the ways that these two governments have pursued this goal are different. They have developed different mechanisms of accountability, with different criteria, and, most importantly, different constitutional principles which are called into application. This point brings us to the fundamental issue which underlies the analysis of this book, namely, what, exactly, are the virtues of each system? In tandem with this question, what are the weaknesses? Also, how can each system learn from the other and improve? These questions highlight the need for comparative research in these two jurisdictions and the choices they have made in structuring their systems and criteria of accountability.

A further point which highlights the need for a comparative analysis refers to the balance between pursuing two different, and largely opposing, values in the Economic Constitution of PPPs. These two values are those of accountability and of economic effectiveness. The issue is necessarily very complicated and, therefore, while we will provide an outline here, its detail will be reserved for each one of the next chapters. Theoretically, it is possible for any given system of institutional design for PPPs to achieve maximum constitutional accountability towards the legislature for the expenditure of public money in PPPs; this can – again, in theory – occur with a project-by-project involvement of the legislature at every stage of every PPP contract. The problem with this approach is that it is likely to hinder economic effectiveness, because it is slow and lumbering: PPPs will take longer to be set into place and they may well be exposed to all kinds of political fluctuations which accompany the organisation of a legislature in a modern democracy. The reverse is also possible; it is theoretically conceivable that the promotion of PPPs will be bestowed to the executive with very limited input by the legislature. This could potentially lead to an increase in the economic effectiveness of the PPPs, because their promotion would be speedier and – to a fair degree – insulated from political challenges. This benefit of economic effectiveness, however, would come at the expense of constitutional accountability. This interplay between the pursuance of economic effectiveness in PPPs and the pursuance of constitutional accountability is unique for each one of the jurisdictions we will examine. The choices that each jurisdiction makes in seeking this balance is interesting, from the perspective of Economic Constitutional Law for PPPs, because it affects institutional design and relationships between institutions, which is one of the areas in which Economic Constitutional Law focuses. For this reason, the interplay between the values of economic effectiveness and accountability will be an underlying theme in our analysis and in the comparison of the systems and criteria of accountability for PPPs in the UK and the USA.

Having provided a basic account of the reasons which explain the significance of a comparison between the UK and the USA with respect to accountability systems for PPPs, we will now advance to the plan of the book.

5.   Plan of the book

As we clarified earlier, a basic distinction which we will follow in our analysis in the present book refers to the importance of legislation in articulating the criteria in which accountability is based on PPPs, as well as its importance in serving as a means of accountability on its own right.

Following this distinction, our first chapter will take the UK as its subject. As we will notice, the basic principle in the case of the UK is that PPPs are promoted by the government largely by virtue of its inherent power to contract, rather than being based on legislation. This legislation could have provided for criteria of accountability specifically for PPPs, could authorise the use of PPPs by the government, and could thus serve as a very powerful mechanism of accountability. The limited use of legislation, however, leads to the use of a system of accountability for PPPs which is the default system of accountability for all financial matters. This was set in the nineteenth century and is focused on the important roles of the NAO and the PAC. This mechanism, largely dedicated to accountability for economic effectiveness, leaves a stark and important gap in the accountability of other matters, such as those which involve the expenditure of public money in PPPs, but which are unrelated to the economic rationale of PPPs: such matters include environmental considerations, the suitability of the private sector to undertake specific government tasks, the amount of integration of the private sector which is desirable, and others. In order to increase accountability in these specific areas, we argue that we have to increase the amount of legislation for PPPs. In order to achieve this result, we propose the recognition of the Concordat of 1932 as a constitutional convention, applicable to PPPs. This recognition will involve the constitutional necessity of the enactment of framework legislation for every government sector which uses PPPs. Such legislation will provide for the need for a statutory instrument for every new PPP project.

The second chapter is dedicated to the USA. As we will observe, the basic principle in the USA is that PPPs have to be based on legislation. This legislation is supposed to authorise the use of PPPs and the commitment of public money and to provide for accountability arrangements and criteria specifically for PPPs. The problem with this, however, is that the basic principle does not provide for the necessity of co-ordinating all the numerous criteria of accountability which are amply provided by the legislation. Because of the absence of a central co-ordination mechanism, these criteria are exposed to a significant degree of subjectivity. The outcome of this is that the Congressional oversight which is provided by the Constitution is hindered, impacting negatively on accountability over PPPs. In order to resolve this issue, we have construed a positive responsibility of the executive and the legislature to systematise the criteria of accountability which the legislation provides for PPPs. The first basis of this duty is the constitutional duty of the President and the members of the Congress to uphold and support the constitution respectively, while the second basis is the institution of due process. The means to fulfil this duty is the enactment of systematising legislation, the adoption of guidelines and the establishment of a specialised agency specifically dedicated to the task.

Following the analysis in the UK and USA chapters we will proceed, in the final, concluding, chapter of the book, to provide an overview of the arguments supported, and we will discuss what has been gained from comparing the UK and the USA. Further to that, we will focus on determining aspects of our research which could potentially be useful in informing broader discussions on the Economic Constitution. A key finding here is that our research has, to a certain extent, demonstrated that the values of economic effectiveness and constitutional accountability need a degree of reconfigurational shaping in order to sit comfortably with each other. Further to that, another central theme which also arises from our work is that the Economic Constitution, apart from constructing novel constitutional principles, can also use adapted versions of existing ones. Such constitutional principles in our research have been those of the Concordat of 1932, which we used for the UK, and the due process, which we used for the USA.

6. Conclusions

Our aim, in this introductory chapter, was to provide the basic framework of our research question, to present the comparative rationale behind it and the methodological pathways taken and which follow in this book. The subject on which this book focuses is the exploration of the systems which have been developed in the UK and the USA for holding the executive to account for its use of public money when it uses PPPs. The specific perspective on which we will focus while exploring these systems is that of the criteria of accountability and the constitutional principles which support their setting in place and operation.

The subject of a government's accountability in its use of public money in PPPs has an interest for public law because of a number of factors which are inherent in these transactions in the UK and the USA: PPPs are used a great deal by both governments, they involve significant amounts of public money, and they bind the government for long periods of time, typically decades. From these characteristics stem the reasons for which, in our inquiry over public accountability, we selected the framework of the Economic Constitution as the most suitable context. The theory of the Economic Constitution, under the first perspective highlighted by Prosser, focuses on institutional arrangements and constitutional principles which are important for the ways that the government manages the economy. PPPs, with their important economic size and their capacity to produce infrastructure which is significant for economic development are one of the ways that the government has to intervene in the economy. Furthermore, the structure of PPPs as economic arrangements of the government is a factor which makes them find their native points of reference in the theory of the Economic Constitution.

The notion of accountability through which we will be pursuing our research question is a narrow one. This narrow perception of accountability, as developed by Bovens, stands for a relationship between an actor and a forum, in which the forum can require the actor to explain his conduct and the actor may face consequences. In our research question, this actor is the government, the forum is the legislature, while the conduct which is the subject of the accountability systems is the use of public money in PPPs. In this context, both the UK and the USA, which recognise – in terms of constitutional principle – the value of the accountability of government for expenditure, each adopt different solutions and use different constitutional principles to achieve this goal. Beyond that, each of them has achieved different balances between the promotion of accountability and the promotion of economic effectiveness in PPPs. The comparison between the two constitutional systems for PPPs, which will be the basic framework of this book, can be informative on the design of institutional structures and the shaping and interpretation of applicable constitutional principles.

Having provided a basic overview of the basic points covered in this introduction, we will now proceed to our first chapter, in which we will be discussing our research question in the constitutional system of the UK.

1 Public-private partnerships in the United Kingdom

1. Introduction

Throughout the introductory chapter we highlighted the purpose of this book, which aims to examine the systems of accountability which have been developed for the use of public money in PPPs. As we have clarified, the perspective on which we will focus is that of the criteria of accountability. In this first chapter, we will be discussing the subject of the criteria of accountability and their impact on the broader accountability mechanisms for PPPs within the Economic Constitution of the UK.

The UK has a rich history in the use of PPPs. Starting in the early 1990s, the UK procured important infrastructure, such as hospitals, prisons, and schools, assigning their financing, building, management and operation to private bodies using PPP contracts. In terms of this process, a major criterion of public accountability, which arose from scrutiny of government's use of PPPs, was that of Value for Money (VfM). The criterion of VfM is used to evaluate important aspects of PPPs, and the organs which are entrusted with scrutinising the government use this criterion in the public accountability process. Given the widespread use, and the predominance of the criterion of VfM as a means of public accountability, an important issue which arises is how well the use of the criterion serves the purposes of public accountability for PPPs in the UK Economic Constitution.

The first point from which we will begin our inquiry focuses on the integration of PPPs to the UK Economic Constitution. Specifically, we might ask why UK PPPs, and their criteria of accountability, are matters that need to be examined by the Economic Constitution. What's special about them? Answering this question will be our purpose in the first section, where we will explore the nature and the scope of PPP transactions, and their integration into the UK Economic Constitution. We will note that the expansion of the PFI, which is the typical PPP in the UK, is promoted predominantly through executive initiatives and with limited use of legislation. From the context of the UK Economic Constitution, it is interesting to seek to evaluate the systems of accountability developed for PPPs, with the limited use of legislation. In other words, PPPs are used too much in the UK for the Economic Constitution to be indifferent when it comes to their accountability, especially given their non-statutory promotion.

The second point on which we need to focus explores the nature of public accountability which is promoted with respect to PPPs in the UK. The answer to this second question is far from straightforward and demands an elaborate discussion of the nature of VfM criterion and the functions of accountability which it is designed to serve. As we will argue, the criterion is mainly one of bureaucratic accountability and, further to that, it is a criterion exposed to a substantial degree of subjectivity. This makes it difficult to handle the issues of constitutional public accountability, especially the absence of statutory criteria. In turn, this gives rise to the exercise of normative functions on the part of organs who have no statutory authority in relation to PFIs.

A solution to these problems of public accountability caused by the use of the criterion of VfM could possibly stem from the recognition of an agreement between the PAC and HM Treasury (Treasury) in 1932 as a constitutional convention. This recognition involves the introduction of a positive rule relating to the government, thereby enabling it to use statutory authorisation in cases of major PFI investment involving the transfer of continuing government functions to the private sector. This, we will argue, could be poised to have a positive impact on relativising the weaknesses which are borne by the current system of public accountability for PFI based on VfM, and on the productive integration of the PFI transactions to the UK Economic Constitution.

2.   The integration of PPPs to the Economic Constitution in the UK

We asserted in the introduction to this chapter that a valid point of departure for our enquiry into accountability for PPPs comes from the Economic Constitution. In this section, therefore, we will discuss the nature and scope of PPPs in the UK and their relationship with the Economic Constitution. The specific perspective of the Economic Constitution which we will be using is that which sees the Economic Constitution as a framework of Constitutional Law analysis which focuses upon 'the key constitutional principles and institutional arrangements which may be relevant to the management of the economy'.[1]

2.1.   Nature and scope of PPPs in the UK

The first reason for which PPPs need to be the subject of an inquiry of Economic Constitutional Law draws from their nature and scope, and involves their expanded use and important integration in the provision of public services. PPPs in the UK have mainly been used under the umbrella of PFI.

---

1 Prosser 8.

The Treasury provides us with a good brief definition of PFI, which will serve as a useful starting point:

> The Government introduced PFI in 1992 as a means of harnessing the private sector's efficiency, management and commercial expertise and to bring greater discipline to the procurement of public infrastructure. Under this policy, the private sector was engaged to design, build, finance and operate infrastructure facilities through a long-term contractual arrangement. PFI was introduced to deliver high quality assets and services and better VfM for the public sector. It aimed to do this through the transfer of appropriate risks to the private sector, a clear focus on the whole of life costs of projects and an innovative approach to service delivery. The payment for PFI projects was structured to ensure that the public sector only paid for the services that were delivered.[2]

As was mentioned earlier, PFI is a species of PPPs.[3] The generic term PPP covers a wide range of types of collaboration between the public and the private sectors[4] such as privatisations and contracting-out. PFI differs from privatisations because, in PFI, the public sector retains a significant role in the operation of the project, and it differs from contracting-out because, in PFI, the private sector provides the capital asset as well as the services. The PFI differs from other PPPs in that, in addition to other services it might provide, the private sector also arranges the finance for the project.[5] In a typical PFI project, in addition to its financing, the private sector is responsible for the design of facilities which are necessary to support the provision of the public service, the building of these facilities, and their operation. The public sector determines the output specifications of the project for the fulfilment of which the private sector is responsible. In terms of a PFI project, the public sector does not own the facilities involved, such as the hospital or school which is being built, but pays the PFI contractor a stream of committed revenue payments for the use of these facilities over a period of time specified in the contract. With the expiration of the contract, the ownership of the facility either passes to the public sector, or it remains with the private contractor, in accordance with the provisions of the agreement.

An illustration of a PFI project would be helpful at this point, and we can usefully return to one related to the construction of a hospital which is already familiar to us from the Introduction. In this hospital PFI contract, a private

2 Treasury, *A New Approach to Public-Private Partnerships* 16.
3 House of Commons Research Paper 03/79, 9.
4 House of Commons – Scrutiny Unit, *Private Finance Initative – its Rationale and Accounting Treatment* (2008) 1.
5 House of Commons Research Paper 03/79, 9.

consortium of companies undertake to finance the relevant facility, and design, construct, and operate it, in order for it to meet the outputs provided by an NHS Trust. The Trust could specify the detail required for various outputs, such as the number of patients that the hospital should be able to accommodate, and the types of health-related incidents that it should be able to handle. The Trust would undertake, pursuant to this contract, to pay to the private consortium a specific amount, which is called the 'unitary charge' for the duration of the contract, which would typically be 30 years. Finance for the facility would originate from bank loans – in percentage terms, amounting to 90 per cent – and from equity for the remaining 10 per cent. The private sector would undertake the relevant borrowing, and it would use the unitary payments received by the government in order to cover the resulting financial responsibilities and make a profit.

PFIs are thus long term contractual arrangements, extending for over 20–30 years, and the fact that the private contractor is responsible for the designing, building, financing and operating of the facilities makes him the principal bearer of the risks that might arise during any of these phases.[6] It should be noted, that this transfer of risk between the public and the private sector refers to a type of risk which is contractual, or economic, and it does not cover the risk over the non-provision of the public service to the citizens; the ultimate business risk of the provision of the public service always remains with the government.[7] It is the government which retains ultimate responsibility towards its citizens for the provision of the public service, irrespective of the means – PFI or otherwise – which it selects to provide this service.

As per 31 March 2014, there were 728 PFI projects in the UK, out of which 671 were operational, with a capital value of £56.6 b.[8] The most active departments in terms of PFI activity are those of Health (with 123 projects, worth £12082.9 m), those of the Department of Education (with 168 projects, worth £7799.5 m), others of the Department for Transport (with 62 projects, worth £7878.8 m) and those of Defence (with 41 projects, worth £9042.8 m).

The last few years have witnessed some of the most significant PFI projects.[9] For instance, the PFI contract for the investment in, and improvement of, 42 (out of 44) waste disposal sites in Greater Manchester was launched by the Department for Environment, Food and Rural Affairs (DEFRA) on April 2009 and is expected to be completed in March 2034. Another PFI project, the widening of three-lane sections of the M25, was launched by the Department for Transport in December 2008 and is a contract due to end in November

---

6 Treasury, *Reform of the Private Finance Initiative* 5.
7 NAO, *Managing the Relationship to Secure a Successful Partnership in PFI Projects* (HC 2001–02, 375) 10.
8 Treasury, *Private Finance Initiative Projects: 2014 Summary Data* 3.
9 Treasury, *Whole of Government Accounts: Year ended 31 March 2010* 133.

2038. Similarly, the Private Sector Resource Management of Estate is a PFI project designed to fully manage the buildings for the Health and Safety Executive and Health and Safety Laboratories. This was launched by the Department for Work and Pensions, with the contract starting in May 2005 and finishing 30 years later, in May 2035. The Department of Health has advanced three important PFI projects during the past decade. The first one, in June 2006, had the aim of delivering hospital facilities for University Hospital Birmingham NHS Foundation Trust, and it is expected to be completed in April 2046; the second one, in May 2009, involved the construction of a new and improved Saint Mary's Hospital in Greater Manchester, and was expected to be completed in April 2047, but it has now been confirmed that the public authority is terminating the PFI; the third one began in March 2010, and involves the redevelopment of cardiac and cancer facilities at St Bartholemew's and the London NHS Trust. Four other projects, organised by the Ministry of Defence over the past 15 years, have also been of great importance. One, begun in October 2003, and with an expected end date in February 2039, aims at the provision of a range of satellite services, including the management of existing Skynet 4 satellites; another, begun in February 2004 and with an expected end date in February 2039, involves the redevelopment, rebuilding and refurbishment of Colchester Garrison; a third, begun in March 2006, and which is expected to be completed in April 2041, aims at the rebuilding, refurbishment, management and operation of facilities for service accommodation at Aldershot, Tidworth, Bulford, Warminster, Larkhill and Perham Down; a fourth project, launched in March 2008, and with an expected completion date in March 2035, involves the provision of modern air-to-air refuelling and passenger air transport capabilities.

Therefore, the first reasons for which the PFI deserves to be the subject of an analysis of Economic Constitutional Law centre around the idea that the PFI represents a growing enterprise, absorbing significant amounts of capital and binding them for many years, involving the private sector in a wide range of sectors, and providing the latter with significant roles in the provision of public services. These first reasons, however, are not enough to explain the intricate relationship between the PFI and the Economic Constitutional Law. Further to that, it is important for us to show, by tracing the history of PFI, how the government has managed it historically, and how it has caused the emergence of public organs. This will be the subject of our next section.

2.2.   *The history of the PFI and the emergence of the principal organs*

We have already described a number of initial features which characterise the integration of the PFI to the Economic Constitution. Further to these points, it is necessary to provide a brief history of the PFI, showing how the government has managed PFI, and how it has caused the emergence of new public organs. As we will observe, the foundation of these organs has been directed towards the achievement of economic effectiveness: it has not been aimed at the establishment of external accountability arrangements to the Parliament for the PFI activity of the government, and the consequent commitment of public money.

The collaboration between public and private sectors in the provision of public services, as a priority government agenda, was announced by the then Chancellor of the Exchequer, Norman Lamont, in his Autumn Statement of November 1992. The announcement itself made clear that it was a collaboration, designed around the principle of risk-sharing between the public and private sectors, and aiming to achieve VfM:

> Secondly, the Government have too often in the past treated proposed projects as either wholly private or wholly public. In future, the Government will actively encourage joint ventures with the private sector, where these involve a sensible transfer of risk to the private sector. Thirdly, we will allow greater use of leasing where it offers good VfM.[10]

It is important to highlight that Lamont's announcement came shortly after a long debate over the involvement of the private sector in a highly sensitive area of government activity, namely the one of detention. The involvement of the private sector in the operation of prisons was discussed in Parliament in the later part of the 1980s[11] and, after the prison disturbances of April 1990,[12] the Criminal Justice Act 1991 was enacted, authorising the Secretary of State to contract out the operation of prisons and remand centres.[13]

The policy of partnership between the public and private sectors, under the principles of risk transfer and VfM, was to be pursued in the next years of that government, and in the autumn of 1993, the then Chancellor Kenneth Clarke announced the creation of the Private Finance Panel. It was a body funded by the Treasury, and it consisted of a panel of eight unpaid non-executives.[14] Among its aims was to stimulate greater participation by both the public and private sectors, and to identify new areas of public activity that the private sector could get involved in. Its members originated from the private sector,[15] and the body, although funded by the government,[16] was to act independently

---

10 HC Deb 12 November 1992, vol 213, col 998.
11 HL Deb 3 May 1989, vol 507, cols 141–4; HC Deb 18 February 1988, vol 127, cols 1132–3; HC Deb 21 July 1988, vol 137, col 1281.
12 Allyson Collins, *Prison Conditions in the United Kingdom* (Human Rights Watch 1992) 3.
13 Criminal Justice Act 1991 s 84.
14 Tony Merna and Cyrus Njiru, *Financing Infrastructure Projects* (Thomas Telford 2002) 117.
15 HC Deb 1 November 1995, vol 265, col 260W.
16 HC Deb 21 July 1994, vol 247, col 426W; Appropriation Act 1995 sch B pt 19 class XVII.

from the Treasury.[17] The focus of the Private Finance Panel was the achievement of effectiveness, through the determination of further areas of participation of the private sector. Its tasks were advisory, and not directed towards establishing a mechanism of external accountability of the government. The difference between the advisory and the accountability processes is that the latter involves the possibility of sanctions to the body being held to account. This last function was absent for the Private Finance Panel, which only had an advisory role. This was a pattern set to continue in the next years of the expansion of the PFI.

The policy of public and private partnership as a main government priority was stressed by the Chancellor in the Autumn Statement of 1994,[18] as well as in his speech to the Confederation of British Industry in 1994.[19] Most importantly, it became clear that the Treasury would only give its approval to projects if the option of private finance had been explored and found uneconomic.[20] This standard, termed 'universal testing of public service' was to remain as the basic standard of Treasury approval up until 1997, when – as we will see in time – it was abolished by the new Government.

Throughout the period 1992 to 1997, which was the first period of the implementation of PFI in the UK, 68 PFI projects, worth around £4 bn.,[21] were signed. The subject of PFI received a considerable amount of Parliamentary interest, particularly in the sectors of education,[22] transport,[23] and health,[24] which were to emerge as dominant areas of PFI activity in the years to come.

The implementation of the PFI programme expanded significantly when the new government was elected in 1997.[25] In May 1997, the Paymaster General Geoffrey Robinson, announced that Malcolm Bates, who was then Chairman of the Pearl Group and Premier Farnell, would conduct a review of the PFI

---

17 Philippa Roe and Alister Craig, *Reforming the Private Finance Initiative* (Centre for Policy Studies 2004) 12 (its functions were transferred to the Treasury Taskforce in 1997).
18 HC Deb 29 November 1994, vol 250, cols 1084–5.
19 Mick Hillyard and Robert Twigger, *The Government Resources and Accounts Bill: Bill 3 of 1999–2000* (House of Commons Research Paper 99/97, 1999) 30.
20 Ibid; Yescombe 33; Jane Broadbent, Jas Gill and Richard Laughlin, *The Private Finance Initiative in the National Health Service: Nature Emergence and the Role of Management Accounting in Decision Making and Post-Decision Project Evaluation* (Chartered Institute of Management Accountants 2004) 10; Committee on Economic Affairs, *Private Finance Projects and off-Balance Sheet Debt: Volume 1* (HL 2009–10, 63-I) 10.
21 Treasury Committee, *Private Finance 2: Volume 1* (HC 2012–13, 97) 2.
22 HC Deb 24 January 1995, vol 253, col 168W; HC Deb 31 October 1995, vol 265, col 141W.
23 HC Deb 10 June 1996, vol 279, col 17; HC Deb 26 November 1996, vol 286, col 156W.
24 HC Deb 28 November 1995, vol 267, cols 606–7W; HC Deb 14 May 1996, vol 277, col 416W.
25 Lorna Booth and Vasilisa Starodubtseva, *PFI: Costs and Benefits* (House of Commons Research Paper 6007, 2005) 4.

process. Further to that, Robinson announced the end of the 'universal testing'[26] since he considered it a mechanism which was placing departments under pressure to find ways to involve the private sector in the provision of public services even in cases where this was not possible. However, Robinson immediately clarified that the end of 'universal testing' did not mean that the departments should not expect any increase in their capital budgets, and that the central government expected that they would be able to produce a high level of suitable projects to achieve the aims of PFI.

Significant changes in the organisational level were achieved under the influence of two reviews published by Sir Malcolm Bates in 1997 and 1999 respectively. The reviews themselves were advisory, continuing the theme which we saw earlier when we described the Private Finance Panel; as such they did not constitute a process in which the government was called to account by an external body. The first organisational change around the reviews was that the Private Finance panel was abolished and replaced by the Private Finance Treasury Taskforce in 1997. The Private Finance Taskforce was set up to be the central point of focus for PFI activities in all areas of government, and it included both a project and a policy wing.[27] Through the Taskforce the government promoted a large number of guidance documents, policy statements, technical notes and case studies. Despite the fact that the creation of the Private Finance Taskforce was a step towards centralisation of PFI procurement, acting as an internal hierarchical structure of accountability, its role also performed a decentralising function, given that the Taskforce was responsible for the promotion of procurement skills across the departmental Private Finance Units.[28]

The project wing of the Treasury Taskforce was replaced, in 2001, with Partnerships UK (PUK), following one of the recommendations of the second review of Sir Malcolm Bates. Special provision was made in section 16 of the Government Resources and Accounts Act 2000, in which the Treasury was authorised to incur expenditure 'in respect of the establishment of a body for carrying on public-private partnership business' as well as for investing to such a body. In 2001, PUK took a public-private partnership form itself, with 49 per cent of its stake retained by the public sector and the remaining by private investors. PUK was designed to collaborate with both public and private bodies in order to help them in the process of negotiation of PFI projects.[29] Again, as it was the case with the Private Finance Panel, the mechanism of the PUK which was discontinued in 2010, was one aiming primarily to ensure the

26 Treasury, *Paymaster General Announces Kick-start to PFI (Public/Private Partnerships) – Review of Private Finance Machinery – End of Universal Testing* (News release 41/97, 8 May 1997).
27 Broadbent, Gill and Laughlin 11.
28 Ibid.
29 Graham Allen, *The Private Finance Initiative (PFI)* (House of Commons Research Paper 01/117, 2001) 17.

effectiveness of the PFI, and not one serving as or establishing an external mechanism of accountability for the government to the Parliament.

A final change at organisational level involved the establishment of the Office of Government Commerce (OGC), which was to replace the policy wing of the Treasury Taskforce. The OGC was established as an office of the Treasury, with a status similar to that of an agency.[30] Its aims were to provide policy standards and guidance on best practice in procurement, to monitor and challenge the Departments towards these standards, to promote collaborative procurement across the public sector, to deliver VfM and to provide innovative ways to develop government's commercial and procurement capability.[31] As was the case with previous reforms which we have already seen, the creation of the OGC was for the purpose of economic effectiveness of the PFI which was to be achieved through an advisory process. OGC, like its predecessor, played no part in the establishment of an external mechanism of accountability for the government to the Parliament.

As we may observe, the reforms which were advanced by the government had, as their primary goal, the increase in the economic effectiveness of the PFI, with the introduction of advisory structures which were usually regulated from the centre. The creation of the Private Finance Panel in 1993, the Private Finance Treasury Taskforce in 1997, the OGC in 2000 and PUK in 2001, were all steps aimed at the improvement of effectiveness through the establishment of advisory institutions. None of these steps, however, established a system of external accountability of the government's PFI, through which the government would have to explain and account for its actions in the promotion of the PFI and the consequent commitment of public money to the Parliament.

The first period which witnessed the materialisation of these changes saw a significant expansion in the use of PFI across government procurement. A total of 563 PFI projects reached their financial close by 2003, with a total capital value of £35.5 bn. From this total capital, £32.1 bn.-worth of projects was signed from 1997 to 2003. This is very vividly reflected in the amount of capital investment per year. In 1995 alone, projects amounting to a total cost of £666.8 m were signed. The average capital investment in PFI projects between 1997 and 2003 amounted to £2.6 bn per year.[32] Continuing the trend which we noted earlier with respect to the first period of the implementation of PFI, the most active departments in terms of PFI investment have been those of Transport, accounting for 22 per cent of projects by capital value, that of Health, with a capital investment of £3.2 bn. and 117 PFI projects, that of Education

30 Treasury, *Managing Public Money* (2013) 60.
31 The National Archives: WebArchive: 'About OGC', <http://webarchive.nationalarchives. gov.uk/20100503135839/http://www.ogc.gov.uk/about_ogc_who_we_are.asp> accessed 10 September 2017.
32 Treasury, *PFI: Meeting the Investment Challenge* 19.

and Skills, with a total of 96 transactions worth a total of £2 bn. and that of Defence, with 46 projects amounting to £2.5 bn.

The PFI programme continued to grow and it reached its peak in 2007–08.[33] Throughout this period, one of the most significant changes in the organisational chart of PFI was the transfer of several of the functions which initially belonged to the Private Finance Unit of the OGC, the Treasury Private Finance Unit. Among these functions, which were related to the implementation of the PFI policy across departments and public bodies, one of the most important was the ownership of the written guidance for authorities on how to agree on PFI projects, a document which is commonly known as 'Standardisation of PFI Contracts'. This has been a document of the utmost significance in relation to the regulation of the broader PFI programme, because it contains model terms which are typically included in all new PFI transactions. The idea of the standardisation of these terms, introduced in 1999,[34] as a mechanism of streamlining PFI projects and dropping their cost due to the decrease of negotiation periods, has been central in the promotion of PFIs.[35]

The financial crisis of 2008 significantly affected PFI investment. The reason behind this rests upon the financial structure of these transactions, which is that they are around 90 per cent dependent upon loans normally provided by banks.[36] The immediate effect of the crisis was that the banks were more reluctant to provide loans for investment, especially ones of such significant size. This economic reality was reflected to the normative level with the introduction of Basel III in 2010–11, which significantly increased the amount of reserves which are required to be held by banks, thereby limiting the capital that it is available to them for investment. In this way, the implementation of Basel III has been isolated as one of the reasons for the decline in PFI investment in the years after the crisis.[37]

The government responded to this crisis by tightening the controls over which PFI projects can be let to the market, especially when they involve larger amounts of required capital.[38] In 2011, the Major Projects Authority was introduced and was intended to serve as an additional layer of assurance for PFI

---

33 Lorna Booth and Vasilisa Starodubtseva, *PFI: Costs and Benefits* (House of Commons Briefing Paper 6007/2015) 4.

34 Treasury, *PFI: Meeting the Investment Challenge* 64 and 98.

35 Ibid 11; Treasury, *Reform of the Private Finance Initiative* 10; NAO, *PFI in Housing* (HC 2010–11, 71) 16; Department of Health, *Liberating the NHS: Report of the Arm's Length Bodies Review* (2010) 20.

36 Treasury, *Reform of the Private Finance Initiative* 17.

37 House of Commons Briefing Paper 6007/2015, 4.

38 The impact of the crisis on PPPs and their regulation has been a subject discussed in my interview with Dr Clare McConnell, Partner at Stephenson Harwood LLP (London, UK, 27 July 2013). The interview confirmed, rather than provided, the factual background of this subject used in this section.

projects.[39] It was established as a joint partnership between the Cabinet Office and Treasury in order to contribute to the improvement of major project delivery through 'robust assurance measures'.[40] Through the assurance processes provided in this context, departments are required to submit an Integrated Assurance and Approval Plan for each major project for validation by both the Major Projects Authority and the Treasury.[41] The creation of the Major Projects has its contribution to make to our theme, focusing on the effectiveness of the PFI within a context which lacks mechanisms of external accountability of the government over the promotion of PFI.

A further measure which was taken at organisational level was an overall reform of the PFI as a model of procurement, with the implementation of PF2. In December 2011, Treasury published a call for evidence for a reform of the PFI[42]; it highlighted the basic characteristics of the PFI, and the main problems which have been noted in its operation, including the impact that its dependence upon the banks had after the crisis. This call for evidence resulted in the PF2 model which was announced by Treasury in December 2012, with a report entitled 'A new approach to PPPs'. The new model involved the participation of the public sector as a shareholder at the Special Purpose Vehicle (SPV) which undertakes the project,[43] as well as attempting to attract institutional investors, such as pension funds, to SPV's equity.[44] Although the use of the PF2 is not yet widespread, there are some exceptions, such as the Priority Building for Schools Programme.

Through this brief account of the history of the PFI detailed here, we may conclude that a further reason for which the PFI needs to be targeted for analysis in relation to Economic Constitutional Law is that the government has responded to it with the creation of many regulatory and controlling organs. These regulatory and controlling organs, as we have noted, were designed to promote the economic effectiveness of the PFI, and none of them was established as a mechanism of external accountability, in which the government would have to explain its promotion of the PFI to the Parliament and face consequences.

2.3. *The promotion of PFI by the government and the limited use of legislation*

Apart from the aforementioned reasons, which would lead us to conclude that the PFI is a viable and substantial subject of the Economic Constitutional

39 Treasury, *Major Project Approval and Assurance Guidance* (2011) 3.
40 NAO, *Major Projects Authority Annual Report 2012–13 and Government Project Assurance* (HC 2013–14, 1047) 5.
41 Treasury, *Major Project Approval and Assurance Guidance* 6.
42 Treasury, *Reform of the Private Finance Initiative.*
43 Treasury, *A New Approach to Public-Private Partnerships* 30.
44 Ibid 34 and 80.

analysis, there is another reason which draws its legitimacy from the ways in which the government has promoted PFI. This third reason is that the way that the PFI has been promoted by the government raises legitimate questions around issues of public accountability.

In the first instance, perhaps the best of these issues to isolate originates from the fact that the government has predominantly promoted the PFI by virtue of its inherent capacity to contract, rather than seeking to advance legislation to substantiate this promotion and the consequent commitment of public money. This legislation would have authorised the participation of the government in PFI projects, and it would have provided accountability arrangements for them. However, instead, the basic trend that the government followed was to promote the PFI and commit expenditure to it utilising its inherent capacity to contract, rather than advancing such legislation.

As we mentioned in an earlier section – in which we examined the nature and the scope of PPPs and PFIs – they are contractual arrangements.[45] For this reason, a requirement for their validity is that the participating parties must have the legal capacity to contract in order to participate in them. The PFI contracts of the central government are contracts of the Crown, in which 'the Crown as the indivisible executive authority of the UK is a party, having engaged itself through the instrumentality of Ministers or officials who are servants of the Crown'.[46] The responsibility of the secretaries of state, who are the agents of the Crown in PPPs and other government contracts, is co-extensive.[47]

The contracting power of the Crown to enter a PFI can be based either on the inherent legal capacity of the Crown to contract, or on authorisation by statute.[48] From the perspective of legal requirements, the Crown is considered to have inherent legal capacity to enter into contracts[49] because it is a corporation[50] and, as a corporation, it has the same ability to contract[51] as an individual of age and capacity.[52] For this reason, the fact that there is no legal requirement that a specific statute authorises the Crown to enter into a PFI Contract is

---

45 NAO, *Financing PFI Projects in the Credit Crisis and the Treasury Response* (HC 2010–11, 287) 4.

46 Colin C. Turpin, *Government Procurement and Contracts* (Longman 1989) 83.

47 Rodney Brazier, *Ministers of the Crown* (The Clarendon Press 1997) 9.

48 A. C. L. Davies, *The Public Law of Government Contracts* (Oxford University Press 2008) 86.

49 Colin Turpin and Adam Tomkins, *British Government and the Constitution: Text and Materials* (6th edn, Cambridge University Press 2007) 348.

50 Frederic William Maitland, 'The Crown as a Corporation' in H. D. Hazeltine, G. Lapsley and Percy Henry Sir Winfield (eds), *Maitland Selected Essays* (Cambridge University Press 1936) 104; Janet M. McLean, 'The Crown in Contract and Administrative Law' (2004) 24 Oxford Journal of Legal Studies 129, 131.

51 Reinier Kraakman and others, *The Anatomy of Corporate Law: A Comparative and Functional Approach* (2nd edn, Oxford University Press 2009) 9.

52 Edwin Peel and G. H. Treitel, *The Law of Contract* (12th edn, Sweet & Maxwell 2007) 590.

maintained.[53] The principle that the Crown can be bound by contracts made on its behalf by either ministers, its servants or agents, also derives from the nature of the Crown as a corporation.[54]

Apart from the common law ability of the Crown to enter into contracts, ministers can also be vested with statutory power to enter into contracts. Examples of this practice are the Crossrail Act 2008,[55] the National Health Service Act 2006,[56] the Immigration and Asylum Act 1999,[57] the Education Act 1996,[58] the Criminal Justice and Public Order Act 1994,[59] and the Supply Powers Act 1975.[60]

Despite the option that the government has to formulate its contracting activity by drawing authority from statutes, this practice is considered the exception, rather than the rule, especially with respect to the PFI.[61] For Mark Freedland, the legal and constitutional basis for the PFI is difficult to identify and it seems to be drawn from the predominantly broad, inherent non-statutory powers for the management of the financial business of the state, in conjunction with some statutory framework. This applies in cases such as the NHS, and in the case of specific powers, such as the power of the minister to make statutory orders granting concessions for toll roads under Pt 1 of the New Roads and Street Works Act 1991. He notes, however, that, particularly in the case of the PFI, that even in cases of legislation which is relevant, this legislation takes for granted the capacity of the government to contract, rather than basing this power on a statutory footing.[62] The limited use of legislation in cases of PFI is also documented by Anne Davies, who notes that novel contractual forms have been used, with very limited input by the Parliament, and that this is partly due to the fact that 'the government possesses important non statutory powers to place contracts which escape ex ante Parliamentary scrutiny completely'.[63] Similar observations are made by Marnix Elsenaar[64] and Colin Turpin.[65]

---

53 Colin C. Turpin, *Government Contracts* (Penguin 1972) 19.

54 B. G. Pettet, *Company Law* (2nd edn, Pearson Longman 2005) 131–2.

55 Crossrail Act 2008 s 6(1).

56 National Health Service Act 2006 ss 211(1) and 223(1).

57 Immigration and Asylum Act 1999 s 149(1).

58 Education Act 1996 s 482(1).

59 Criminal Justice and Public Order Act 1994 ss 7(1) and 96(1).

60 Supply Powers Act 1975 s 1(1).

61 The limited use of legislation for PPPs has been one of the subjects discussed in my interview with Professor David Howarth, Professor of Law and Public Policy at the University of Cambridge (Cambridge, UK, 14 March 2016). The interview confirmed, rather than provided, the factual part of this section.

62 Mark R. Freedland, 'Public Law and Private Finance – Placing the Private Finance Initiative in Public Frame' (1998) Public Law 288, 292–3.

63 Davies 86.

64 Marnix Elsenaar, 'Law, Accountability and the Private Finance Initiative in the National Health Service' (1999) Public Law 35.

65 Turpin, *Government Procurement and Contracts* 83; Davies 86.

It is important to note that some legislation which authorises the government to participate in certain PFI projects and which provides for accountability arrangements does exist, and we will discuss its nature later. What we claim here, however, is that the government has predominantly promoted the PFI using its inherent capacity to contract, rather than by advancing such legislation.

The practice of government to contract without seeking the establishment of its contractual authority in a statute can be traced back to a memorandum written in 1945,[66] and which only became available to the public as late as 2003. The memorandum to which we refer here is one written by the then First Parliamentary Counsel, Granville Ram, who, in 1945, highlighted the issue of how far legislation is necessary to authorise any extension of the existing powers of a government department. According to Ram,[67] ministers do not share the same position as a statutory corporation, which is a creature of statute and has no powers except the ones conferred upon it by the statute. Even if a statute has authorised its appointment, a minister may, as an agent of the Crown, 'exercise any powers which the Crown has power to exercise, except in so far as he is precluded from doing so by statute'.[68] He proceeds by arguing that, despite the fact that a minister does not need a statute to exercise his powers, he is only able to pay for any obligations he has undertaken if Parliament votes in favour of payment, as is the case with votes on the Appropriation Act.

The opinions expressed in Ram's memorandum, which has come to be known as 'Ram's doctrine', were used in this way for a period of over 60 years to substantiate the contractual activity of the government without the need for authorising legislation, including the PFI. After the memorandum became public in 2003, it created a considerable amount of academic debate with many differentiated and opposing views. For Lord Anthony Lester and Matthew Weait,[69] 'it is inappropriate for the executive to seek to base the exercise of ministers' and civil servants' powers without Parliamentary authority on medieval concepts of the Crown as a corporation sole'. In supporting their argument, they distinguish government powers into two categories: powers exercised by virtue of government's dominium and powers exercised by virtue of government's imperium. The traditional way in which government exercises its power is by virtue of imperium, which refers to the exercise of government's coercive power. This way of governing, according to Lester and Weait, is appropriately exercised

---

66 Granville Ram, *Memorandum* (1945). The original full text of the memorandum is contained in the Joint Committee on Statutory Instruments, *Eighth Report of Session 2007–08* (HL 2007–08, 47 and HC 2007–8, 38-viii) 16–19. Subsequent page references to the text of the Memorandum will refer to the page number of the report of the Joint Committee.

67 Ram 16.

68 Ibid.

69 Matthew Weait and Anthony Lester, 'The Use of Ministerial Powers without Parliamentary Authority: The Ram Doctrine' (2003) Public Law 415.

through legislation, which is enforceable in the courts. On the other hand, the use of resources by the government, such as money gathered through taxation, in order to advance policies by the government refers to the power of dominium. The aforementioned writers argue that the exercise of coercive powers of dominium without Parliamentary authority, as Ram's doctrine is interpreted to suggest, is unconstitutional and inappropriate.

If we look closely at the argument of these writers, we note that they criticise the practices of the government which proceed without Parliamentary authorisation, but this criticism is focused on the exercise of coercive dominium powers. As for the non-coercive dominium powers of the Crown, however, which include government contracts such as the PFI, they claim that the government may exercise them by virtue of the parcel of freedoms which are provided to any private or public person by the common law,[70] and they do not mention the need for authorisation by law or similar involvement of the Parliament. Margit Cohn,[71] however, disagrees with this view in her own contribution on the subject. She notes that the problem of the exercising of government powers without Parliamentary authorisation is general, and not merely limited to cases of coercive powers; it 'threatens three basic values of proper administrative practice-participation, clarity and accountability'.[72] The legislative process, on the contrary, she claims, has the potential to promote participation of additional interest groups, and it requires that the decision-makers justify their choices to the public. In this way, although Cohn agrees with the conclusions of Lester and Weait – which criticise the practice of the executive not relying on statutory instruments for the exercise of merely the executive coercive functions – she differs from them by suggesting that the dominium powers in general should be the object of legislation, given their extensive use in modern government.[73]

In keeping with Lester, Weait and Cohn, other, subsequent writers have contributed to the discussion of the use of contracts by the government. For Janet McLean, the problem is rooted in the distinction between a public law view of the government, which focuses on constructing state in terms of relationships between organs, and a contract law view of the government which constructs government as a contracting entity.[74] For Turpin there is no need for a specific statute to authorise the Crown to enter contracts[75]; he states simply 'whatever the Crown may lawfully do it may do by means of contract'.[76] For

---

70 Ibid 419–20.
71 Margit Cohn, 'Medieval Chains, Invisible Inks: On Non-Statutory Powers of the Executive' (2005) 25 Oxford Journal of Legal Studies 97.
72 Ibid 102–3.
73 Ibid 111.
74 McLean 129.
75 Turpin, *Government Procurement and Contracts* 19.
76 Ibid 84.

T. C. Daintith, writing on the subject before the New Public Management reforms, the government has discovered means of using its economic strengths to promote policies which should normally be promoted with legislation, without involving the Parliament.[77] When writing on the same subject in 1994,[78] however, he classified the government contracting as belonging to the power of dominium, related to the ability of Government to secure its policy objectives through the use of public wealth.

A further perspective related to the problems of public accountability associated with the extensive outsourcing of government, through contracts or by other means, focuses on the re-examination of the role of law in general, rather than the use of specific authorising statutes in the new system. As we will see later in this chapter, PFI has been utilised as one of the instruments used as part of a broader reform of the government, termed New Public Management (NPM). This has involved a broad outsourcing of government powers, through the creation of agencies, and non-departmental bodies, to name but two. Several interested commentators discuss the problems of accountability in modern administrative and constitutional reality, and the role and function of law. Three particularly significant voices in these debates are Mark Freedland,[79] David Feldman,[80] and Tony Prosser.[81] The analyses promoted by these writers are closer to the framework which we employ in our present work because they seek to determine what are the properties of operation of contemporary governance, as a whole, both in terms of basic principles and constitutional unity. Their focus differs from ours around the issue of context; the context for our discussion over accountability is specifically oriented towards the operation and role of criteria of accountability. A further difference of focus is that they examine, from a holistic perspective, the problem of public accountability in the modern system, while our contribution is directed specifically to considerations of public accountability relevant to PFIs.

For Freedland, writing as early as 1994, when the NPM system had only been implemented for a few years, there are major concerns around whether the contractualised government could protect individual rights as completely as the existing Public Law framework. A detailed expression of his concerns, which span from employment law and extend to the offering of high standards of services, Freedland proposes that these issues are solved through an extended understanding of the concept of the Rule of Law.

77 Terence Daintith, 'Regulation by Contract: The New Prerogative' 32 Current Legal Problems 41, 41–2.
78 Terence Daintith, 'The Techniques of Government' in Jeffrey Jowell and Dawn Oliver (eds), *The Changing Constitution* (3rd edn, Oxford University Press 1994) 209–36.
79 Mark R. Freedland, 'Government by Contract and Public Law' (1994) Public Law 86.
80 David Feldman, 'The Limits of Law: Can Laws Regulate Public Administration?' in B. Guy Peters and Jon Pierre (eds), *The SAGE Handbook of Public Administration* (SAGE Publications 2012) 279.
81 Tony Prosser, *The Economic Constitution* (Oxford University Press 2014).

In Feldman's contribution to the discussion, he lays down seven key principles which could serve as a point of reference in the contemporary system: norms are an important aspect of the idea of bureaucratic rationality; we should not assume that administrators always treat legal norms as having greater authority over other norms; not all legal norms are judicially enforceable; virtually all power-conferring rules must be legal, because a non-legal rule cannot make lawful the action of a public authority which interferes with people's legal rights and freedoms; law may exercise different functions; for administrative law to be effective in fostering good administration it must command respect and support from administrators; legality and respect for rights are two important bases for legitimacy of all governmental action and of public administration. By Feldman's reckoning, although the courts are supposed to play a role in the operation of the system, this role could in some cases sit uneasily with the goal-driven principles of good administration.[82] Judicial review would serve, according to Feldman, in setting the general standards over which the administrative systems would operate.

We have provided a basic overview of Prosser's theory in the Introduction.[83] He discusses the problems of accountability related to modern government in terms of the framework which we also employ in the present chapter, in other words, the framework of Economic Constitution. In discussing the dynamics of the Economic Constitution in the UK, Prosser makes a map of institutions which compose the network of economic governance, and he assesses the functions of Parliament and the courts in holding the government to account. In the normative perspective of his work, apart from assessing how well the network of institutions succeed in promoting the values of scrutiny and accountability,[84] he assesses the values of accountability, transparency and deliberation in the institutions themselves, as well as the external accountability of these institutions to Parliament, the Courts and to other forms of administrative justice. The focus of his enquiry into the Economic Constitution is achieved within the context of the broader machinery of government, and is analysed in networks and organs of accountability, such as the Treasury, the Parliament, the Courts, and other, different agencies.

As we mentioned earlier, these commentaries focus on a holistic evaluation of public accountability within the system of contemporary governance. Our present focus is purely the PFI, which – as we will see – is an instrument of NPM. Alongside this, our interest lies in examining the impact that the criteria of accountability have upon the public accountability of the PFI. It is a controversial assertion that the challenges to public accountability, which are caused by the practice of the government contracting without statutory authorisation, are more critical in the case of PFI contracts than in other governmental contracts. The reasons for this are found in the wide use of PFI which involves – as

82 Feldman 351–2, 357.
83 See our Introduction pp. XXX–XXX[orig. 7–9].
84 Prosser 18–19.

we have seen – a more substantial involvement of the private sector in the provision of public services than in other government contracts. With the absence of statutory authorisation in PFI contracts, a very important means of public accountability is lost, due to the absence of the substantial weight wielded by legislation as a tool of public accountability.

This exposition completes our account of the reasons why the PFI needs to be researched from the perspective of Economic Constitutional Law, which processes and protects issues of public accountability in the economic organisation of government. The government has promoted PFI on a large scale, and it has involved large amounts of money as well as an important and unprecedented integration of the private sector in the provision of public services. This promotion has resulted in the creation of a number of important government organs which were founded in order to regulate and control the PFI, focusing primarily upon the promotion of economic effectiveness rather than upon the creation of external mechanisms of accountability. Further to that, the government predominantly promoted the PFI using its inherent capacity to contract, rather than by seeking to found this promotion on legislation.

3.   PFI and the notion of public accountability

In order to explore the issues of public accountability which arise from the limited use of legislation for the promotion of PPPs, it is necessary to refer to the concept of public accountability itself. As we discussed in the Introduction, the notion of public accountability is one of the most discussed and contested in existing literature. From this context, we selected a narrow perspective of accountability which, according to Bovens, is defined as 'a relationship between an actor and a forum, in which the actor has an obligation to explain and to justify his or her conduct, the forum can pose questions and pass judgement, and the actor may face consequences'.[85] As we clarified in the Introduction, the actor is the government, the forum is the legislature and the conduct is the use of public money for PFI by the government.

The voting of legislation is a process in which the government, having the position of an actor, when introducing the respective bill, will have to answer Parliament's questions. Parliament has the position of the forum. The government will be required to answer the questions of the Parliament, and explain its rationale in giving the specific content of the bill. If this rationale does not convince Parliament, or the forum of accountability, the government, or the actor, will have to face the consequences, which are the rejection or modification of the bill by the Parliament when enacting it into law. These are important consequences for a government, because they reflect something significant, which is its political status. Therefore, it can be asserted that the

---

85 Bovens, 'Analysing and Assessing Accountability: A Conceptual Framework' 450.

voting of legislation qualifies as a form of accountability, in which the government has the position of the actor, while the Parliament has the position of the forum.

The main aspect of accountability involved in the voting of legislation is the political form of public accountability, which is defined by Bovens as the accountability exercised by the political representatives to the cabinet of ministers.[86] In its constitutional dimension, political accountability focuses on preventing the unaccountable exercise of power by the elected leaders, and aims to limit and control the tendency of the executive to concentrate more and more power.[87]

As we have seen, the limited use of legislation in the promotion of the PFI impacted in precisely this way upon the constitutional dimension of political accountability for these transactions. The reason why is that, with the predominant use of the inherent contractual powers of the Crown – instead of the statutory authorisation – the Parliament lost an important means of constitutional public accountability, namely, the enactment of legislation. In this way, the doctrine of the inherent contractual capacity of the Crown permitted the government to make a large number of PFI contracts, to commit important public expenditure to them, and even to construct a complete machinery dedicated to tracking the effectiveness of these transactions, with limited input by the Parliament in the form of legislation.

We have already argued that legislation has a limited role in the promotion of PFI, and we may now proceed in our exploration of the system of accountability which is typically used in PFI.

3.1. PFI and the accountability structures of the NPM

We have noted, in the previous subsection, that the PFI does not use legislation as a basic mechanism for its public accountability. The question which we are left with refers to the determination of the mechanism of public accountability used instead of the legislation. The determination of this mechanism for PFI requires that we view the PFI as one of the instruments of the NPM.

PFI is one of the instruments of the NPM,[88] which, as we detailed earlier, was introduced as a progressive move towards the end of the 1980s in the UK to replace the older system of governance, which has often come to be referred to as 'bureaucratic'. A fundamental distinction which can therefore be made

---

86 Ibid 455.

87 Bovens, Schillemans and Hart, 'Does Public Accountability Work? An Assessment Tool' 225.

88 Mark Bovens, 'The Integrity of the Managerial State' (1996) 4 Journal of Contingencies and Crisis Management 125, 131; R. A. W. Rhodes, 'The New Governance: Governing without Government' (1996) 44 Political Studies 652, 658; Michael Brereton and Michael Temple, 'The New Public Service Ethos: An Ethical Environment for Governance' (1999) 77 Public Administration 455, 460.

from the outset is of that between PFI as an instrument of NPM and traditional procurement methods, as means of procurement used by the bureaucratic system of governance.

The NPM was based on seven concepts. These were the hands-on professional management in the public sector, the establishment of explicit standards and performance measures, greater emphasis on output controls, the gradual disaggregation of units in the public sector, greater competition in the public sector, emphasis on private sector styles of management practice, and emphasis on greater discipline and parsimony in resource use.[89] These broad concepts were implemented through a set of specific policies, which focused on the ideas of achievement of objectives; efficiency, adaptation, direction, innovation, effectiveness, self-interest and profit.[90] In contrast to those NPM policies, the bureaucratic model was focused on the ideas of compliance with rules, adherence to a Due Process, anticipation, assumption of responsibilities, formalism, legality, vocation, and public interest.

The distinction between the two systems, as described in the previous paragraph, materialises a distinction between the concepts of public administration and public management. The former focuses on rules, the latter on objectives. The former focuses on due process, the latter on efficiency. The former focuses on legality, the latter focuses on effectiveness.

The first point which readily attracts our attention in this distinction relates to the role of law in the bureaucratic system: the law provides the backbone of accountability in this model, because most of the concepts which we mentioned, such as the adherence to due process and legality, presuppose a legal system which establishes rules for their operation. In contrast to that, the concepts on which the NPM is based depend more on the idea of economic efficiency and effectiveness and less upon the idea of following established procedures and legal rules. Public administration focuses on rules, while public management focuses on objectives.[91] Public administration focuses on due process, while public management focuses on efficiency. Public administration focuses on legality, while public management focuses on effectiveness. This distinction reveals the basic question on which people and organs are held accountable in each one of the two systems. In the bureaucratic system, the basic question of accountability would be 'Did you follow the rules?' while in an NPM system, the basic question of accountability would be 'Did you operate achieving effectiveness and efficiency?'

89 Christopher Hood, 'A Public Management for all Seasons?" (1991) 69 Public Administration 3, 4–5.
90 Jan-Erik Lane, 'Will Public Management Drive Out Public Administration?' (1994) 16 Asian Journal of Public Administration 139, 144.
91 Ibid.

Inextricably linked with this important distinction is the distinction of the role that the audit performs in each system, as a means of accountability. In the bureaucratic system, where, as we have seen, the idea of adherence to rules is dominant, the audit will seek to establish whether the public funds were spent appropriately, in other words, whether the amount spent is equal to the amount authorised by the law and whether it was spent following the spending intentions authorised by that law. In an NPM system, where the idea of achieving effectiveness is dominant, the audit as a means of accountability will seek to establish whether the public funds were spent effectively. In this way, the bureaucratic system will use audit as a means of accountability, but it is typically an audit of propriety. So, to summarise, while the NPM system uses the audit as a means of accountability, this is primarily as a performance audit.

The importance of the effective use of capital in the NPM is also manifested in case law from the 1990s, in which decade the NPM reforms were advanced in the UK. One example of a characteristic decision is that of the *Pergau Dam* case.[92] The substantive issue of the case was whether the Secretary of State acted lawfully, by deciding to provide economic assistance for the construction of a hydro-electric facility in Malaysia, despite the fact that the project was uneconomical. This aid was to be based on a provision of the Overseas Development and Co-operation Act 1980 which provided, in its section 1(1) that:

> The Secretary of State shall have power, for the purpose of promoting the development or maintaining the economy of a country or territory outside the UK, or the welfare of its people, to furnish any person or body with assistance, whether financial, technical or of any other nature.

Among other matters, the court processed the issue of whether the intention of the minister to grant aid based on the grounds that a refusal would be damaging for UK credibility, was relevant. The court held that 'whatever the Secretary of State's intention or purpose may have been, it is, as it seems to me a matter of the courts and not the Secretary of State to determine whether on the evidence before the court, the particular conduct was, or was not, within the statutory purpose'.[93] In this way, it did not matter – according to the court – whether the minister was moved by considerations aiming at the economy of the transaction or by political considerations which were related to the credibility of the UK. What mattered to the court was whether the contribution that the minister authorised was put towards an investment which was 'sound'. The fact that the Act did not provide directly for the purposed development to be 'sound' was irrelevant, according to the Court, given that if Parliament had intended

---

92 *R v Secretary of State for Foreign and Commonwealth Affairs, Ex parte World Development Movement Ltd.* [1995] 1 W.L.R. 386.
93 Ibid 401 H.

to grant authorisation to the minister to provide aid on development which was unsound, it would have been expected to have clearly provided so.[94] The court held that:

> Accordingly, where, as here, the contemplated development is, on the evidence, so economically unsound that there is no economic argument in favour of the case, it is not, in my judgment, possible to draw any material distinction between questions of propriety and regularity on the one hand and questions of economy and efficiency of public expenditure on the other.[95]

Given that the investment in this particular case was unsound, the act of the minister to authorise the government aid was unlawful. Ian Harden argues that the decision of the court to provide a rule of constitutional principle, according to which 'the proposed spending by the executive of money voted by Parliament is unlawful if, in relation to the object for which the money has been provided, no reasonable minister could think that the proposed spending represented VfM'.[96] Harden clarifies that the principle does not signify that the public law principles require that every spending decision is the best VfM; however, according to him, the principle lies on a minimum which has to be achieved in government action.

The court-decision of *Pergau Dam* did not result, as Prosser notes,[97] in a quick expansion of judicial review of economic decision-making, and the courts did not return to the principle of illegality because of lack of VfM. In our view, the significance of the case lies in the fact that it mirrored the changing reality between the traditions of the bureaucratic and the NPM systems. This is, as we have mentioned, the transition between a system which would have its accountability arrangements based on the idea of adherence to rules, and a system which would focus its system of accountability on the economic performance achieved. The case of the *Pergau Dam* is, in some sense, a hybrid between the two different rationales: the court attempted to project the values of the previous system (adherence to rules) and the values of the new (achievement of economic effectiveness).

There exists, we have shown, a marked distinction between the mechanisms of public accountability in the bureaucratic system and in the NPM. Accountability differs fundamentally between a traditional procurement project, which is a creature of the bureaucratic model, and a PFI project, which is an instrument of NPM. In the traditional forms of procurement, the subject of

---

94 Ibid 402 A.
95 Ibid 402 D.
96 Ian Harden, 'Value for Money and Administrative Law' (1996) Public Law 661, 662.
97 Prosser 252.

accountability would be whether the rules and the procedures have been followed, and audit would tend to verify whether the sums which were spent were spent appropriately. On the other hand, on a PFI setting, performance audit as a means of accountability would seek to establish whether the monies which were spent on the project were so spent achieving the maximum possible effectiveness.

But what are the specific questions which the performance audit would seek to establish in a PFI project? The answer to this requires us to delve a little deeper into the concept of performance audit as it is defined by the auditors themselves. According to The International Organisation of Supreme Audit Institutions (INTOSAI),

> Performance Auditing is concerned with the audit of economy, efficiency and effectiveness and embraces: a. Audit of the economy of administrative activities in accordance with sound administrative principles and practices, and management policies; b. Audit of the efficiency of utilisation of human, financial and other resources, including examination of information systems, performance measures and monitoring arrangements, and procedures followed by audited entities for remedying identified deficiencies; and c. Audit of the effectiveness of performance in relation to the achievement of the objectives of the audited entity, and audit of the actual impact of activities compared with the intend impact.[98]

As we notice from the definition, crucial for the measurement of performance audit are the ideas of economy, efficiency and effectiveness. These three concepts compose the notion of VfM, and each one of them has its own definition. Economy is defined by the NAO as 'minimising the cost of resources used or required (inputs) – Spending less'. Efficiency is defined as 'the relationship between the output from goods or services and the resources to produce them – spending well'. Finally, effectiveness is defined as 'the relationship between the intended and actual results of public spending (outcomes) – spending wisely'.[99] For the Treasury, 'PFI should only be pursued where it represents VfM in procurement'.[100]

---

98 INTOSAI Auditing Standards 1.0.38 and 1.0.40.
99 NAO, 'Assessing Value for Money' <https://www.nao.org.uk/successful-commission ing/general-principles/value-for-money/assessing-value-for-money/> accessed 10 September 2017.
100 Treasury, *Value for Money Assessment Guidance* (November 2006) 7. The dynamics of the use of VfM have been discussed in my interview with John Garrity, Head of the Central Private Finance Unit at the Department for Communities and Local Government and with Mr Paul Sadgrove, Senior Official at the Department for Communities and Local Government (London, UK, 5 December 2012). The interviews confirmed, rather than provided, the factual part of this section.

VfM is a compendious term covering a wide range of features within the PFI project, beginning from the strategic analysis, all the way through the tendering, the contract completion, the pre-operational implementation, the early – and late – operational phases, with all the steps that these phases involve.[101] In this way, it will be used to verify the economy, efficiency and effectiveness of the decision to proceed with the project, and the validity of the reasons for choosing the PFI route over a more traditional procurement structure. It will be used in determining both qualitative and quantitative rationales for the project. Additionally, it will be used to assess the quality of the governance arrangements which are in place and for the establishment of a required form of consultation over the project, as well as for the establishment of the need for the use of external advisers. In the tendering phase, VfM will inform the output specifications of the project, and it will be used by the Authority to clarify the balance between the flexibility and price of the proposed deal. It will inform the Authority over the need for innovation and the range of solutions which will be considered. It will be used to assess the skills that a team will need to maintain throughout the tendering, and will be the point of reference in the criteria assessing the quality of the bids. In the phase of contract completion, VfM criteria will be used to assess whether the contract meets the business requirements of the authority, and to ensure that the project strategy and outcome are still in line with the business needs of the authority. It will inform the evaluation of which alternatives have been re-evaluated and eliminated, as well as the standard this re-evaluation will operate from. It will assess the contract management techniques, and the procurement management. In the pre-operational implementation phase, VfM will inform the baselining of service provision, as well as that a good standard of post-procurement evaluation has been carried out. It will be a standard of reference to the assessment of the effective oversight exercised, as well as guaranteeing that the skills transfer within the public sector has been correct. In the early operational phase, VfM will inform the evaluation of whether the use of the asset fits the purpose of the contract, and the Authority will use it as a point of reference in maintaining that the procurement route is still the optimal. Similarly, it will be used to assess the operation of governance structures and the appropriate skills level for the Authority's team. Finally, in the mature operational phase, VfM will be the point of reference in the improvement of performance through the previous operational phases, and will ensure that the governance skills are still appropriate.

As we noted in the previous sub-section, the UK government practice of establishing PFI contracts without Parliamentary authorisation has a negative impact in the political accountability for the PFI, in its constitutional, democratic

---

101 NAO, *A Framework for Evaluating the Implementation of Private Finance Initiative Projects: Volume I* 8–9.

and learning functions. With the observation that VfM is the predominant criterion for public accountability for PFI, the question this begs is how well this criterion operates to serve the goals of public accountability. It is to this issue that we will now turn.

3.2. *The operation of VfM as a criterion of public accountability in PFI*

VfM – as we saw earlier – is used as the predominant means of accountability in the system of public accountability for the PFI. The issue is of particular significance, given that the government promotes PFI with limited use of authorisation by the law, markedly impacting on the public accountability of these transactions.

The first significant factor which should be noted about the criterion of VfM is that, as a criterion of audit, it is classified under the administrative or bureaucratic species of public accountability. According to Bovens, the various mechanisms of financial accountability which have resulted from the audit explosion of the NPM belong to the administrative function of public accountability which aims to provide 'regular financial and administrative scrutiny',[102] and which, exactly like the criterion of VfM, includes not only 'the probity and the legality of public spending, but also its efficiency and effectiveness'.[103] This means that there is an incompatibility between the gap which is created with the limited use of statutory authorisation and the use of VfM as a predominant criterion of accountability. The foundation for this incompatibility depends upon the fact that the limited use of authorisation by the statute impacts on the political and constitutional form of accountability, while the criterion which is used cannot – theoretically – fill this gap, because it is designed to address an administrative form of accountability.

Apart from this, however, the criterion of VfM is a highly unstable one, and we can readily observe this if we look closely at the way in which it is constructed and the history of its use. We have already seen how VfM is considered to encompass three notions, those of economy, efficiency and effectiveness. These three concepts were first used as the components of a notion which is broader in the reform of local government in 1982. The Local Government Finance Act 1982, which established the Audit Commission, provided in its section 27 that the Audit Commission will undertake or promote studies 'on the economy, efficiency and effectiveness in the provision of local authority services and of other services provided by bodies whose accounts are required to be audited (. . .) or on the financial management of such bodies'. The trend for perceiving economy, efficiency and effectiveness as one concept, the concept of VfM, is

---

102 Bovens, 'Analysing and Assessing Accountability: A Conceptual Framework' 456.
103 Ibid.

also apparent in US practice of the same period and the work of the US General Accounting Office was the first to analyse VfM in the three components of economy, efficiency and effectiveness.[104] The National Audit Office Act 1983 used the same three terms to assign to the C&AG the task of performing VfM evaluations and the Treasury and the NAO, in their reports, refer to the three points of economy, efficiency and effectiveness as one: VfM.[105]

The importance of the concept of VfM behind the promotion of the PFI programme has been fundamental,[106] not only on the previously-described level of public accountability, but also because it has contributed a great deal to the shaping of the government's basic argument with respect to PFI. It was argued that this, PFI, promised to be an instrument of procurement better able to secure VfM than traditional procurement methods.[107]

The construction of the criterion of VfM refers to six determinants which fulfil the three components of efficiency, effectiveness and economy.[108] These determinants are the risk transfer, the long-term nature of contracts, use of output specifications, competition, performance measurement and incentives and private sector management and skills. The possibility of achieving a satisfactory level in these six determinants is calculated in PFI with a twofold analysis which includes, first, the calculation of a benchmark cost of providing the specified service under traditional procurement (this is known as public sector comparator, or PSC) and, second, the comparison of this benchmark to the cost of providing the service under PFI.

104 Rowan Jones and M. W. Pendlebury, *Public Sector Accounting* (4th edn, Pitman Publishing 1996); Kathryn Hollingsworth, Fidelma White and Ian Harden, 'Audit, Accountability and Independence: the Role of the Audit Commission' (1998) 18 Legal Studies 78, 79; R. Glendinning, 'The Concept of Value for Money' (1988) 1 International Journal of Public Sector Management 42.

105 Treasury, *The Green Book: Appraisal and Evaluation in Central Government* (2003); Treasury, *PFI: Meeting the Investment Challenge*; NAO, *Highways Agency – Procurement of the M25 Private Finance Contract* (HC 2010–11, 566).

106 Jane Broadbent and Richard Laughlin, 'The Role of PFI in the UK Government's Modernisation Agenda' (2005) 21 Financial Accountability & Management 75, 86; Jane Broadbent and Richard Laughlin, 'Control and Legitimation in Government Accountability Processes: the Private Finance Initiative in the UK' (2003) 14 Critical Perspectives on Accounting 23, 39–40; Istemi Demirag and Iqbal Khadaroo, 'Accountability and Value for Money: a Theoretical Framework for the Relationship in Public–Private Partnerships' (2011) 15 Journal of Management & Governance 271, 274.

107 Allyson M. Pollock, David Price and Stewart Player, 'An Examination of the UK Treasury's Evidence Base for Cost and Time Overrun Data in UK Value-for-Money Policy and Appraisal' (2007) 27 Public Money & Management 127; Allyson M. Pollock and David Price, 'Has the NAO Audited Risk Transfer in Operational Private Finance Initiative Schemes?' (2008) 28 Public Money & Management 173; Darrin Grimsey and Mervyn K. Lewis, 'Are Public Private Partnerships Value for Money? Evaluating Alternative Approaches and Comparing Academic and Practitioner Views' (2005) 29 Accounting Forum 345.

108 Grimsey and Lewis 354.

The PSC includes four components: the Raw PSC, which is the cost of the capital, the transferable risk, the retained risk, and subtraction of competitive neutrality (in effect, the return of part of the capital by the private sector to the public through taxes). Once the Net Present Value (NPV) of both PSC and PPP has been prepared and adjusted to a comparative basis, then a comparison of the two is made and VfM is considered to exist in the PPP option when the net present value of private sector supply is less than the net present value of the base cost of the service, adjusted for the cost of risks to be retained by the government, cost adjustments for transferable risk and competitive neutrality effects.

A decision on whether VfM exists or not tends to depend on the result of the comparison between the two NPVs: the NPV of the PSC and the NPV of the cost of providing the service under PFI, as the relevant critical literature has highlighted.[109] There is a considerable amount of fluidity in these calculations. This derives mainly from the following factors: first, in contrast to the cost of PFI, which is the price given by the private bidder, the PSC is a hypothetical construction and it can be subjective[110]; second, the PSC component of 'risk transfer' is especially vulnerable to subjectivity since there is no generally accepted method to calculate it[111] and this feature has been criticised on the grounds that the consequential fluidity in its construction has led to its use in covering over differences between the real costs of the projects[112] in the VfM comparison. Third, the NPV as a measure is theoretically subjective because of its high mathematical exposure to discount rates. While in PPPs, the Government has attempted to cover the theoretical problems associated with the reliance on discount rates by providing a fixed percentage of them, this has resulted in a great deal of capitalisation of the differentiations among the varied discount rates in the calculation of risks retained and/or transferred, because the variation of the discount rates are risks of the project.[113] The valuation of risks is, however, a fluid construction, with no generally

109 Jane Broadbent, Jas Gill and Richard Laughlin, 'Evaluating the Private Finance Initiative in the National Health Service in the UK' (2003) 16 Accounting, Auditing & Accountability Journal 422, 426.

110 Grimsey and Lewis 358; John Quiggin, 'Risk, PPPs and the Public Sector Comparator' (2004) 14 Australian Accounting Review 51, 52; Akintola Akintoye and others, 'Achieving Best Value in Private Finance Initiative Project Procurement' (2003) 21 Construction Management and Economics 461, 463.

111 Allyson M. Pollock, Jean Shaoul and Neil Vickers, 'Private Finance and "Value for Money" in NHS hospitals: a Policy in Search of a Rationale?' (2002) 324 British Medical Journal 1205, 1208.

112 Malcolm Sawyer, 'The Private Finance Initiative: the UK Experience' (2005) 15 Research in Transportation Economics 231, 237.

113 This issue has gathered a considerable amount of literature. See indicatively: Edward J. Zajac and Cyrus P. Olsen, 'From Transaction Cost to Transactional Value Analysis: Implications for the Study of Interorganisational Strategies' (1993) 30 Journal of Management Studies 131, 137; James F. Oehmke, 'Anomalies in Net Present Value Calculations' (2000) 67 Economics Letters 349; Broadbent, Gill and Laughlin, 'Evaluating the Private Finance Initiative in the National Health Service in the UK' 428; Declan Gaffney and others, 'PFI in the NHS – Is There an Economic Case?' (1999) 319 British Medical

accepted mathematical method to calculate it and therefore the use of NPVs is a factor which increases fluidity in the judgement of whether VfM has been achieved.

These observations would not be of value if the difference between the two NPVs was generally substantial. The reality – instead – is that, in PPPs, the numerical values of the two NPVs tend to be very close,[114] and therefore slightly different estimations can substantially influence the decision over who will provide the project: the public sector or a private contractor.

Having highlighted the main characteristics of the use of the criterion of VfM, we will turn our attention to the resulting consequences arising from the public accountability of PFI.

4.   The impact of the use of VfM as a basic point of reference in the public accountability for PFI

The use of the criterion of VfM as a basic point of reference for the accountability of PFI, as we saw previously, raises two issues: the first is that it is a criterion designed for the administrative function of public accountability, while the predominant problem in the public accountability for PFI is in the constitutional dimension of accountability. The second is that, even as a criterion of the administrative function of public accountability, it is highly unstable and subjective. In this section, we will analyse the consequences of these two issues in the public accountability for PFI.

In order to determine and evaluate these consequences, the first step which we need to take is to construct an institutional map of the basic organs which participate in the auditing system of accountability for PFI.

4.1.   *The basic organs of public accountability in*
PFI and their functions

The basic mechanism of public accountability for the PFI in terms of performance, or VfM, audit is based on the predominant role of the C&AG. The C&AG is considered an officer of the House of Commons[115] and he exercises his activities heading the NAO. The NAO comprises of nearly 880 staff[116] who are independent of the government, and their basic task is to help the C&AG to perform his functions.[117]

Journal 116, 118; Paul Grout, 'The Economics of the Private Finance Initiative' (1997) 13 Oxford Review of Economic Policy 53.

114 Grimsey and Lewis 362.
115 National Audit Office Act 1983 s 1(2); Budget Responsibility and National Audit Act 2011 s 12(2).
116 NAO, *Cabinet Office – Managing Early Departures in Central Government* (HC 2010–12, 1795) 1.
117 Budget Responsibility and National Audit Act 2011, sch 3, s 2(2). The importance of the NAO for PPPs has been one of the subjects discussed in my interviews with Sadgrove and

The C&AG, which is the basic instrument for the VfM auditing system of accountability, is responsible for reporting his findings and conclusions to a committee of the Parliament known as the Public Accounts Committee (PAC). His responsibilities include certifying that the money voted by Parliament to be spent by the government for the PFI has been spent as intended by the Parliament, and also that this money is spent in a way which safeguards VfM.[118] With the latter authority, in other words, the verification that the money has been spent with VfM, which is statutory, the C&AG acquires the role of the basic performance auditor for the PFI, and he exercises this authority writing reports. These reports about VfM examine the activities of a government department which has used PFI; they are presented to the PAC. The PAC will then use the findings of these C&AG reports to hold the government (usually through an Accounting Officer) accountable.[119]

Both the C&AG and the PAC are envisioned by the legal instruments which established their powers as organs of scrutiny and audit. With respect to the NAO, Section 6 of the National Audit Act of 1983 provides that:

> The C&AG may carry out examinations into the economy, efficiency and effectiveness with which any department, authority or other body to which this section applies has used its resources in discharging its functions.

This section is invoked uniformly by the NAO in the introduction to its reports on PFI, which state:

> [The C&AG] has statutory authority to report to Parliament on the economy, efficiency and effectiveness with which departments and other bodies have used their resources.[120]

With respect to the PAC, the basic properties of its power to hold the executive to account are provided on the standing order[121] of the committee:

> There shall be a select committee to be called the Committee of Public Accounts for the examination of the accounts showing the appropriation

Garrity (see note 166) and Mrs Pamela Gachara of the Association of British Insurers (London, UK, 19 June 2013). The interviews confirmed, rather than provided, the factual background of this subject.

118 National Audit Office Act 1983 s 6; Government Resources and Accounts Act 2000 s 6; NAO, *Annual Report 2012* (2012) 8–9; Oonagh Gay, *Comptroller and Auditor General* (House of Commons Briefing paper SN/PC/4595, 2008).

119 See for example: NAO, *The Performance and Management of Hospital PFI Contracts* (HC 2010–11, 68); PAC, *PFI in Housing and Hospitals* (HC 2010–11, 631).

120 NAO, *Financing PFI Projects in the Credit Crisis and the Treasury Response* I (unnumbered).

121 Standing Order No 148, HC 2015–16.

of the sums granted by Parliament to meet the public expenditure, and of such other accounts laid before Parliament as the committee may think fit, to consist of not more than sixteen members. The committee shall have power to send for persons, papers and records, to report from time to time, and to adjourn from place to place.

We may conclude from the above use of key operative phrases ('may carry out examinations', which is used for the NAO, and 'for the examination', which is used for the PAC), these two bodies are envisioned by the legislation and the Parliament respectively to be organs scrutinising the activity of government. They are expected to examine and analyse the accounts of public bodies which are using PFI as means of procurement, and ask these public bodies to explain their actions. They illustrate, in other words, 'a relationship between an actor and a forum, in which the actor has an obligation to explain and to justify his conduct, the forum can pose questions and pass judgment, and the actor may face consequences'.[122]

The system described above, based on the central role of the C&AG to perform VfM audit, is the central point for reference of the auditing system of accountability for the PFI, and there are a large number of the C&AG's reports on PFIs which have led to PAC examinations of accounting officers, and which we will examine in detail later. It has to be noted that it is the typical, default system for accountability over financial matters in general, and that it has been in operation since the latter half of the nineteenth century. The Office of the C&AG was established with s.1 of the Exchequer and Audit Departments Act of 1866. Similarly, the PAC, was established in the same decade, in 1861, with Standing Order No. 90. In this way, although the C&AG-PAC are a predominant system of accountability for the PFI, they are not a system of accountability which was designed and created for it.

4.2.   The use of VfM audit for the exercise of a normative regulatory function

As we showed earlier, both the NAO and the PAC are envisioned by the instruments which created them as organs of audit scrutiny. The C&AG, as a performance auditor, must examine the PFI activities of government departments, then write a report and present it to the PAC. As an organ of scrutiny, the PAC must process this report and on its basis, hold government departments accountable for their use of the PFI.

This function of examination and scrutiny is largely descriptive and evaluative. An indicative example of this descriptive and evaluative function is the 2010 NAO report on the financing of PFI projects in the credit crisis.

---

122 Bovens, 'Analysing and Assessing Accountability: A Conceptual Framework' 449.

A description of the way that the credit crisis has affected the PFI opens this NAO narrative:

> In late 2007, market confidence in the providers of this credit insurance collapsed, leaving PFI projects in the UK without access to capital markets. (. . .) The bank loan market, however, continued to function. (. . .) The collapse of Lehman Brothers in September 2008 led to a halt in loan syndication, continuing throughout 2009. This limited the ability of banks to make new PFI loans.[123]

The NAO goes on to describe how – in relation to PFI – the Treasury acted towards the changing conditions of the crisis:

> The Treasury's initial response was to evaluate the extent of the impact of financial 1.2 market disruption on PFI projects (. . .) Departments were, therefore, already being advised to seek a right to bring about a refinancing and obtain an increased share of any gains. In October 2008, this was made a formal amendment to standard contract terms.[124]

Accompanying these descriptive goals, the NAO evaluated how well the Treasury promoted VfM in PFI in the first years of the crisis:

> The Treasury intervention on the Greater Manchester Waste project was timely and helped to reactivate the market. The Treasury chose this project because it clearly met its lending criteria. (. . .) Although helpful in moving projects in the pipeline towards contract closure, Treasury lending created increased risks for the public sector parties.[125]

These patterns of the descriptive and evaluative role of the NAO are present in most of his reports related to PFI, both general and specific. In similar ways, in the 2012 report dedicated to the equity investment in privately financed projects, the NAO described the government's utilisation of equity in PFI projects[126] and evaluated it in terms of VfM.[127] Similarly, in another important general study of the NAO in 2011, which focuses on the lessons from PFI and other similar projects,[128] the report describes how the government has acted with respect to recent PFI projects[129] and evaluated how effectively VfM has

---

123 NAO, *Financing PFI Projects in the Credit Crisis and the Treasury Response* 5.
124 Ibid 14.
125 Ibid 17–18.
126 NAO, *Equity Investment in Privately Financed Projects* (HC 2010–12, 1792) 6, 14, 15, 21, 22, 23.
127 Ibid 8, 9–10, 15, 21.
128 NAO, *Lessons from PFI and Other Projects*.
129 Ibid 5, 8, 19, 20, 21, 24.

been promoted.[130] On similar grounds, in the report of 2001 dedicated to the management of the relationship between the public and the private sector in PFI,[131] the NAO describes[132] and evaluates[133] how authorities manage their relationship with private contractors.

In an earlier sub-section, we developed our argument that there are two negative properties of the criterion of VfM with respect to its use as a main point of reference for the PFI. The first of these properties is that it is a criterion designed to cover administrative accountability, while the main weakness of the promotion of the PFI is in the area of political accountability. The second negative property is that it is fairly unstable and subjective. As we will see, these two properties lead the C&AG and the PAC – both of which have been envisioned as organs of audit scrutiny and examination – to perform, beyond the descriptive function that their role involves. This means that they also demonstrate a normative function.

4.2.1. *The concept of normativity*

The descriptive and evaluative function of the NAO and the PAC and the distinction from the normative role of these bodies, corresponds largely to the distinction proposed by H. Kelsen, in his classic text 'The Pure Theory of Law', between the terms 'sein' (meaning 'is') and 'sollen' (meaning 'ought to'):

> The difference between is and ought cannot be explained further. We are immediately aware of the difference. Nobody can deny that the statement 'something is' – that is, the statement by which an existent fact is described – is fundamentally different from the statement 'something ought to be' – which is a statement by which a norm is described. Nobody can assert that from the statement that something is, follows a statement that something ought to be, or vice versa.

In this way, the reports of the NAO and the PAC contain not only a dimension of 'what it is', which as we saw earlier makes them better attuned to the audit role, but also a dimension of 'what ought to be'.

4.2.2. *The normative function of the NAO*

Before passing to the detailed examination of the normative function of the NAO with respect to the shaping of the criterion of VfM in PFI, it is essential that we focus our attention on the analysis of the basic position of this body

---

130 Ibid 5, 6, 7, 8, 18, 23.
131 NAO, *Managing the Relationship to Secure a Successful Partnership in PFI Projects.*
132 Ibid 2, 4, 5, 7, 9.
133 Ibid 3 and 33.

in relation to the criterion. These basic positions are developed in the report entitled 'Review of the VfM Process for PFI', which was written for the consideration of the House of Commons' Treasury Select Committee in 2013. Despite the fact that the report does not contain any explicit normative points, it is of fundamental importance because it provides the framework within which these normative points are developed; we will give closer scrutiny to these later in this section.

The first point made by the report is that the model used by the government to assess PFI[134] has a number of features which favour PFI in comparison with traditional procurement options.[135] The reasons for its strength relate to the mathematical construction of the model, which stresses advantages of PFI which are due to the fact that it can spread payments over time,[136] and that it does not take into account the cost of government borrowing.[137] The NAO has suggested that 'to assess whether it would be cheaper to use government borrowing rather than PFI on individual projects would require structural change to the model'.[138] Given that the choice of model on VfM matters,[139] the report suggests that transparency is important: the stakeholders have to be clear on which questions they want any given model to answer.[140]

A further fundamental point with respect to the criticism of the model of VfM in PFI used by the Treasury rests upon the fact that there is not adequate data to support key assumptions of the model.[141] The model provides an adjustment of the optimism bias of the evaluating teams, based on the premise that evaluating teams tend to be over-optimistic about the prospects of the project they are procuring. A further adjustment to the model for VfM of PFI provided by the Treasury was related to tax. Given that, under the assumption of the model, the SPV which undertakes the PFI will have to pay its taxes in the UK, the model for the calculation of PFI had to take into account this tax, which would be paid to the government. An additional adjustment made to the calculations of PFI under the Treasury approach, relates to changes which were reasonably expected to occur in projects with long procurement times, and this is referred to as flexibility adjustment. The final adjustment provided by this specific model of VfM focuses on the residual value of the asset. In cases where the public sector comparator produces a result which is significantly lower than the PFI option, then the residual repair costs are added to this result to reflect the cost of bringing the asset to PFI standards of quality at the end of

134 See earlier section 3.2.
135 NAO, *Review of the VFM Assessment Process for PFI* 5.
136 Ibid 9.
137 Ibid.
138 Ibid.
139 Ibid 28.
140 Ibid 5.
141 Ibid 30–31.

the project. According to the report of the NAO, the assumptions on which these adjustments of the VfM model of the Treasury are based can have a significant impact on the decision to use PFI. However, they depend, as the NAO argues, on the estimations of the evaluating teams, and they are not founded on empirical evidence, and departments have failed to gather the necessary data to substantiate them.[142]

A further point of criticism that the NAO exercises on the application of the model of VfM by the government is that the evaluation teams over-rely on it.[143] They treat the model as a pass-fail test on whether they should use PFI, instead of using the model as *one* of the means with which to inform their decisions. The roots of this rationale are provided by the reasons for which the Treasury implemented what is, in the opinion of the NAO, a simplified model of estimating VfM. These reasons are that the Treasury intended to ensure a simple model was present to ensure that economic analysis would take place; to focus the efforts of the authorities in their questioning of the assumptions of the model; to reduce the cost that a more complicated model would involve due to the predicted need of over-reliance of public authorities to advisers; and to promote consistency in the way that the public sector evaluates PFI.[144]

The following raft of characteristics provide a picture of this model of simplicity advocated by the Treasury. This NAO report envisions how the determination of VfM might be achieved:

> Along with the Treasury, we would like to see modelling used more intelligently. This requires models to be designed in such a way that they aid a project teams' understanding of their project and allow the team to explore the relationships between the project's various elements. (. . .) In accordance with Treasury guidance, we would like to see project teams treat models as just one element, set alongside other factors, which informs their judgement about which contracting approach offers best VfM.[145]

But precisely which are those factors that the NAO would like the government to include in the construction of the VfM model? The answer to this question is complicated and it can be approached through a collective estimation of the patterns which can be distinguished in the normative points made by the NAO in its reports on PFI, both the general and the specific ones. We will now move on to consider the determination of these normative patterns.

A predominant category of normative points in the NAO reports focuses on prescribing directions of financial policy which need to be followed for the achievement of VfM in PFI. The first tendency which can be observed in these

142 Ibid 5.
143 Ibid 31.
144 Ibid 13.
145 Ibid 36.

normative points centres around the NAO's belief that VfM can be achieved with the evaluation of many procurement and finance options:

> Where there are material changes, such as project costs increasing by 15 per cent, the Treasury should require that the department re-evaluate the project. This re-evaluation should assess all the benefits, and potential loss of benefits, of continuing the project in its current form, compared to other available options, including other forms of procurement.[146]

Evidence of this tendency can be found in many points across the reports of the NAO on PFI. In this way, the departments are prescribed to 'assess a range of financing options, including all public finance or part public and part private finance' during procurement,[147] and the Treasury 'should continue to consider how a greater mix of finance sources (. . .) can be used to finance infrastructure projects'.[148] At the same time, the Treasury is prescribed to use its review of PFI 'to consider alternative models of PPPs'.[149] It is asked to 'work with departments in identifying a range of alternative methods for delivering infrastructure and related facilities services, building on the lessons learnt from PFI, to maximise VfM for Government'.[150] The Department of Defence is urged to undertake 'a more robust appraisal of alternative options at the point where it makes the decision to programme the funding', where PFI is an option.[151] In similar terms, the Department of Transport is prescribed to explore all the reasonable options when designing its procurement and to 'include a full evaluation of the benefits and disadvantages of credible options', without being exclusively anchored to the PFI model.[152]

A second theme which can be distinguished in the prescriptions of the NAO to the Treasury and the Departments is one related to the adoption of a centralised approach to PFI. This centralised approach is expressed in a variety of ways, extending from the central guidance of contracting activities to the adoption of a framework of understanding all the different PPPs contracts by all bodies of the public sector as a portfolio. The following are just a selection of examples:

> The centre, working together with projects, should develop a timetable for when key actions and decisions are needed on both sides and should keep this under review during procurement.[153]

146 NAO, *Financing PFI Projects in the Credit Crisis and the Treasury Response* 12.
147 Ibid 12.
148 Ibid.
149 NAO, *Equity Investment in Privately Financed Projects* 9.
150 NAO, *Lessons from PFI and Other Projects* 10.
151 NAO, *Ministry of Defence – Delivering Multi-Role Tanker Aircraft Capability* (HC 2009–10, 433) 9.
152 NAO, *Highways Agency – Procurement of the M25 Private Finance Contract* 11.
153 NAO, *PFI in Housing* 10.

The Department needs to balance its cost of providing central support with the effective management of risk to the VfM achieved by the Trusts. The Trusts are capable of managing the contacts day-to-day but the Department's Private Finance Unit is best placed to provide them with support on complex issues and coordinate activities by Trusts. The Department should (. . .).[154]

The Treasury should adopt a portfolio approach to refinancing, with input from the relevant departmental team, so that individual authorities do not exercise any right to a refinancing on a piecemeal basis.[155]

The theme of stressing centralised models of regulation and planning as a way to achieve VfM is pursued in various other points across the NAO's reports. The Treasury is prescribed to prepare guidance for departments on 'how to challenge bidders' proposed equity returns more rigorously at the procurement stage'.[156] Beyond this, it also prescribes that the Treasury should analyse the lessons from the crisis and 'it should use these lessons to prepare a contingency plan for how departments should handle future market disruption affecting procurement plans'.[157] Keeping with this same theme, the NAO prescribes that, when there is departmental sponsorship at the local level, the departments 'should set out, at the earliest stage, the roles and responsibilities of all parties and the criteria for central intervention'.[158] Furthermore, the Departments and the Treasury are prescribed to 'be proactive in identifying those local authorities that have the potential to secure savings and offer them the support they need to bring savings into fruition'.[159] Similarly, the NAO prescribes for the OGC – a central body which was responsible for the implementation of policy in PFI – that it 'should take forward its plans to consider further guidance on contract management issues'.[160] Apart from the points that we outlined in the previous paragraph, the portfolio approach is also promoted in the recommendation to the Treasury, which must work with the cabinet office to determine 'what changes should be made to harness the Government's buying power'.[161] The same approach is advanced by the NAO, which prescribes that the department should ensure that its collection of data should 'ensure it caters to the needs of the PFI portfolio'.[162]

A further theme in the prescriptions of the NAO to the Treasury and departments relates to the view that VfM can be achieved with the adoption of a

154 NAO, *The Performance and Management of Hospital PFI Contracts* 9.
155 NAO, *Financing PFI Projects in the Credit Crisis and the Treasury Response* 13.
156 NAO, *Equity Investment in Privately Financed Projects* 9.
157 NAO, *Financing PFI Projects in the Credit Crisis and the Treasury Response* 12.
158 NAO, *Lessons from PFI and Other Projects* 11.
159 NAO, *Savings from Operational PFI Contracts* 8.
160 NAO, *Managing the Relationship to Secure a Successful Partnership in PFI Projects* 6.
161 NAO, *Lessons from PFI and Other Projects* 11.
162 NAO, *The Performance and Management of Hospital PFI Contracts* 10.

skills, knowledge and expertise transfer model. The NAO asks the government to ensure that there is constant development of the commercial skills of the public sector, and that there is appropriate transfer of skills by the private to the public sector:

> The Cabinet Office and departments should urgently report on progress in implementing our previous recommendations to improve commercial skills and expertise in central government.[163]
>
> The Treasury, working with the Cabinet Office and other government departments with policy responsibility in this area, should consider how the positive disciplines which investors have brought to PFI projects, such as taking immediate steps to enforce contracts and/or resolve problems, could be applied to publicly managed projects.[164]

This idea of prescriptions focusing on the improvement of skills as a means to achieve VfM appears in many other points within the reports. In this way, the NAO provides that, throughout the procurement stage 'authorities must develop a staffing and training plan to ensure that they have staff with the right skills and experience to manage the contract after it has been let'.[165] Furthermore, according to the NAO, the departments and the authorities 'should adopt a spend-to-save approach by devoting skilled resources to actively managing their operational contracts'.[166] Remaining with this theme of focus on skills, the Department of Defence is also prescribed to continue maintaining the knowledge and skills needed to manage the Future Strategic Aircraft contract in the future. In order to achieve this 'the Department must continue its succession planning activity to ensure that knowledge is retained within the team, by implementing document handover processes and ensuring the availability of staff with appropriate experience and expertise'.[167] Similarly, the Department of Health is requested to 'ensure it retains its expertise and makes that expertise available to all Trusts'.[168] The Department of Transport is also requested to 'build its in-house commercial and technical capability for considering alternative technical solutions, procurements and contract management, and reduce its reliance to advisers'.[169]

An additional pattern which can be distinguished in the exercise of the normative role of the NAO relates to the importance of frequent and intensive monitoring, collection and distribution of data as a means to achieve VfM in

---

163 NAO, *Lessons from PFI and Other Projects* 10.
164 NAO, *Equity Investment in Privately Financed Projects* 10.
165 NAO, *Managing the Relationship to Secure a Successful Partnership in PFI Projects* 6.
166 NAO, *Savings from Operational PFI Contracts* 8.
167 NAO, *Ministry of Defence – Delivering Multi-Role Tanker Aircraft Capability* 9.
168 NAO, *The Performance and Management of Hospital PFI Contracts* 9.
169 NAO, *Highways Agency – Procurement of the M25 Private Finance Contract* 11.

PFI. The policy promoted by NAO with respect to management of data is based on the ideas of transparency and dissemination of information across the public sector. It is unequivocal about this in the following report:

> Too often, Government has failed to identify, collect and use the data it needs to help support decision-making and secure the best VfM. Greater focus should be given to the types of data that should be gathered to improve decision-making, who should collect them and the cost of collection.[170]
>
> [Trusts] need transparency and clarity over contractors' costs and activities. They should seek to obtain and use open book accounting arrangements.[171]
>
> [The department should increase] the frequency of monitoring returns from local authorities during the construction phase to at least quarterly, rather than six monthly, from contract award until asset construction is complete and all facilities are operational.[172]

The same theme of the focus on the improvement of data monitoring, collection and distribution as a means to increase VfM is reinforced in further points of NAO reports. The NAO prescribes that 'the Treasury should establish with investors a standard form of disclosure so that, on each change of shareholder, authorities become entitled to equity sales data sufficient to judge the rate of return to the seller'.[173] The NAO also prescribes the prerequisites of data collection, insisting that: 'Data should be collected where it adds demonstrable value, and supports decisions but only where the benefits clearly outweigh the costs and burden of collecting data'.[174] The Departments and authorities in general 'should maintain up-to-date corporate records and knowledge of their contracts to support effective contract management'.[175] With respect to transparency, 'the Treasury should ensure transparency in public reporting of operational PFI-related savings'.[176] The Department of Defence is prescribed to 'mandate an appropriate degree of openness and transparency from the bidders in its tender documentation, including access to key supply data'.[177] Developing this theme of monitoring, the Department for Communities and Local Government 'should develop a framework for collecting and using data which will aid

170 NAO, *Lessons from PFI and Other Projects* 9.
171 NAO, *The Performance and Management of Hospital PFI Contracts* 10.
172 NAO, *Department for Environment, Food and Rural Affairs – Managing the Waste PFI Programme* (HC 2008–09, 66) 8.
173 NAO, *Equity Investment in Privately Financed Projects* 10.
174 NAO, *Lessons from PFI and Other Projects* 9.
175 NAO, *Savings from Operational PFI Contracts* 8.
176 Ibid 9.
177 NAO, *Ministry of Defence – Delivering Multi-Role Tanker Aircraft Capability* 10.

evaluation of the programme and help local authorities benchmark their projects'.[178] Similarly the NAO prescribes that the Department of Health 'should require contract and site specific data, and improve its quality of data collection, to ensure that it caters to the needs of the PFI portfolio'.[179]

In this way, we can now answer the question which we set earlier, relating to the ways that the NAO envisions the structuring of a VfM model of PFI. It is a model which takes into account many alternative procurement models and financing options and one which is largely centralised, treating government contracting as a whole, and governmental activity shaped with a significant centralised role. It is also a model which uses a portfolio approach in projects. Furthermore, it is a model based on the development of commercial skills by departments and their transfer among the different contracting organs, as well as between the public and the private sector. Finally, it is a model which is very demanding in terms of data, and which is required to permit the ample monitoring needed by the different organs controlling each other, based on the principles of open-book accounting.

Having developed the main themes of the normative preposition of the NAO with respect to the understanding of the promotion of VfM in PFI, it is now time to turn our attention to the normative preposition of the PAC on the same subject.

4.2.3. The normative function of the PAC

A role which is similarly normative to the one of the NAO is exercised by the PAC, and we will now see the patterns of the normative prepositions of this organ with respect to PFI.

One distinct pattern which can be distinguished relates to the PAC's conviction that private contractors should not make excessive profits from the PFI. When excessive profits are being made, this is considered an important indication for the PAC that the government is receiving poor VfM, and that there should be mechanisms to share these profits with the government. The PAC commentary on this is unequivocal:

> Partial information we have seen suggests initial investors can quickly make high profits from selling on their shares in PFI projects, indicating that the taxpayer may be getting a poor deal in the original PFI contracts. The Treasury should introduce arrangements for sharing gains on the sale of PFI equity shares in new PFI projects.[180]

---

178 NAO, *PFI in Housing* 9.
179 NAO, *The Performance and Management of Hospital PFI Contracts* 10.
180 PAC, *Lessons from PFI and Other Projects* 5.

The focus on profits made by private contractors is a theme running through many other normative points of the PAC reports. The PAC prescribes that 'the Treasury should introduce standard contractual arrangements to recover excess cash left after contractors have met bank requirements; and share in other investor returns above defined levels'.[181] The Treasury is also prescribed to 'review whether investors are systematically realising gains on share sales, as well as refinancing debt'.[182] Concentrating on the same theme, the PAC provides that the OGC 'should complete its current review of contractors' returns as a matter of priority'[183] and that it 'should introduce its new guidance on refinancing as quickly as possible to ensure that authorities have contractual rights to share in refinancing gains'.[184] The departments are prescribed to 'look at the scope for more ways to share the savings from efficiency gains with contractors'.[185] Furthermore, the departments are prescribed that they 'should not agree to high returns unless high risks are actually being borne'.[186]

A further theme which can be distinguished in the reports of the PAC on PFI relates to the idea of centralisation. As was the case with the same concept in the NAO reports, the notion of centralisation – as advanced by the PAC – covers both the increased role of central organs in the regulation of PFI, as well as the handling of the PFI projects as a portfolio:

> The Treasury should identify groups of projects which could be refinanced at the same time. This portfolio approach would enhance the public sector bargaining position, reduce transaction cost and increase potential gains.[187]
>
> The Treasury should take ownership and responsibility for overseeing the government portfolio. It should ensure that decisions about whether, and how, individual projects should proceed are based on each project's impact on the total portfolio's value and risk, and the relevant department's delivery capability and existing portfolio projects.[188]
>
> The Treasury, in consultation with investors, should identify and address the sources of cost and delay. The Treasury should consider whether best value would be secured by greater centralisation of the procurement of PFI projects.[189]

---

181 PAC, *Equity Investment in Privately Financed Projects* (HC 2010–12, 1846) 6.
182 PAC, *Financing PFI Projects in the Credit Crisis and the Treasury's Response* (HC 2010–11, 553) 6.
183 PAC, *Managing the Relationship to Secure a Successful Partnership in PFI Projects* (HC 2001–02, 460) 6.
184 Ibid.
185 PAC, *Contracting out Public Services to the Private Sector* (HC 2013–14, 777) 8.
186 PAC, *PFI Construction Performance* (HC 2002–03, 567) 13.
187 PAC, *Financing PFI Projects in the Credit Crisis and the Treasury's Response* 5.
188 PAC, *Major Projects Authority* (HC 2014–15, 147) 5.
189 PAC, *Equity Investment in Privately Financed Projects* 6.

The PAC has also noted that 'central government's management of private sector contracts has too often been very weak',[190] and it prescribes the Cabinet office 'to provide guidance on departments on how to ensure that contractors, of any size, have effective governance and internal controls over all aspects of their operations'[191] and to 'provide governance and support to ensure the terms of contracts properly protect both the taxpayers' interest and the service users' legitimate expectations'.[192] Similarly the Treasury is prescribed to 'intervene after any significant changes in costs to assess whether PFI deals should go ahead'.[193] The same concept of centralisation is advanced, with the important role of the Major Projects Authority which 'should work with departments to improve their project planning, and ensure that they have devoted sufficient attention to the planning phase before seeking approval'.[194] Even more indicative of the importance of centralisation in the PAC's normative patterns relates to the content of the Major Project Authority's reviews and the importance they should wield. In this case, the PAC prescribes that 'the Authority's reviews should clearly set out whether the project should continue, be stopped or reset, and Treasury should ensure the recommendation is adhered to'. With respect to the Health Trusts and PFI, the relevant report stresses that 'local authorities will be at a disadvantage compared to the private sector if the Departments do not provide sufficient central support. Central departments need to have adequate resources to: (. . .) offer support to them'.[195] Remaining with the theme of stressing the vital importance of centralised guidance, the PAC prescribes that the DEFRA 'should make better use of its position and expertise to support local authorities in negotiating PFI contracts and achieve VfM for local taxpayers'.[196]

An additional normative pattern which can be distinguished in the PAC's reports relates to the tendency to prescribe the consideration of traditional procurement methods rather than the extensive use of the PFI. For the PAC, the default procurement position should never be the PFI; instead, the default position for procurement should be the conventional type, and PFIs should only be used when certain requirements are fulfilled. The committee expresses this in many ways, including the promotion of what is known as the unbundling PFI model, in which the private sector is only involved with the construction of the asset, but not with its operation.

190 PAC, *Contracting out Public Services to the Private Sector* 6.
191 Ibid 7.
192 Ibid.
193 PAC, *Financing PFI Projects in the Credit Crisis and the Treasury's Response* 5.
194 PAC, *Major Projects Authority* 6.
195 PAC, *PFI in Housing and Hospitals* 6.
196 PAC, *The Department for Environment, Food and Rural Affairs: Oversight of three PFI Waste Projects* (HC 2014–15, 106) 6.

The use of PFI has been based on inadequate comparisons with conventional procurement which have not been sufficiently challenged. The justification of proceeding with PFI in the future needs to have regard to a range of important factors. Assessment of new projects should include: (. . .) the potential for improvements in the delivery of conventional projects.[197]

The Treasury must consider unbundling the service delivery from PFI contracts or find ways to lower the cost of financing the operating period.[198]

The Treasury should consider separately the procurement process for building the asset from that for providing a service to ensure that operation and maintenance are based on actual requirements.[199]

The tendency to support the role of conventional procurement methods rather than the PFI is also expressed with the link clearly being made between the high returns of the investors and the perceived inadequacy of the PFI: 'The excessively high returns being made by the investors in PFI projects are further evidence that the previous emphasis on using PFI is inappropriate for the future'.[200] For this reason, the PAC prescribes that the Treasury 'should ensure that all new business cases demonstrate whether private finance is used because it is better than a conventional procurement and not because it is the only financing alternative'.[201] Enlarging on this, the PAC urges departments that 'any decision to use PFI should be taken after careful analysis of the advantages and disadvantages of each form of procurement for the particular project'.[202] In addition, the PAC stresses to the Department for Communities and Local Government and to the Department for Health that 'there is no clear evidence to conclude whether PFI has been demonstrably better or worse VfM for housing and hospitals than other procurement options'.[203] The PAC prescribes them to 'prepare whole-programme evaluations which assess PFI against alternative procurement routes using clear VfM criteria'.[204] Similarly, with respect to the Department for the Environment, Food and Rural Affairs, the PAC criticises its insistence in promoting PFI in waste management, and requires it to consider 'other forms of support (. . .) to ensure that local authorities are not locked into projects that provide more capacity than required and are very expensive'.[205]

---

197 PAC, *Lessons from PFI and Other Projects* 5.
198 PAC, *Financing PFI Projects in the Credit Crisis and the Treasury's Response* 5.
199 PAC, *Equity Investment in Privately Financed Projects* 6.
200 Ibid 5.
201 Ibid.
202 PAC, *PFI Construction Performance* 13.
203 PAC, *PFI in Housing and Hospitals* 6.
204 Ibid.
205 PAC, *The Department for Environment, Food and Rural Affairs: Oversight of three PFI Waste Projects* 4.

A further theme in the prescriptions of the PAC relates to the request for transparency and an open-book approach in contracting. A focus on transparency can be found in various normative points of within PAC's reports, and it reaches new heights with its insistence that the Freedom of Information Act 2000 (FOI) is applied to as much of the contractors' data as possible, receiving priority over concerns around commercial confidentiality:

> The Treasury and the Cabinet Office must also reconsider how private companies providing public services, whether or not in the form of PFI, can be bound by the provisions of the Freedom of Information Act.[206]
>
> Transparency on the full costs and benefits of PFI projects to both the public and private sectors has been obscured by departments and investors hiding behind commercial confidentiality. Freedom of information should be extended to private companies providing public services. The Treasury should define commercial confidentiality and the exceptional circumstances where it applies.[207]
>
> Open-book accounting needs to be standard practice in government contracts and needs to be used.[208]

The normative theme of transparency is stressed in various other points of the reports of the PAC related to PFI. The PAC prescribes that the 'Cabinet Office should: (. . .) explore how the FOI regime could be extended to cover contracts with private providers, including the scope for an FOI provision to be included in standard contract terms'.[209] It prescribes that 'neither the Cabinet Office nor departments should routinely use commercial confidentiality as a reason for withholding information about contracts with private providers' and that 'a clear explanation for any exceptions must be provided and the Cabinet Office should check that departments are treating disclosure as their default position'.[210] Additionally, the PAC prescribes that 'in future all contracts should have appropriate mechanisms, such as (. . .) open-book accounting'[211] and that 'assessments of new projects should include a more transparent and complete comparison of alternative funding'.[212] The theme of transparency is also promoted in relation to the activities of the Major Projects Authority from which 'the Committee expects the complete and transparent disclosure of information on project status, (. . .) and will expect to receive annual updates on the performance of projects in the Authority's portfolio'.[213] The prescription to the MPA

---

206 PAC, *Equity Investment in Privately Financed Projects* 5.
207 PAC, *Lessons from PFI and Other Projects* 5–6.
208 PAC, *Contracting out Public Services to the Private Sector* 5.
209 Ibid 5–6.
210 Ibid 6.
211 PAC, *Managing the Relationship to Secure a Successful Partnership in PFI Projects* 6.
212 PAC, *Lessons from PFI and Other Projects* 5.
213 PAC, *Assurance for Major Projects* (HC 2012–13, 384) 6.

to publish more information on the projects is so important for the PAC that it stands 'even if this means reviewing the government's transparency policy'.[214] Following the same theme of transparency the Department for Communities and Local Government is prescribed to 'ensure that the choice of procurement route, PFI or otherwise, is based on clear and transparent VfM criteria'.[215]

The final normative theme which can be distinguished in the prescriptions of the PAC focuses on the skills which are required for the public authorities to effectively manage their PFI projects. According to the PAC, the cultivation of these skills will lead to a decrease of the reliance of the authorities upon private advisors and will, as a consequence, improve the VfM of PFI transactions. They state that:

> The Major Projects Authority and the Treasury should identify and publish lessons from PFI experience to improve the public sector's commercial skills across all projects.[216]
>   Staff responsible for managing PFI projects must be equipped with the appropriate skills.[217]

Whilst focusing on skills, the PAC prescribes that the OGC (which is now abolished) 'should introduce further guidance and training on the key principles of contract management'[218] and that the departments should pursue 'staff continuity between the procurement and the subsequent management of the contract'.[219] The Cabinet Office and the departments are also prescribed to 'invest in developing experience and expertise in commercial issues and contract management'[220] and the former 'should explicitly require departments to ensure that those who are responsible for day-to-day contract management have sufficient authority, commercial skills and expertise'.[221] Similarly, with respect to the role of the Major Projects Authority, the PAC prescribes that the Executive Director of the Authority 'should be responsible for co-ordinating the (. . .) deployment of staff with relevant project management skills across government',[222] while the MPA as a whole is prescribed to 'develop and implement a tailored approach to improving the project delivery skills and awareness of ministers, shadow ministers, and permanent secretaries'.[223] Insisting on the importance of skills, the PAC also prescribed the Agency responsible for

---

214 PAC, *Major Projects Authority* 7.
215 PAC, *PFI in Housing and Hospitals* 5.
216 PAC, *Lessons from PFI and Other Projects* 6.
217 PAC, *Managing the Relationship to Secure a Successful Partnership in PFI Projects* 6.
218 Ibid 7.
219 Ibid.
220 PAC, *Contracting out Public Services to the Private Sector* 10.
221 Ibid.
222 PAC, *Assurance for Major Projects* 5–6.
223 PAC, *Major Projects Authority* 6.

procuring the M25 PFI contract 'to develop its own commercial skills so that, in major procurements, it can challenge its advisers effectively, evaluate the quality of the advice received, and engage only those advisers who provide good VfM'.[224]

In a way which echoes our approach to the normative patterns of the NAO in the previous section, we will now move on to use them to construct the basic normative proposition of the PAC towards the construction of the concept of VfM in PFI. The promotion of VfM for PFI involved, at the outset, an understanding of PFI as an exceptional procurement path, with the conventional procurement methods as the standard. Secondly, it must involve the avoidance of excessive private sector gains, as the PAC considered these indicators of poor value for the public. Further to that, pursuing VfM must involve focus on transparency and open-book accounting, as well as the prioritisation of transparency over concerns of commercial confidentiality. Finally, a condition for the promotion of VfM should involve the cultivation of appropriate skills in the public sector, thereby increasing the likelihood of effective negotiation with private contractors, and thus obviating or limiting dependence on private advisors.

With the completion of the normative account of the PAC, we are now in a position to fully weigh up our findings around this examination of the role of the VfM criterion of evaluation over the system of accountability for the PFI.

4.2.4.   *The impact of the use of VfM as a criterion of accountability and the role of other Parliamentary committees*

As we saw earlier, the government's practice to contract with limited use of Parliamentary authorisation has a negative impact on the political and constitutional species of public accountability for PFI, which focus on the accountability of the executive to the representatives of the citizens and the prevention of unaccountable exercise of power by the government. The predominant system of public accountability in PFI is based on the utilisation of performance audit with the criterion of VfM, and it fails to address the weakness of public accountability resulting from the limited use of legislation. There are two reasons for this: the first is that the criterion of VfM is one of bureaucratic, and not constitutional, accountability. It was designed to focus on the evaluation of economic performance. The second reason is that, even as a criterion of bureaucratic accountability, it is exposed to a substantial degree of subjectivity. These two reasons lead the two basic organs of public accountability for PFI – the C&AG and the PAC – to exercise a normative function. This normative function is not expressly authorised by the legislative instruments, which merely provide a role of scrutiny for both organs of accountability.

224 PAC, *M25 Private Finance Contract* (HC 2010–11, 651) 5.

In this way, the accountability of the PFI is directed towards economic performance, neglecting other areas which might otherwise be facilitated by a fully functioning system of political accountability. Such areas would address issues which, although they are not associated with economic performance, are important for the PFI. The following issues are among them: the sensitivity of particular government activities, such as defence and detention, to private involvement; the suitability for projects involving important access to citizens' private data for private operation; the acceptable level of control of the private sector over the determination of public policy through the delivery of PFI services; the impact of the involvement of the private sector in the level of trust of the citizens towards the government; the acceptability of the expanded use of alternative means of resolution towards the role of the courts which is promoted by the PFI; the role of the banking institutions in accumulating information over a wide array of government services assigned to companies which these institutions finance in PFI arrangements; the environmental commitment of the PFI as opposed to traditional procurement methods, such as in the cases of waste facilities or the involvement in nuclear operations and anti-flooding projects.

All these issues, and many more which might be included under the umbrella of a process of constitutional accountability, are lent limited status and importance due to the fact that the predominant system of accountability for the PFI through VfM audit mainly focuses on economic performance. Given that the two predominant organs of public accountability for the PFI – the C&AG and the PAC – are organs directed to the evaluation of economic performance, the major question remains as to whether or not there are other committees in Parliament which have a positive role in addressing the issue of constitutional accountability of the PFI resulting from the limited use of legislation.

Despite the fact that, out of all the Committees in Parliament, the PAC is the singular one to have focused on the PFI issue, there are two committees which have also examined PFI, albeit in a comparatively minor way. The first of these is the Treasury Committee, which has produced three relevant reports since 1999. The other, the Economic Affairs Committee of the House of Lords, has produced one report on PFI. As was the case with the PAC, both of these Committees have, as we will see in detail, focused on the aspects of PFI related to accountability for economic performance and not upon the broader issues which we detailed earlier, and which would be fully discussed in a proper setting of political accountability, such as the voting of legislation. Furthermore, both these committees are significantly dependent upon the NAO, something which could potentially skew their focus on economic performance.

The role of the Treasury Committee of the House of Commons is, according to the Standing Order No. 152, HC 2015–16, 'to examine the expenditure, administration and policy' of the Treasury, the Board of the Inland Revenue and the Board of Customs & Excise. The Treasury Committee has produced three reports on the PFI, in 2001, 2011 and again in 2014, all of which are key to the determination of its role as an instrument of public accountability.

There are two basic themes underpinning the three reports. The first theme is that of the dependence of the Committee to the NAO. The findings of the NAO have been used to substantiate the conclusions of the committee in subjects such as the transfer of risk in PFI contracts,[225] the possibility of VfM gains,[226] the detailing of the advantages and disadvantages of the PFI,[227] the incentives of the use of the PFI,[228] the viewpoint on VfM in the use of PFI in the crisis,[229] the consideration of the whole-life costs,[230] the broader evaluation of the performance of the PFI,[231] the reliability of VfM assessments,[232] and the burden which reliance upon external advisors signifies.[233] The importance that the findings of the NAO have for the Committee reaches its culmination in the report of 2014,[234] in which the Committee uses the findings of an NAO report which it had requested and which provided an analysis of the VfM assessment process.[235] This report[236] is the same one which we explored earlier and which made the case for many important aspects of the views of the NAO on the VfM audit. The Committee made extensive use of the report to substantiate its conclusions on the qualitative and quantitative nature of the VfM assessments.[237]

Another key area in the examination of PFI by the Treasury Committee is a focus on the aspects of the PFI related to economic performance and the achievement of economic effectiveness. Vital features in the evaluations of the committee related to the economic performance and the VfM of the PFI include the following: first, that 'the main justification [for the use of PFI] should now be the prospect of obtaining VfM',[238] and not any budgetary and accounting incentives which would promote its use, irrespective of VfM considerations.[239] In this way, in all three reports, the Committee criticises the government for the budgetary and accounting incentives which continue to exist and which help bias decision-making, favouring the use of PFI rather than traditional procurement methods.[240] A further underlying pattern in the examinations of

225 Treasury Committee, *The Private Finance Initiative* (HC 1999–2000, 147) para 27.
226 Ibid para 43.
227 Treasury Committee, *The Private Finance Initiative: Volume I* (HC 2010–12, 1146) 5.
228 Ibid 10.
229 Ibid 15.
230 Ibid 22.
231 Ibid 25.
232 Ibid 36.
233 Ibid 49.
234 Treasury Committee, *Private Finance 2: Volume I*.
235 Ibid 25.
236 NAO, *Review of the VFM Assessment Process for PFI*.
237 Treasury Committee, *Private Finance 2: Volume I* 25–29.
238 Treasury Committee, *The Private Finance Initiative* para 23.
239 Ibid paras 66–73; Treasury Committee, *The Private Finance Initiative: Volume I* 8–14; Treasury Committee, *Private Finance 2: Volume I* 8–14.
240 Treasury Committee, *The Private Finance Initiative* paras x–z; Treasury Committee, *The Private Finance Initiative: Volume I* 12–13 and Q3, Q5 and Q1; Treasury Committee, *Private Finance 2: Volume I* 9, Ev w12, 12–14, Qq 79–83.

the committee is the one of proper risk allocation and its role in the achievement of VfM.[241] With respect to the concept of risk transfer, the committee has expressed its concern that the private sector might attempt to minimise risk by limiting its adherence to contract specifications[242]; that the main risk is the construction risk which does not have to be transferred for the full duration of the PFI project[243]; that the PF2 reform of the PFI will involve less transfer of risk to the private contractor, reducing the overall VfM.[244] An additional pattern in the evaluations of the Committee over the VfM of the PFI lies in the importance of transparency. The Committee has discussed the PSC under the framework of transparency and supported that the PSC 'should contain a clear statement of the risks which have been quantified and included in it'.[245] Again on the subject of transparency, the Committee recommended that 'far more transparency is required'[246] in project data and that the 'Treasury should consider whether' the information published 'should extend to publishing data and costings on existing contracts where commercially possible, in addition to what is already published'[247]; the Committee also advised that transparency should cover 'the requirement for private sector investors to provide actual and forecast equity return information'.[248] Another focus of the committee towards the achievement of effectiveness is one related to flexibility. Around this issue of flexibility, the Committee has argued that PFIs are inherently inflexible because of the length of their term, and also because their financing structure involves negotiations between many stakeholders in order for changes to occur.[249] Also with regard to the notion of flexibility, the Committee highlights that another cause of inflexibility derives from the fact that the PFI contracts were very detailed and binding for extensive periods of time.[250] The Committee questions whether the means that the government has envisioned to address this problem through the splitting of soft services are adequate, particularly due to the inevitable increase in complexity that these means involve.[251]

These patterns, which include, in summary, the insistence on a level playing field between the PFI and traditional projects, proper risk allocation between public and private sectors, transparency of investors' returns and other data, and flexibility, collectively highlight an economic focus on the approaches of the Treasury Committee. As was the case with the system of accountability between

---

241 Treasury Committee, *The Private Finance Initiative* paras 27–30.
242 Ibid para 30.
243 Treasury Committee, *The Private Finance Initiative: Volume I* 21.
244 Treasury Committee, *Private Finance 2: Volume I* 23.
245 Treasury Committee, *The Private Finance Initiative* para 38.
246 Treasury Committee, *The Private Finance Initiative: Volume I* 48.
247 Ibid.
248 Treasury Committee, *Private Finance 2: Volume I* 30.
249 Treasury Committee, *The Private Finance Initiative: Volume I* 29.
250 Treasury Committee, *Private Finance 2: Volume I* 31.
251 Ibid 32–33.

the PAC and the C&AG, the Treasury Committee also focuses on economic performance and not on broader issues of the use of PFI, such as the ones that a system of political accountability – like the voting of legislation – would discuss. The focus on this discussion of the aspects of the PFI related to its economic performance is further enhanced by its major dependence on the NAO. Through this dependence, the Committee adopts the normative standpoints of the NAO, and together with them, an analysis of the PFI from the perspective of economic performance, with the consequent marginalisation of the broader issues related to the use of private finance.

The same features relating to dependence on the NAO, and the focus on the analysis of PFI from the perspective of economic performance, can also be noted in the workings of another committee which participates in Public Accountability for the PFI. This is the Economic Committee of the House of Lords, which has produced one report on the subject in 2010. This report is concerned with the subject of the contribution of the PFI and PPPs in the public infrastructure and their accounting treatment.[252]

On the subject of the reliance on the NAO, the Committee has used the NAO findings to substantiate its conclusions in a variety of contexts. Some of them are ones related to the optimism bias,[253] evaluation of the Public Sector Comparator in the determinations of VfM,[254] and on the robustness of the VfM tests[255] on the accounting treatment of the PFI.[256]

As was also the case with the Treasury Committee, apart from the subject of the reliance to the NAO, a further shared area for consideration is the focus on the economic performance of the PFI and the achievement of effectiveness and VfM. The central points of focus with respect to this theme include the following: the first is based upon the importance of cost comparisons, as exemplified in borrowing costs, discount rates and optimism bias in the calculation of VfM. With respect to borrowing costs, the committee stressed that even if the cost of debt finance might potentially be higher than traditional procurement, 'this factor alone does not rule out the use of private finance',[257] due to the potential advantages of the PFI and the fact that the higher cost 'reflects risks carried by the private sector and a margin of profit'.[258] With respect to the notions of discount rates and optimism bias, which are treated as interlinked subjects,[259] the committee suggests an alternative method of calculation, adopting an approach which is rare in reports: 'we recommend that, in order to

252 Committee on Economic Affairs, *Private Finance Projects and off-Balance Sheet Debt: Volume 1* (HL 2009–10, 63-I).
253 Ibid 13–14.
254 Ibid 14.
255 Ibid 15.
256 Ibid 17–18.
257 Ibid 33.
258 Ibid.
259 Ibid 13.

reach a fairer basis of comparison, where a percentage uplift for optimism bias is added to the estimated Net Present Value of Public Sector Comparators, an appropriate rate of uplift should also be added to estimates of the NPV of the cost to the client under PFP'.[260] A further point of focus lays on the accounting treatment of the PFI for which the Committee highlighted the need of greater clarity over the 'financial liabilities arising from the PFI', and the inclusion of the 'PFP liabilities in departmental balance sheets'. Together with other measures, these features promote the removal of 'institutional bias in favour of private financing of public procurement, so that public authorities can select it, or another procurement method, on a case-by-case basis according to value for money'.[261] The Committee discussed the concept of risk, highlighting the need to stress the sharing of risks between the parties,[262] for which the Committee stressed the importance of the bundling of risks in groups.[263] A further point of significance for the Committee over the promotion of effectiveness is based on proper monitoring and commercial skills for which it notes that 'monitoring and managing private finance contracts has long been a weakness of the public sector (. . .). We recommend that public authorities should do more to maintain and improve commercial skills of staff dealing with private finance projects, with emphasis on long-term contract management as well as contract negotiation'.[264]

These Committee foci, which include the emphasis on cost comparisons (borrowing costs, discount rates and optimism bias) in the calculation of VfM, the suggestion of an alternative method of calculation, the accounting treatment of the PFI, the promotion of a level playing field between public and private finance, of risk sharing between parties, and the proper monitoring and transfer of skills, suggest an analysis of the PFI based on economic effectiveness. As was the case with the C&AG and the PAC, and also in the case of the Treasury Committee, the Lords Economic Committee focused itself upon the performance aspects of the PFI, not discussing broader issues such as those which would be discussed in terms of the voting of legislation. Its dependence on the workings and conclusions of the NAO further stress this economic approach to PFI, which – as we have seen – the NAO promotes.

In this way, both the Treasury Committee and the Economic Affairs Committee of the House of Lords have their focus on the accountability of PFI based on economic performance. If we return, at this point, to our original inquiry around whether the UK Parliament exercises a mechanism which fills the gap of political accountability left by the limited use of legislation in the promotion of the PFI, the answer is resoundingly in the negative. Both of these

260 Ibid 14.
261 Ibid 18.
262 Ibid 21.
263 Ibid 32.
264 Ibid 25.

Committees which have examined the PFI are focused on its economic performance, as was the case with the PAC and the NAO. They do not approach and consider issues related to broader questions that a more complete system of political accountability, such as the one involved in the voting of legislation, would be able to discuss.

It needs to be noted for reasons of consistency that – despite the fact that these Committees are those which have produced reports specifically on the PFI programme at a broader level – there are references and more minor inquiries around the role of private contracting at the level of other departmental Committees, such as the Defence Committee[265] and the Health Committee.[266] None of these reports has, however, discussed the PFI as their main subject nor approached it in a broader way, even within the remits of their individual sectors, and the occasional nature of their references to PFI precludes a distinction of stable patterns of accountability comparable to the ones examined earlier.

4.3. *The problem of accountability captured and summarised*

As we saw in the first section of this chapter, the practice of the government in contracting without Parliamentary authorisation has had a negative impact on the political/constitutional species of public accountability of the PFI. The basic structure which serves as the main mechanism for public accountability for the PFI is built around a criterion which is designed as an instrument of the administrative kind of public accountability and which cannot – for this reason – fill the gap resulting from the absence of statutory authorisation. This leaves a gap in the accountability of other matters which are related to the PFI, but not those related to the pursuit of economic effectiveness. Such matters largely unaccounted for include issues such as certain environmental concerns over the use of PFI, and broader issues relating to the integration of the private sector to the machinery of government and to the provision of public services, as well as the suitability of a public service to be offered through PFI, among others.

---

265 Defence Committee, *Defence Equipment 2009* (HC 2008–09, 107); Defence Committee, *Defence Equipment 2010* (HC 2009–10, 99); Defence Committee, *Major Procurement Projects* (HC 2001–02, 779); Defence Committee, *Defence Acquisition* (HC 2012–13, 9); Defence Committee, *Major Procurement Projects* (HC 2000–01, 463); Defence Committee, *Strategic Lift* (HC 2006–07, 462); Defence Committee, *Defence Procurement* (HC 2002–03, 694).

266 Health Committee, *Public Expenditure on Health and Care Services – Volume I* (HC 2012–13, 651); Health Committee, *2012 Accountability Hearing with Monitor* (HC 2012–13, 652); Health Committee, *Annual Accountability Hearing with Monitor* (HC 2010–12, 1431); Health Committee, *Social Care – Volume II* (HC 2010–12, 1583-II) especially Ev 1; Health Committee, *Commissioning – Volume II* (HC 2010–11, 513-II) Ev 120, Ev 163.

The unsuitability of the criterion to address concerns of political public accountability and its exposure to a notable degree of instability and subjectivity has led two organs – the C&AG and the PAC – to exercise a role incompatible with their primary functions. As we have shown, the C&AG is an organ which is designed by legislation to be an organ of audit scrutiny and it is not authorised to exercise a role of setting norms. And yet, it exercises normative functions and shapes its own agenda over the promotion of the PFI, which encompasses political goals. Similarly, the standing order which established the PAC envisions it as an instrument for the scrutiny of government. Yet, the PAC – rather like the C&AG – exercises a function which is not only one of scrutiny, but shapes its own agenda over the promotion of the PFI, which also involves political choices.

This is a situation which we have seen is caused by the lack of suitability of the criterion of VfM to be used as an instrument of political public accountability, and by its exposure to instability and subjectivity. This permits the C&AG and the PAC to define it as they see fit, and, due to the fact that their role is based on the scrutiny of VfM, by defining the criterion, they also have considerable freedom to define their own roles. This would perhaps be acceptable if the way that each defined their role was in harmony with the legal instruments which provide that role. But, as we have clearly seen, this is not the case: the law envisions these organs as organs of scrutiny, and not as organs authorised to set norms and perform political functions.

The points of view which we put forward here bring us into a position of conflict with a significant part of the body of literature on the subject of performance audit.

An indicative example of this literature is that authored by Jan-Eric Furubo,[267] which focuses on forming a definition of performance auditing and on discussing its multi-faceted relationship with accountability. Furubo argues that accountability exists not only in a related chain of accountability, but that it can also be about the need by a party to establish the credibility and reliability of information.[268] The complicated construction of the subject matter – he asserts – often requires the involvement of a specialist, such as the auditor, who needs to be independent from investigatory and reporting constraints. He develops this by explaining that the need for classical audit derives from the fact that we accept that human nature can be weak, and that we, therefore, need a system of control. This need does not cease to exist, according to Furubo, when the purpose with which people are entrusted is to improve things. For this reason, he states, 'if we accept that there are weaknesses in human nature which makes

---

267 Jan-Eric Furubo, 'Performance Auditing: Audit or Misnomer?' in Jeremy Lonsdale, Peter Wilkins and Ton Ling (eds), *Performance Auditing – Contributing to Accountability in Democratic Government* (Edward Elgar Publishing 2011) 22.
268 Ibid 29.

auditors necessary for discovering behaviour in pecuniary matters, also economy, effectiveness and efficiency will be under threat of dishonest behaviour'.[269] The holding to account for these three notions, which, as we stated earlier, represent the main components of the concept of VfM, is the objective of the performance auditor. In this way, Furubo defines performance auditing as 'an evaluative activity which produces assessments regarding performance or information about performance, of such a reliable degree and with such freedom from investigatory and reporting constraints, that they can be used in the realm of accountability'.[270] Based on this definition, Furubo builds on the idea of independence that the auditor should enjoy. According to him, this independence includes the right of the auditor to choose what to audit, but also the right to decide by precisely which methods this audit will be carried out, and that 'it is a democratic necessity'[271] that the auditor must autonomously define what he himself is doing.

The aforementioned position of Furubo is one with which we disagree, within the parameters of this book. We assert that the NAO's ability to independently define the methods that it will follow when carrying out the performance audit, by defining the properties of the VfM, is the instrument which permitted it to veer away from a purely auditing role and perform a role which is political and which is outside the parameters that the National Audit Office Act 1983 laid out for the NAO's function. Furubo comments on the relationship between the performance, the VfM, audit and the exercise of a political role by the auditor. He argues that to claim that political decisions are a no-go area for the performance auditor and that the scope of his tasks will be limited to the scrutiny of purely technical implementations, is appropriate. To argue – as we do – in opposition to this is to suggest that the auditor will have a political role.

Two further commentators sharing a similar standpoint to Furubo are Vital Put and Rudi Turksema.[272] Our argument, once again, also sits at odds with both. The two of them begin from the premise that the ability of the supreme audit institutions to freely select the topics of their audit permits them to ask inconvenient questions, focus on the issues that they consider important and, most critically, to ensure that the central auditing bodies are political players. Based on this position, they examine the methods by which the NAO and the Government Accountability Office (GAO) select the topics of their audit. They distinguish these methods into formal and informal. In the formal category, they describe that a first dimension is institutional, which refers to the constitutional position which is held by each audit institution in the constitutional model of

---

269 Ibid 32.
270 Ibid 35.
271 Ibid 43.
272 Vital Put and Rudi Turksema, 'Selection of Topics' in Jeremy Lonsdale, Peter Wilkins and Ton Ling (eds), *Performance Auditing – Contributing to Accountability in Democratic Government* (Edward Elgar Publishing 2011) 51.

each country. The second one is the operational dimension which mainly contains risk analysis based on outcomes that the auditing institution tries to achieve.[273] The informal factors which impact upon the decision of the supreme audit institutions over the topics of their audit are those of the professional judgement of auditors, political taboos, organisational structure of the auditing institutions, their publishing policy and reporting practices.[274] Both authors comment on the fact that the risk analysis, which is a widespread means by which auditors base their decision on which topics they will focus their audit upon, is a technique which has neither been confirmed nor invalidated empirically.

In keeping with Furubo, however, the authors do argue that the auditors should enjoy complete freedom over the selection of their techniques and the definition of their role. They begin with the assumption that the freedom of auditors to select their topics freely assures that they are political players. Once again, this is a position with which we will disagree in this book. As we argue, the exercise of a political role by the NAO with respect to PFI is outside the remit which the law prescribes for this body. Furthermore, the authors point out the weaknesses of techniques – due to issues of subjectivity – which allow that the supreme audit institutions pick their subjects. This concern is in keeping with our conclusions, given that the criterion of VfM is exposed to a considerable degree of instability and subjectivity.

Having highlighted the points in which our conclusions differ from those expounded by other commentators, it is now time to proceed to the remaining unexplored areas of this subject, in order to complete our examination of the impact of the use of the criterion of VfM in the public accountability of the PFI. This issue relates to the examination of the means through which the gap in public accountability – which remains due to the absence of statutory authorisation in PFI – can be filled.

5. The recognition of the Concordat of 1932 as a constitutional convention and as a means of addressing the issues of political accountability for the PFI

As we have shown in the present chapter, there has been limited use of legislation in the promotion of the PFI. This limited use refers primarily to statutory authorisation for government contracting, as well as to the absence of a general framework governing the PFI programme as a whole. The limited use of legislation has a negative impact on the constitutional accountability for the PFI, by which the representatives of the people hold the executive to account. The gap of constitutional accountability which is created leaves unanswered important questions related to the use of PFI. These relate to the broader political aspects

---

273 Ibid 55–57.
274 Ibid 58.

of these transactions, including factors such as their suitability and desirability for specific government activities, and those around environmental concerns. The broader system of accountability for the PFI fails to address these issues because it is predominantly focused, through the utilisation of the criterion of VfM, upon economic productivity and bureaucratic effectiveness. The unsuitability of the criterion to address concerns of constitutional public accountability and its exposure to a significant degree of instability and subjectivity has led two organs, the C&AG and the PAC, to exercise a role incompatible with their primary functions. Although they are perceived to be organs of scrutiny and audit, they actually exercise functions which are normative and which are better suited to the function of regulation. As we have also seen, the workings of other committees in Parliament, such as the House of Lords' Economic Committee and the Treasury Committee, do not manage to fill the gap of constitutional accountability, because their activities are again focused on the economic productivity of the PFI, and not upon their broader political aspects. Similarly, departmental committees, which would be expected to discuss aspects of the PFI more oriented to the political aspects of the PFI, seem to discuss the PFI on an occasional, infrequent and unsystematic basis. In this way the gap in constitutional accountability, which sets aside the discussion of the broader political aspects of the PFI, remains.

At this point in our argument, it would add strength to illustrate these considerations with some potentially possible scenarios. Supposing that the government, through the Department of Health, decided to undertake a PFI project related to a hospital in London which is dedicated to the treatment of patients suffering from a specific kind of disease. We may distinguish two groups of considerations for the project: from the one side, there are considerations of economic effectiveness, such as the cost of the project, how rigorously market testing will be carried out, how it will be commissioned and with which contractor. From the other side, there are certain considerations of broader political aspects of the project, such as whether it is desirable that a hospital of this kind opens in London, instead of York or Leeds, for example, or whether the private sector is the best suited to undertake the operation of a facility of this specific kind. They may consider whether the project will impact negatively on the broader environmental condition of the specific neighbourhood, or whether the private sector provides the necessary guarantees for the protection of the sensitive data of the patients, to name but a few concerns. For the first group of considerations, which relate to economic performance, there is a well organised system which exists for the accountability of the department to Parliament: most likely, the NAO and the PAC will discuss these considerations, and, if not, they would likely become the preserve of one of the other Parliamentary committees. However, we should question what happens with the second group of considerations, related to the broader political aspects of the project. A comparable system is not in place for the accountability of the department over this second group of considerations. The NAO and the PAC will not discuss these issues, neither will the Treasury Select Committee nor the Lords' Economic Affairs

Committee, and discussion in the other select committees will be occasional and limited. As for the involvement of the full Houses of Parliament, the government is not perceived as being required to submit the contract of the PFI hospital to it, nor does it follow this practice.

Through the enactment of legislation, the Parliament would be able to hold the government accountable with the involvement of all of its members, and not only of the members of a specific Parliamentary committee, and this would bring to the surface the broader political aspects of the use of the PFI. As we will argue in the next section, such a requirement could be construed through the recognition of the Concordat of 1932, between the Treasury and the PAC, as a constitutional convention.

5.1.   *The Concordat of 1932 as a constitutional convention*

The background context against which the Concordat of 1932 arose has been helpfully provided by numerous sources, such as the Managing Public Money of the Treasury and the Memorandum of Granville Ram, to which we referred earlier.[275] In the mid-nineteenth century, it was a common practice for the government to gain Parliamentary authority for some areas of expenditure through the use of the Contingencies Fund.[276] In its earliest days, the PAC protested against this practice and it stressed, in 1862, that the recourse to the mechanism of Contingencies Funds should only be made in cases where there was pressing need for the expenditure in a given year, and that otherwise, such expenditure should be sanctioned in terms of the Estimates process. Later, in 1885, the PAC became concerned that the mechanism of the Estimates and the Appropriation Act was not sufficient either, and it argued that it made little legal and financial sense that the distinct terms of an Act of Parliament might be overridden by the Appropriation Act. It stressed that 'the matter . . . is one of great importance from a constitutional point of view'.[277]

Although the Treasury agreed in principle, the matter arose again in 1908, when the PAC noted that:

> while it is undoubtedly within the discretion of Parliament to override the provisions of an existing statute by a vote in Supply confirmed by the Appropriation Act, it is desirable in the interests of financial regularity and constitutional consistency that such a procedure should be resorted to as rarely as possible, and only to meet a temporary emergency.[278]

---

275 See p 29 [orig. 36].
276 Treasury, *Managing Public Money*, Annex 2.3. The original text of a number of reports to which we refer here are provided by the Treasury report. Reference to them will be made by citing the relevant passage of the said Treasury report.
277 Ibid A2.3.3.
278 Ibid A2.3.4.

However, the matter arose again with a greater intensity in the 1930s, given that, throughout the decade of the 1920s, there had been instances of government practice in which the Departments had obtained money based on the Votes and the Appropriation Act to materialise expenditure which had not been provided in a specific Act. The PAC drew attention to these instances numerous times, in 1930, 1931 and 1932, and, in the last case, the report of the Committee criticised the practice of the Ministry of Labour in obtaining money by means of Votes for the training and resettlement of the unemployed, exceeding the powers conferred to the Minister by statute. The PAC's words are forthright and unequivocal, urging that:

> Your Committee consider also, as a matter of general principle, that, where it is desired that continuing functions should be exercised by a Government Department, particularly where such functions may involve financial liabilities extending beyond a given financial year, it is proper, subject to certain recognised exceptions, that the powers and duties to be exercised should be defined by specific statute.[279]

The subject was mentioned in Parliament after the report,[280] and the Treasury replied to it by admitting that 'there have been in the past many instances where continuing services which have never been dealt with by statute – some of them of considerable importance – have been provided for with no more permanent authority than that given by an Appropriation Act, and some of those services continue today, without the propriety of the means of providing for them having been called in question'.[281] It proceeded by arguing that, although the Treasury must be allowed some flexibility and discretion in asking the Parliament to exercise its legislative power, the practice should normally be that 'where it is desired that continuing functions should be exercised by a Government Department (particularly where such functions involve financial liabilities extending beyond a given year) it is proper that the powers and duties to be exercised should be defined by specific statute'.[282]

In the relevant debates of the Parliament, the subject arose yet again in 1933, this time with the Department of Health, in the discussion of the Supplementary Estimate. The Department of Health asked that £500,000 be provided to it by the Supplementary Estimate. The sum was to be spent, according to the White Paper, 'subject to such conditions as the Minister of Health, with the approval of the Treasury, may determine'.[283] When a member of the Parliament rose and

---

279 As provided by Ram in 17.
280 HC Deb 11 July 1932, vol 268, cols 1019–1020.
281 As provided by Ram in 17–18.
282 As provided by Ram in 18.
283 HC Deb 10 July 1933, vol 280, col 895.

argued against the practice of getting the authorisation for money without an Act of Parliament, the then Minister of Health responded by recognising the principle outlined by the PAC the previous year, albeit disagreeing on its application in the particular case:

> The principle of this matter has been extremely well put, if I may say so without assumption, in the last report of the Select Committee on Public Accounts, published in June of this year. I will read the relevant passage, because I feel that it will put Hon. Members in possession of the principle which ought to govern matters of this sort. The words are these: 'The committee of 1932 also expressed the opinion, as a matter of general principle, that, where it is desired that continuing functions should be exercised by a Government Department, particularly where such functions may involve financial liabilities extending beyond a given financial year, it is proper, subject to certain recognised exceptions, that the powers and duties to be exercised should be defined by specific statute. Your Committee are assured by the Treasury that they agree that practice should normally accord with this view, and will continue to aim at the observance of this principle.' The House will observe that we are dealing with a case which does not fall within that principle. We are dealing here with expenditure which is not concerned with 'continuing functions,' and which will not last beyond the present financial year.[284]

Again in the same year, 1933, the PAC returned to the views that it had expressed the previous year, referring to them as 'a general principle', and mentioning that: 'certain further examples if continuing expenditure not covered by specific legislative function' and, specifically, that the annual Exchequer grant for police expenditure had 'no statutory basis whatever'.[285] They proceeded by saying that:

> It has been represented that a number of other important services of a continuing nature are supported solely by the authority of the annual Appropriation Act, but in the opinion of Your Committee this circumstance does not furnish adequate ground for the abandonment of attempts to place such expenditure on constitutional basis.[286]

The most authoritative sources on the subject, including the memorandum of Glanville Ram, and the Treasury Report on the Management of Public Money,[287]

---

284 HC Deb 10 July 1933, vol 280, col 897.
285 As provided by Ram in 18.
286 Ibid.
287 Treasury, *Managing Public Money*, Annex 2.3.

as well as the relevant 2013 report of the House of Lords,[288] hold the agreement of the Concordat to be contained in the 1932 interchanges between the PAC and the Treasury to which we referred earlier, and they term the agreement 'the 1932 Concordat'. It is the wording of this agreement which we will use for our analysis in the next section.

The Concordat of 1932 is not currently explicitly recognised as a constitutional convention. However, its recognition as a convention applicable to the PFI is very important for the increase of the constitutional accountability over the PPPs. As we showed earlier, the root of the problem of constitutional accountability in the PFI is in the limited use of legislation. As we will see in detail, the recognition of the Concordat as a constitutional convention, and its modern application to the PFI, means that it is in a position to lead to more cases in which the Parliament will be able to participate in the production of legislation on the PFI. In order to verify whether the Concordat of 1932 ('the Concordat') it is necessary that we discuss it with reference to the criteria produced by Ivor Jennings in 1946 for constitutional conventions. There are three and they are as follows:

> First, what are the precedents; secondly, did the actors in the precedents believe that they were bound by a rule; and thirdly, is there a reason for the rule? A single precedent with a good reason may be enough to establish the rule. A whole string of precedents without such a reason will be of no avail, unless it is perfectly certain that the persons concerned regarded them as bound by it.[289]

The reason why we selected to follow this set of criteria is that, due to their judicial recognition by the courts of Canada[290] in the 1980s, they are considered fairly uncontroversial by the relevant literature.[291]

5.2. *Precedents followed by the belief of binding by a rule*

The criteria laid down by Jennings begin from the precedents in the practice of the constitutional actors associated with the potential convention, as this practice is determined through their perception that, while engaging in it, they follow a binding rule.

---

288 Committee on the Constitution, *The Pre-Emption of Parliament* (HL 2012–13, 165, 2013) 8–9.

289 Sir Ivor Jennings, *The Law and the Constitution* (5th edn, University of London Press 1959) 136.

290 See the landmark case *Reference re Amendment of Constitution of Canada* [1981], 1, S.C.R. 753, 888 (S.C.C.).

291 Geoffrey Marshall, *Constitutional Conventions: The Rules and Forms of Political Accountability* (Oxford University Press 1984) 10.

There are a number of features which can aid our understanding of the establishment of this practice, which is accompanied with the element of opinio juris, signifying the belief of the constitutional actors that they follow a binding rule. The Welfare Reform and Pension Act 1999, section 82, provides that the Secretary of State may incur expenditure on preparing for legislative changes within his responsibilities, provided that he has the consent of the Treasury and the approval of the House of Commons. The explanatory note of section 82 clarifies that the ability to exclusively seek for Parliamentary approval instead of waiting for Parliamentary legislation is given exceptionally by the Secretary of the State in this case. The explanatory note describes the Concordat as follows:

> Under a 1932 PAC Concordat, any functions of a Government Department that continue beyond a given year — particularly where there are financial liabilities — should *normally be defined by specific statute*, rather than rely solely on the authority of the annual Appropriation Act.[292]

To the same extent, and echoing the previous case, the Explanatory Note for the Loans to Ireland Act 2010 highlights that the definition by a specific statute is the normal and the required way through which functions are transferred. The importance of this feature is emphasised by the italicised text as follows:

> The Act authorises Treasury to make payments in respect of loans to Ireland out of money provided by Parliament. Statutory authority for such expenditure *is required* in accordance with the Concordat of 1932 between the Government and the PAC.[293]

The Electricity (Miscellaneous Provisions) Act 2003 provides authorisation to the Secretary of State to engage in transactions related to British Energy (BE). In the associated debate in the House of Lords, Lord Sainsbury of Tureville claims that:

> Clause 1 gives the Government explicit Parliamentary authority to provide financial assistance to a BE company. The rescue aid which has been extended to British Energy is currently authorised under the Appropriation Act. However, under the Concordat with the PAC which has been in place since 1932, *it is usual that any significant or long-term expenditure* should have additional specific statutory authority. Clause 1 provides that authority.[294]

292 Explanatory Notes to the Welfare Reform and Pension Act 1999, 122.
293 Explanatory Notes to the Loans to Ireland Act 2010, para 3.
294 HL Deb 3 March 2003, vol 645, col 607.

Here, Lord Sainsbury refers precisely to this 'usual', normal, character of the application of the Concordat. In this way, both of the first two criteria of Jennings are fulfilled in the Concordat of 1932.

The case *R v Secretary of State for Work and Pensions ex parte Hooper and others*,[295] is one of the very few in which reference is made by the government concerning the way that it perceives the Concordat of 1932. It is clear from one of the points made therein that the government in this instance perceived the Concordat as a constitutional convention. The argument of the representative of the Secretary of State is clearly delineated as follows:

> As a corporation sole, the Crown has the same right to deal with its property as any other legal person. It needs no statutory authority to do so. There are constitutional conventions in the relationship between the Crown and the Parliament as to when the Crown will spend money voted by Parliament without a specific statutory authority to do so.[296]

The court does not answer the specific point and, therefore, it cannot be argued that – this is case – the law is supporting the nature of the Concordat as a constitutional convention. The value of this point, though, is that, in this case, the government recognised the Concordat as a constitutional convention.

These examples should not be taken as evidencing that the government has consistently followed the prescriptions of the Concordat. The most indicative example is the whole system of criminal injuries compensation schemes, which operated from 1964 to 1995 on the basis of the prerogative. It is worthwhile looking at this matter in closer detail both because it sheds light on the perceptions of the executive's ability to expand funds in the exercise of continuing functions (being solely based on the Appropriation Act) but also to witness the perceptions of the judiciary.

The Criminal Injuries Compensation Scheme was established in 1964 with the purpose of providing compensation from the state for victims of crimes of violence.[297] Until 1964, victims who suffered injuries caused by a crime had no right of compensation beyond the right to sue the party which caused the injury. In 1964, a scheme for the compensation of victims of crimes of violence came into force. It was a non-statutory scheme, established on the basis of the prerogative, and payments to victims were made ex gratia. In 1978, the Pearson Commission on Civil Liability and Compensation for Personal Injury recommended that the scheme be put on a statutory basis. This was achieved with

---

295 *R v Secretary of State for Work and Pensions ex parte Hooper and others* [2005], Pens LR 337.
296 Ibid [47].
297 Mary Baber, *Criminal Injuries Compensation* (House of Commons Research Paper 95/64, 1995) 1.

the Act of 1988 which codified the existing scheme with some amendments. Section 171 of this Act provided that the statutory framework for the compensation of victims of crime would only come in force on such a date that the Secretary of State would appoint by means of a statutory instrument. This construction, which was operational from 1964 on a prerogative basis – even if it involved the occurrence of continuing expenditure by the Crown – and which should, theoretically, be covered by the Concordat of 1932, reached the courts in 1995, with the *Fire Brigades Union*[298] case.

In this case, a problematic key issue was that the Secretary of State for the Home Office announced his intention not to bring into force sections 108–117 of the Criminal Justice Act 1988, which contained the amended framework for compensations, but, instead, introduced a new scheme. The Fire Brigades Union sought a judicial review of this decision, using the argument that the Secretary of State, by failing or refusing to bring into force the enacted provisions, had acted unlawfully in breach of his duty under the Act of 1988. Furthermore, they argued that, by implementing the new scheme, he had acted unlawfully in breach of his duty under the Act and had abused his prerogative powers. Finally, the House of Lords, held that the Act had provided the Secretary of State with discretion on when to introduce the statutory scheme. The Act, however, did not give him the power to decide on whether the statutory scheme would be implemented. Consequently, according to the House of Lords, his decision to introduce a new scheme which was not consistent with the scheme contained in the statute was an abuse of the prerogative power.

What is particularly interesting in this case, which, together with the *Pergau Dam* case, is considered to provide limits to the discretion of the executive to shape its intervention in the economy, is that the Lords, in numerous instances, seem not to recognise the need for a statute authorising the exercise of continuing functions when it involves expenditure. The paying of compensation to the victims of crime is a function which was assigned to the Home Office, and it signified continuing expenditure extending beyond a given year by that department. Theoretically, this falls in the normative content of the Concordat, and, as such, it should be accompanied by a statute which would authorise this expenditure. However, we read that, in the opinion of Lord Keith of Kinkel,

> The scheme based on compensation analogous to damages in tort which operated from 1964 operated by virtue of the Royal Prerogative. (. . . .) I can see no valid ground upon which it might be held that that a payment under the tariff scheme would be unlawful. At the present time the prerogative in this field exists unimpaired'.[299] And he adds that 'If sections 108

---

298 *R v Secretary of State for the Home Department, Ex parte Fire Brigades Union and Others* [1995] 2 AC 513.

299 Ibid 545 B.

and 117 had never been enacted, it would have been open to the Secretary of State to discontinue making payments under the 1964 scheme and to start making payments under the tariff scheme'.[300]

In addition, through the contributions of Lord Mustill and Lord Nicholls of Birkenhead, we may observe that they consider that it would be valid for the Secretary of State to discharge his continuing functions, signifying the occurrence of expenses without the requirement of a statute, but rather by virtue of the prerogative. Lord Mustill claims 'thus, if in the present case Part VII had been brought into force there would have been no room left for the exercise of that aspect of the prerogative which had enabled the Secretary of State to establish and maintain the scheme'.[301] Similarly, Lord Nicholls concurs, 'There would be no difficulty if sections 108 to 117 were repealed. The field of compensation for victims of criminal injuries would then be wide open for the prerogative power. The position in law would become as it was before the Act of 1988 was passed. There could then be no question of a statutory impediment to setting up and making payments under a new, tariff scheme in exercise of the prerogative'.[302]

The picture with respect to legislation directed towards the PFI is equally mixed. There are cases of legislation which authorises the participation of government in PFIs, but it is unclear whether the government adopted this legislation due to a perceived constitutional obligation to do so or for other reasons. We will now proceed with an examination of this legislation.

An example worth exploring here, in which the government sought to adopt a legal foundation for its PFI activity, is that of section 223 of the National Health Service (NHS) Act 2006 which provides that:

> Public-Private Partnerships: (1) The Secretary of State may form, or participate in forming, companies to provide facilities or services to persons or bodies exercising functions, or otherwise providing services, under this Act.

This NHS Act section covers the formation of companies, but it does not mention participation in PPP contracts. Furthermore, the Act neither provides for accountability mechanisms nor for accountability criteria with respect to the performance of these companies. Similarly, the National Health Service (Private Finance) Act 1997 established the power of NHS Trusts to enter into agreements. The 1997 Act makes direct mention of PFI only in its title, and its section 1 refers to the concept rather fleetingly, as follows: 'The powers of a National Health Service trust include power to enter into externally financed development agreements'.

---

300 Ibid 545 D.
301 Ibid 564 F.
302 Ibid 574 B.

The section continues to focus on, and develop this subject, establishing that these agreements need the certification of the Secretary of State. However, it is argued that (s.1. 6) even if this certification is not provided, the validity of the agreement between the Trust and the private party is not affected. As was the case with the previous (2006) Act, the National Health Service (Private Finance) Act 1997 does not provide for the accountability of the Trusts to Parliament, nor does it establish criteria for this accountability. The background of the Act can be traced to the much commented upon case, *Crédit Suisse v Allerdale Borough Council*,[303] which was decided in the same year of the enactment of the aforementioned legislation. The case is considered a leading one by the relevant literature,[304] and its subject focused upon the powers of a local authority to contract. In brief, the council had decided to provide a swimming pool and it created a company to develop the project, one which was based on the powers provided by section 111 of the Local Government Act 1972. In order to finance the project, it was loaned £6 m by a bank. The council attempted to repay the loan by selling time-shares, something which proved unsatisfactory and, subsequently, the company went to liquidation. When the bank attempted to recover the money owed to it by the company, via the council, they argued that the council did not have authority, by law, to enter in such a contract in the first place.

The court recognised that it is 'an unattractive feature of the council's case that it is seeking to assert the illegality of its own action in entering into a contract of guarantee in order to resist the bank's claim to enforce the guarantee'.[305] Despite this fact, the court held that the claim of the council was valid, and that the bank could not enforce the guarantee. It reasoned that the authorities are creatures of statutes, and they therefore only have the contracting powers that the statutes recognise. The situation was summed up thus:

> Accordingly in my opinion the bank's argument on the statutory powers point fails at each stage. The establishment of the company and the giving of the guarantee were part of an ingenious scheme designed to circumvent the no doubt irksome controls imposed by central government. The council, however, could only do what it was empowered to do by statute. Neither the establishment of a company nor the giving of a guarantee fell within the express or implied powers of the council.[306]

In the aftermath of this influential case the National Health Service (Private Finance) Act 1997 was enacted. In this way, arguably, the provision sought to

303 *Crédit Suisse v Allerdale Borough Council* [1997] Q.B. 306.
304 Craig 143; Davies 97, 106, 108.
305 *Crédit Suisse*, 344 E.
306 Ibid 332–333.

repair the trust of the financing sector to the contractual commitments of the government, a trust which was – to a degree – shaken by the *Crédit Suisse* case. It is doubtful that the government promoted this legislation because it felt obliged to do so by matters of constitutional principle, such as the Concordat.

A further Act which provides authorisation for the use of PPPs is the Greater London Authority Act 1999. According to s 210, the PPPs to which it applies are those relating to at least one of the following parties, London Regional Transport, Transport for London, or a subsidiary of these bodies. As was the case with the previous Acts, the relevant sections of this Act (210–239) do not provide for accountability to Parliament throughout the relevant PPP agreements nor for criteria of accountability. It does, however, provide a bureaucratic mechanism of accountability with the creation of the institution of the PPP arbiter, which is appointed (and can be removed) by the Secretary of State, to which matters related to the contract can be referred (225–235).

An additional example of legislation which provides the foundation of the PPP activity of government is that of the Criminal Justice Act 1991, which provides, in its s 84, the following observation on potential contracts relating to prisons:

> The Secretary of State may enter into a contract with another person for the provision or running (or the provision and running) by him, or (if the contract so provides) for the running by sub-contractors of his, of any prison or part of a prison.

As has already been noted,[307] the enactment of legislation with respect to the contracting-out of prisons has been a necessity both because it touches on a highly sensitive area of governance around human rights, detention and police powers, and because, if this provision was not enacted, the government would have been restricted in its options, and would have had to proceed to prisons PFI because of the Prison Act 1952. Once again, it is difficult to ascertain whether government promoted the Criminal Justice Act 1991 due to some perceived constitutional obligation connected with the Concordat. It is worthy of note, however, that the Criminal Justice Act 1991 provides for a certain degree of accountability to the Parliament in s 86B, in which it requires the Secretary of State to make orders by means of a statutory instrument in order to enable officers of contracted-out prisons to carry out specific tasks of enforcement.

The four examples which we have detailed thus far in which legislation was used document a marginal tendency with respect to the promotion of the PFI. The regular practice of promoting PFI by the central government – as the

---

307 Freedland, 'Government by Contract and Public Law' note 33.

critical literature has also highlighted – is mostly non-statutory and is – in the main – based on the inherent common law non-prerogative powers of the Crown. Our illustrative examples also captured this complexity; in many cases the government had other incentives to promote this legislation rather than a perceived obligation to do so by virtue of the Concordat.

A further characteristic of the existing legislation which potentially has relevance for PFI is its facilitative, rather than coercive, nature. This means that the intention of the said legislation is to facilitate the outsourcing of public functions to the private sector, rather than provide obligatory frameworks of accountability which the government is prescribed to follow. A characteristic example of a facilitative statute is the Deregulation and Contracting Out Act 1994 (Contracting Out Act). The Act provides, in its s 69, a minister or office holder with the capacity to transfer certain functions to other persons or their employees. The functions which can be transferred by virtue of this provision must be those which the minister or office holder can exercise by virtue of an existing enactment, and not functions which are exercised based on common law. Furthermore, they must be functions which can be exercised by an officer of his. If a minister or office holder intends to use this provision, he will have to do so through statutory instrument, which is submitted to the affirmative resolution procedure (s 77).

The Contracting Out Act is considered a very good example of a facilitative Act. It aims to facilitate the government when using contracting out, rather than providing an element of coercion. In this way, the Contracting Out Act 1994 cannot be read as obliging the government to use the s 77 affirmative resolution procedure for every PFI project under consideration, but it can exercise its own judgement with regard to this. A survey of cases – undertaken by Catherine Donnelly[308] and Anne Davies[309] – in which it has been used, betrays limited use of the statutory instruments provided by s 77 of the Act, and, most crucially, limited applicability to the PFI. One illustration of a case where the prescriptions of the Act have been used in relation to the PFI is the SI 2001/3698, which authorised private firms to provide court staff, thereby facilitating PFI schemes to build court facilities. Other examples bear little relation to the PFI, such as the SI 1999/2128, which provided that the function of posting jury attendance summonses can be performed by private contractors. A further example is the SI 2004/1975, which empowered Ofcom to contract out its functions in relation to the regulation of advertising.

The existing legislation which has potential relevance to PPPs is largely facilitative; it does not usually provide for coercive procedures of accountability. The

---

308 Catherine Donnelly, *Delegation of Governmental Power to Private Parties: A Comparative Perspective* (Oxford University Press 2007) 198.
309 Davies 256.

facilitative nature of the existing limited legislation on the PFI serves to reaffirm rather than provide the foundation of the contracting power of the Crown. In addition, it remains uncertain, in many cases – such as those of the National Health Service (Private Finance) Act 1997 and the Criminal Justice Act 1991 – whether the government enacted them fulfilling the prescriptions of the Concordat or for other, entirely unrelated, reasons.

The nature of this legislation, in tandem with its varied application, and uncertainty around government motivations, thus fails to give us a clear definition; despite the fact that there are some instances of the practice of the constitutional actors which consider the agreement of the Concordat as binding, there are occasions when this is not the case.

5.3. *The criterion of 'reason' in the recognition of the Concordat of 1932 as a constitutional convention and the modern adaptation of the Concordat to the PFI*

The final requirement set by Jennings is that there is a reason for the recognition of a practice as a constitutional convention. As we analysed earlier, the government has not followed the practice of using legislation as a means of establishing a means of accountability for the PFI. This has produced a gap of constitutional accountability over the broader political considerations of the use of PFIs; these broader considerations include the suitability of an activity for exercise by the private sector, the environmental concerns related to the project, the degree of suitable access to citizens' private data by the private contractor, and, generally, all these considerations which are largely unrelated to the economic productivity of the PFI project. The recognition of the Concordat as a constitutional convention would require the government to use legislation as means of accountability for PFI projects. The discussion of the relevant bills would inevitably mean that the complete Parliament having to explore the detail and discuss each individual PFI project in question, and this discussion would be able to include all the aforementioned broader political considerations related to the project, completing the gap of constitutional accountability. This is arguably a reason for the recognition of the Concordat as a constitutional convention, in keeping with the requirement of 'reason' as provided by Jennings.

However, we require further elaboration with respect to the applicability of the norm contained in the Concordat to the PFI. The reason sitting behind this is that the Concordat was agreed more than 80 years ago, many years before the imposition of the NPM reforms which gave rise to the PFI. For this reason, when we claim that the Concordat should be a principle of the Economic Constitution towards the PFI, we need to discuss how the Concordat will be applied in a setting at such a distance, historically-speaking, (and yet, as we will see, in another sense, so close and recognisable) to the setting around which the Concordat was agreed.

The original text of the Concordat provides the following:

> where it is desired that continuing functions should be exercised by a government department (particularly where such functions involve financial liabilities extending beyond a given year) it is proper that the powers and duties to be exercised should be defined by specific statute.[310]

It may be observed, in the first instance, from our earlier analysis of the background of the Concordat, that the parties which agreed it, in other words, the PAC and the Treasury, intended to provide a rule which could be applied beyond merely the specific context of their interchanges, such as the provisions by the Ministry of Labour and the expenditure of the Home Office. The wording that was used, such as 'continuing functions exercised by a government department' and 'matter of general principle', shows that their purpose was to regulate, in more general situations, which powers are assigned to a department, and in particular where there is a creation of financial liability.

The wording which the PAC and the Treasury used when constructing the Concordat reflects the structure of the government which they could see operating around them. It was a government organised on the basis of departments, echoing the writings of Max Webber, who just 10 years previously, in 1922, had published his influential essay 'The Nature, Conditions, and Development of Bureaucratic Herrschaft'.[311] Each department would be assigned its own budget, and, through this budget, it would commit the public sector to financial liabilities as it delivered the public function. As part of a process begun at the end of the nineteenth century, the PAC agreed an important parameter with the Treasury: the limitation thus set out would be that, when the government intended to restructure its activity, as is an inevitable part of responsive governmental evolution, legislation other than that of the Appropriation Act should shape the re-assigning of functions to government departments, particularly in instances when this would involve financial liabilities.

In a modern PFI setting, however, there are three basic differences to this basic model: the first difference is that a PFI project can be agreed between a department and a private contractor, as typically happens with the department of Defence. Alternatively, it can be agreed between an agency and a private contractor, as, for example, in dealings with the Ministry of Transport. In cases of PFI activity by an agency, it will be the agency committing itself to financial liabilities towards the private sector, and not a department, as the Concordat, in its original form, would require. Any agency, such as the Highways Agency in the case of a PFI project such as the M25, would be committed to pay the

---

310 Ram 17.
311 Max Weber, 'Bureaucracy' in Roth Gunther and Claus Wittich (eds), *Economy and Society: An Outline of Interpretive Sociology* (University of California Press 1979).

private consortium periodic payments for the project. In other words, the agency, whether funded by the department or not, would be the one creating the financial liabilities towards the private sector.

The second difference is that, in the 1932 setting, the roles of the exercise of functions assigned and the role of the creation of financial liabilities were both united in one body. This body was a department, and it would be both the body exercising the function which was assigned (to use the original phrases from the Concordat), and, simultaneously, the body which created financial liabilities for the public sector. Today, in an NPM structure such as the PFI, these two roles are performed by different bodies, being, respectively, the department or agency on one side and the private contractor on the other. In a PFI setting, the department or agency creates the financial liability, but the exercise of continuing functions is provided by a different body, namely the private body which undertakes the provision of the service.

Alongside these two differences there is a third one, which relates to the consequences of the application of the Concordat. The original text of the Concordat refers to legislation which is required, in case continuing functions are assigned to a department. However, today, the system has many other instruments apart from the law, while the law – as Feldman pointed out – performs many functions which are different and more varied, highlighting that norms are an important aspect of bureaucratic rationality and that they are not all judicially enforceable. Consequently, it is reasonable to ask questions around which of the legal instruments of the new age, and which of their functions, we should understand in relation to the Concordat in its application to the PFI.

An important guiding point in our attempt to construe the Concordat in the modern context of the PFI, which differs from the original environment of 1932 in at least these three points which we have distinguished, is provided by its rationale towards the kind of financial liabilities that it was originally intended to address. The background of the Concordat – in tandem with the wording used when the Treasury and the PAC agreed – point to an important characteristic which underlies this agreement: this is the significant character of the expenses involved by government in the shaping of its organisation. In other words, what the PAC had attempted to do, in all the years that it pushed for the recognition of the need for legislation, and what the Treasury had come to agree on in 1932, was simply that, when the government is about to change its structure ('functions assigned to a department'), involving significant public expenditure ('particularly where such functions involve financial liabilities extending beyond a given year'), this should be done with the enactment of legislation other than the Appropriation Act. Furthermore, financial liabilities extending beyond a given year do not merely mean liabilities which are insignificant or comparatively rather trivial, such as the acquisition of office supplies or the painting of a Ministry's offices: it would be difficult to suppose that the PAC and the Treasury agreed that legislation might be necessary in such conditions. On the contrary, it is more likely that they meant that legislation *is* needed when important liabilities are created for the public sector, such as was the case in the liabilities created by the training and relocation of the unemployed or the deployment and organisation of police forces, in which two cases the PAC had protested to the Treasury.

This point is a crucial one in our examination of the extent to which, and how, the Concordat would be applied to the PFI. It is well acknowledged that a PFI project, as a structure, is a source of financial liabilities for the public sector, especially if it extends over long periods of time, such as 30 years. This is the case, irrespective of which form the public money takes as it is channelled to the private sector, and irrespective of whether the public function will be exercised by government itself or by a private party on behalf of the government. With respect to the expenditure, it may be the case that the agency, instead of a department, commits itself to the expenditure involved in the payment to the private contractor during this 30-year period, but the fact is that if the department stops making its payments to the agency, then the agency will not be able to pay for the service involved in the PFI. The money, in other words, will still come from the government, exactly as was the case in 1932, even if it comes channelled through an agency. With respect to the private exercise of function, we should stress, here, that – according to the reports of both the NAO and the PAC – the ultimate responsibility of the public function in cases of the PFI always rests with the authority, and consequently, it is accurate to describe the private party as exercising a public function on behalf of the authority.

It needs to be noted, therefore, that the Concordat should be applied both to PFI projects which are being agreed between a department and a private contractor, but also to PFI projects which are agreed between an agency and a private contractor, as long as the money for the operation of the PFI is provided by the department. These are monies which are public, they are significant in size, and they accompany the exercise of a public function. Given that, as we showed earlier, the PAC and Treasury had intended that cases fulfilling such criteria should be based on legislation other than the Appropriation Act, there seems to be no reason why we should not conclude that agency PFI projects should be covered by the Concordat. In this way, it should not be the case that a department only finances agency PFI activity by means of the Appropriation Act. There should be additional legislation, because this would bring the activity within the normative prescription of the Concordat.

With respect to the entities which are covered by the Concordat, we have, up to this point, distinguished two. These are the departments, which provide the clearest case of application of the Concordat, and the agencies, which receive their funding for their PFI activities from the departments. The questions to which we will now turn are concerned with two more marginal, but existing, cases. The first of these is around what happens to agencies or other public bodies which are not departments, and which do not receive support for their PFI activity from departments. These entities can be of three kinds: entities which are financed directly by Parliament, entities which are participating in PFI projects via their own means, and entities which are participating in PFI projects which are financially self-sustaining and do not need any support from the government or the entity itself.

Using the same analytical approach as we employed earlier, which considers the significant expenditure as the underlying rationale of the Concordat, it would be helpful to discuss the applicability of the Concordat in such cases with reference to the concept of public money. The concept of public money has been central to the construction of the auditing system of accountability, and was substantially analysed by Lord Sharman in his influential 2001 report entitled 'Audit and Accountability in Central Government', to which we referred earlier. Lord Sharman distinguishes between classic and modern definitions of public money. According to him:

> Classic thinking on what constitutes public money concentrates on how revenue is raised and on Parliamentary authorisation of expenditure. On the first of these bases, public money will consist of tax revenues and government borrowings, as well as income generated by public bodies from fees and charges. On the second, public money would consist largely of money voted in estimates, but would also cover cases where money was raised under statutory powers (for example, through levies on particular industries).[312]

However, as he clarifies, these existing definitions are not able to provide a comprehensive view in the current climate. Later in Lord Sharman's argument, he concentrates his analysis upon the subject of public money from a subjective perspective, examining the organs which manage public money, among which are government departments (including agencies and trading funds), NDPBs, Public Corporations, Devolved Administrations, Local Authorities, Parliamentary Bodies (such as the NAO), Bodies connected to the Monarchy, and Local Public Spending Bodies, as well as the contractors of PFI contracts.

The criteria provided by Lord Sharman can provide us with a point of reference to the problem of the application of the Concordat in the aforementioned marginal cases, which include those entities receiving their budget directly from Parliament without the involvement of a department, those entities which participate in PFI projects by their own means, and entities which are participating in PFI projects which are financially self-sustaining and do not need any support from either the government or the entity itself. All these cases should be included in the Concordat on a case-by-case basis as long they are among the entities which manage public money, and as long as the public part of the money that they manage is involved in PFI projects. It should be stressed that the characteristic of the expenditure of public money as *significant* expenditure is always present in PFI, given that both the NAO and the PAC have ruled that the PFI procurement option should only be considered for large-scale projects.

---

312 Lord Sharman of Redlynch 9.

Having discussed the applicability of the Concordat to the PFI activities of departments, agencies and other entities, we will now proceed to the most challenging part of its application to the PFI, which is the norm outlined by the prescription of the Concordat itself. As we highlighted earlier, the original 1932 Concordat refers to the need for legislation as the consequence of its application: it states that 'it is proper that the powers and duties to be exercised should be defined by specific statute'. However, as Feldman has distinguished, the NPM is based on a much more complicated normative activity of government, while the law itself serves many different functions. It is, therefore, important to isolate the principles to which reference needs to be made so that we properly construe the prescription of the Concordat requiring legislation. In accordance with our argument, these two principles should be those of constitutional accountability and bureaucratic effectiveness, and the proper construction of the normative part of the Concordat should be based on a proper balance between these two principles, which – as we will see – are in opposition to each other.

The requirement of the existence of a specific statute, can be interpreted as meaning two different things: in one sense, it can mean that there will be a new statute every time a PFI project is to become operational and that this statute will provide for the powers and duties transferred to the private contractor. Fundamentally, this is a construction in which enabling legislation will be required for every PPP project, establishing the procedures which have to be followed when government intends to exercise its discretion and commit expenditure to a PPP project. In another sense, the requirement of the existence of specific statute can also mean that there will be a broad statute covering the PFI projects of a specific sector in general, and then there will be authorisation by Parliament (by means of statutory instrument) for every PFI project within this specific sector, providing for the powers and duties transferred to the private contractor. This construction is based on the enactment of framework, rather than enabling legislation, which will establish the basic mechanism of accountability for every PPP project, and which requires the adoption of a statutory instrument.

The first construction of the prescription of the Concordat poses many advantages as it seems to offer to fill up the gap of constitutional accountability over the PFI. Indeed, as we have explained, the gap itself has been caused by the limited use of statutory authorisation by the contracting government. This first construction of the Concordat would require legislation on every single PFI contract, and the government would be held accountable in the process by the representatives of the people, as constitutional accountability requires. The involvement of the complete Parliament and the time-consuming, serious and thorough debate which the enactment of legislation involves would surely serve to evolve discussion of the broader political aspects of the PFI, irrespective of whether they are related to economic productivity. Then the NAO and the PAC, as well as the other committees of Parliament which produce material on the economic performance of the PFI could continue their habitual focus on the economic aspects of the PFI, with limited space to exercise a normative role, given that there would be ample room for the exercise of this normative role with the authority of legislation.

However, this first construction of the Concordat negates one of the basic principles of the NPM, which is the principle of effectiveness. The sheer number of PFI projects which are being advanced every year would paralyse Parliament, because it would necessarily have to hurriedly discuss each new statute over the PFI, thus potentially reducing the quality of the legislation produced. Furthermore, PFI projects would take longer to come into operation, something which would inevitably increase their cost, because the private contractor would remain exposed to uncertainty for a longer period of time. This cost increase would also be undesirable from the perspective of their effectiveness, because, necessarily, the public sector would have to pay more. For these reasons, we may conclude that, despite the fact of the first construction of the rule of the Concordat, ironically, effectiveness of the PFI may be compromised.

The second construction of the Concordat would interpret the meaning of the phrase 'specific statute' of the Concordat as one which is closer to the notion of authorisation by statute. Following this construction, there will be the need for a framework statute for every PFI sector, which will provide that, for the authorisation of expenditure on every PFI project, Parliament will need to be presented with a statutory instrument related to the PFI project in question. The use of a statutory instrument would safeguard an important feature. Parliament would be informed about departments' PFI projects and it would thus have the opportunity to discuss them, holding each Ministerial decision to approve a PFI project accountable.

The properties of a statutory instrument, which we have offered in the previous construction, and to which we will now turn, determine how it might be used. There are statutory instruments which are subject to the negative resolution procedure, and which become law unless there is an objection from the House. In the first kind of statutory instrument of the negative resolution procedure, the instrument is produced in draft form, and cannot be advanced if the draft is disapproved within 40 days. In the second kind of instrument of the negative resolution procedure, the instrument is produced and can be annulled if a motion to annul – known as 'prayer' – is passed within 40 days. In addition to the negative resolution procedure, there are also instruments of the affirmative resolution procedure, which cannot become law unless approved by both Houses. The first kind of these instruments is produced in draft and cannot be made unless the draft is approved by both Houses (or, for financial statutory instruments, by the House of Commons). The second kind contains the instruments which are produced but cannot come into force unless or until they are approved. The instruments of the third kind will come into effect immediately after having been made, but cannot remain in force unless approved within a statutory period (usually either 28 or 40 days). Further to these procedures for both the instruments of the negative and the affirmative resolution procedure, there are also instruments of other procedures. In the first of these other procedures the instrument is required to be produced before Parliament after being made but it does not require Parliamentary scrutiny, while in the second procedure, the instrument is not required to be produced in this way at all.

In order to select which one of these procedures will be required for the modern application of the Concordat in the PFI, it is necessary to find a balance between the two poles of constitutional accountability and bureaucratic/economic effectiveness. In the one extreme, the one in which bureaucratic effectiveness is intensively focused upon, while constitutional accountability is of considerably less significance, there is the option provided by the procedure which requires that the instrument is presented to Parliament after having been made without the requirement of Parliamentary scrutiny. Such an extreme would safeguard the bureaucratic effectiveness of the promotion of the PFI, but it would not promote constitutional accountability, which aims at the scrutiny of the executive by the representatives of the people. At the other extreme we have the version of the affirmative resolution procedure which would require the instrument to be established in draft, but not to be made, unless the draft was approved by both houses (or the House of Commons, in cases of financial statutory instruments). Such an extreme would safeguard the constitutional accountability of the executive with respect to the promotion of the PFI, but it would come at the cost of the effectiveness of this promotion, because it would signify significantly less speedy awards of contract. It is undeniable that one could argue for almost all types of procedures described earlier in this paragraph, using arguments drawn from the two opposing poles of constitutional accountability and economic/bureaucratic effectiveness.

Our preferred position is that a healthy balance is struck between these two opposing poles, with the version of the affirmative resolution procedure which requires that the instruments are laid immediately after having been made, but with the proviso that they cannot remain in force unless approved within a statutory period (either 28 or 40 days). This option is fairly balanced, because, from the perspective of constitutional accountability, it ensures that every new PFI project is laid and discussed in Parliament, and that it cannot be concluded unless Parliament provides its approval. This ensures that the government will be held accountable by the representative of the people, as constitutional accountability requires. From the perspective of economic/bureaucratic effectiveness, this procedure makes certain that a fair price is paid because effectiveness to accountability is ensured. For the effective establishment of a PFI contract with a 30-year term, insisting upon an additional 28 or 40 days for Parliament to provide its consent is not such an unreasonable burden: it marginally but fruitfully slows the speed of the transactions.

A further point to which we need to refer relates to the content of the secondary legislation which will be produced. A starting point of the argument which we have followed in the present section has been the importance we ascribed to the significant character of the expense which accompanies the exercise of the continuing function. The fact, however, that the application of the Concordat is triggered by a financial matter, which is the significant financial liability undertaken by the government, either directly or through an authority, does not signify that the legislation produced will solely address these financial aspects. Instead it will, both at the primary level, in which broad pieces of legislation are drawn up by departmental sector, around PFI activity, and at the secondary level, in which secondary legislation will be made on a project-by-project basis, legislation which will include provisions related to all aspects of a PFI project, ranging across the complete spectrum of subjects that might be of interest to particular PFI projects, and which cannot be completely discussed in terms of the auditing system of accountability. One reason which is important to highlight is that, if this legislation is only financial, then two problems are created: first, we will be constructing a double system, with the auditing system of accountability sharing the same goals as the system of accountability involving the voting of legislation – something which will result in the unnecessary waste of resources, and can lead to incompatibility. Second, a purely financial construction of the legislation would involve the exclusion of the House of Lords from its debate and voting. This would, however, have a negative impact on the quality of constitutional accountability which is created with the Concordat for the PFI, because it would limit dialogue to only one part of Parliament, the House of Commons. For both these reasons, we may conclude that, despite the fact that the application of the Concordat to the PFI is triggered by the intensely significant financial nature of the PFI, the resulting legislation needs to be legislation extending way beyond the financial aspects of the PFI.

In summary, our argument is that the Concordat needs to be adapted to the present economic reality of the PFI if it is to play a meaningful role in filling the gap of constitutional accountability left by the practice of the government in failing to use legislation in the promotion of the PFI. This adaptation would strike a good balance between the values of constitutional accountability and economic effectiveness. Too much Parliamentary involvement would signify sound constitutional accountability at the expense of economic effectiveness. Too little Parliamentary involvement would signify expedient promotion of the economic effectiveness in the promotion of the PFI at the expense of constitutional accountability. A good balance between these two values is achieved if we construct the Concordat to require that a framework statute is enacted for each PFI project department, which will provide that, for the authorisation of expenditure for every new PFI project, the Secretary of State for the said department will need to provide a statutory instrument for affirmation by Parliament. This statutory instrument will be in force immediately after its making, but it will be invalidated in cases where the Parliament does not affirm it within a stipulated period of between 28 and 40 days.

The position which we have advocated is designed to address the concerns of a number of commentators whose ideas we introduced in the first part of this chapter. For Margit Cohn, the exercise of government powers without Parliamentary authorisation in cases of both imperium and dominium, is problematic in terms of proper administrative practice, participation, clarity and accountability. At least for this part of the government's exercise of dominium powers, which are exercised in the form of PFI, our construction provides a solution which will permit the authorisation of the government through legislation. Our position towards Turpin is that of partial difference, because she advocates a lack of need for a specific statute to enter contracts. In our view, the recognition of the applicability of the Concordat to the PFI requires a statute, from a perspective of Constitutional Law at least, to authorise the contracting activity of the government. Similarly, we partially differ from Lord Anthony Lester and Matthew Weait, both of whom construct the obligation of the government to use legislation only for the exercise of coercive powers. For us, this obligation also exists for the part of the non-coercive dominium powers which is exercised through the use of PFI.

The recognition of the Concordat as a constitutional convention enables it to operate as a standard of criticism inside the Economic Constitution with respect to the PFI. This is because, with this recognition, it becomes a rule of positive morality of the constitution[313]; it refers, as such, not so much to what the participants of the Constitution perceive is required from them, but what these participants ought to perceive as required from them. Therefore, with the Concordat of 1932 being recognised as a constitutional convention, it becomes a standard of criticism, in case the Treasury breaches its procedural requirements. For this to materialise however, we have shown that the Concordat cannot be applied in a modern setting such a PFI, in its original form, but needs updating in certain areas.

In addition to that, it needs to be noted that the significance of constitutional conventions, such as the Concordat of 1932, has been recently enshrined in the recent case of *Miller*.[314] One of the subjects that the Supreme Court in *Miller* examined related to the properties of application of the Sewel constitutional convention, which requires that the UK government abstains from legislating on devolved matters. The Lords argued that 'it is well established that the courts of law cannot enforce a political convention',[315] such as the Sewel convention in this case.

Despite that, they recognised that conventions have a value in the UK Constitution, highlighting that:

> In reaching this conclusion we do not underestimate the importance of constitutional conventions, some of which play a fundamental role in the operation of our constitution. . . . But the policing of its scope and the manner of its operation does not lie within the constitutional remit of the judiciary, which is to protect the rule of law.[316]

---

313 Marshall 10–12.
314 *R (on the application of Miller and another) v Secretary of State for Exiting the European Union* [2017] UKSC 5.
315 Ibid 141.
316 Ibid 151.

Miller, in this way, illustrates that, although the courts would not be likely to apply the Concordat, it could still be recognised as a constitutional convention which, as such, could be important for the operation of the Economic Constitution.

6.   Conclusions

In this chapter, we have focused the examination of our research question to the UK. More specifically, we have examined the systems of accountability which are developed for PFI and the use of public money within it, from the perspective of the relevant criteria and constitutional principles. The conclusions of this examination can be summarised as follows.

We began by examining the integration of the PFI to the Economic Constitution in the UK. Referring to the nature and the scope of the PFI in the UK, we pinpointed three characteristics of this integration: the first characteristic is that the PFI has been widely used as a means of providing public services. By its very nature, it substantially involves the private sector. The second characteristic is that the promotion of the PFI has been accompanied by the creation of a substantial number of organs, whose aim lies primarily in improving the effectiveness of the PFI, and less in the creation of structures for holding the government accountable for this promotion. The third characteristic is that the government has based its contractual activity over the PFI predominantly with the non-prerogative powers of the Crown, rather than to the use of statute.

As we have seen, the limited use of statute over the promotion of the PFI has had a negative impact on the constitutional species of public accountability of the PFI, which means that the opportunities for representatives of the people to hold the government accountable for its decisions on the PFI are limited. The reason for this is that the use of legislation is one of the most powerful means of constitutional accountability, because it gives the representatives of the people the chance to be informed on governmental PFI activity and to hold it accountable over its decisions and the consequent commitment of public money. However, despite the fact that the gap of public accountability is located in the constitutional species of public accountability, the existing mechanism of accountability over the PFI is predominantly based on a criterion of the bureaucratic species of public accountability, that of VfM. The aim of performance or VfM accountability is to evaluate the economic productivity of the promotion of the PFI, and not to discuss broader political considerations of the PFI, such as the suitability of any particular, individual public activity to be undertaken by the private sector, the desirability of the degree of involvement of the private sector the possible danger to private data of citizens, and environmental concerns, amongst others. Such considerations would be opened up for discussion in a healthy system of constitutional accountability, involving the full participation of Parliament, are outside the remit of the activities of the NAO and the PAC, which are the basic organs of performance, VfM, and accountability, and which focus wholly upon economic performance. Similarly, such considerations are left outside the scope of other Parliamentary committees, such as the Lords' Economic Affairs Committee and the Treasury Select Committee, which, again, focus their accountability role on the evaluation of the economic productivity of the PFI. Other Parliamentary Committees demonstrate a very marginal association to the PFI and to the discussion of its broader political aspects.

The fact that the predominant weakness of the system is in the constitutional species of public accountability, while existing mechanisms are focused on the bureaucratic species of public accountability aiming at the evaluation of economic performance, has important consequences for the role of the NAO and the PAC. These two organs, which are provided by the legislative instruments which establish their role as organs of scrutiny and audit, exercise a normative role, which does not appear to have been envisioned for them. The VfM audit, in other words, develops normative and regulatory dynamics through the activities of the NAO and the PAC instead of being an instrument of mere scrutiny as was intended when these two organs were created. The factors which led to this outcome are, first, that the criterion of VfM is unsuitable to address concerns of constitutional accountability, being itself a criterion of bureaucratic accountability and, second, that it is exposed to a significant degree of subjectivity. The combination of these two factors led the NAO and the PAC to use the criterion of VfM as an instrument establishing norms, and not purely as an instrument of scrutiny.

Given that neither the activities of the NAO and the PAC nor those of the other select committees can address the gap of constitutional accountability which is left by the limited use of legislation for the PFI, we proceeded by inquiring if there could be an alternative mechanism which could address this gap. Such a mechanism, we argued, involves the recognition of the Concordat of 1932 between the Treasury and the PAC as a constitutional convention. This recognition imposes a positive obligation upon the government to involve Parliament more in the promotion of the PFI. An inherent part of this involvement must be an appropriate balance between the values of bureaucratic effectiveness and the need for the improvement of constitutional accountability. These exist in diametric opposition: at one extreme, an intense involvement of Parliament in the PFI would improve constitutional accountability, but it would lead to an increase of the timeframe required for new PFI projects, and, therefore, it would have a negative impact in terms of bureaucratic effectiveness; at the other extreme, the marginalisation of the role of Parliament would lead to speedier awarding of PFI contracts, thereby improving bureaucratic effectiveness, but it would lead to weaker constitutional accountability. The solution which we proposed for the modern construction of the Concordat and its application as a principle of the Economic Constitution to the PFI is based on the following requirement: the government would be required to introduce a framework of Acts covering the PFIs of each sector, which would provide for the need of secondary legislation for every new PFI project. This statutory instrument would be in force immediately after its making, but it would be invalidated in cases when the Parliament did not affirm it during a period of either 28 or 40 days after it had been laid.

The solution which we have proposed seeks an appropriate balance between the co-ordinates of bureaucratic effectiveness and constitutional accountability; if adopted, it would involve the participation of the Parliament in the PFI with all the weight, time-consumption and seriousness that the enactment of legislation involves, without having a heavy impact on the bureaucratic effectiveness of the PFI. With the gap of constitutional accountability filled, which would be achieved with the participation of Parliament through the enactment of legislation, the system of accountability over the PFI would be more complete, and would be able to cover the broader political considerations associated with the use of PFI. Such broader political considerations, related to all these subjects which we analysed, such as suitability of public service for outsourcing to the private sector and environmental concerns, would become the subject of debate and accountability when all of Parliament, instead of purely specialised economic committees, participates in the shaping of the normative framework of the PFI. Such participation forms the backbone of the solution which we advocate, which, through the recognition of the Concordat as a constitutional convention, regards this participation both as a standard of criticism for the practice of the government and as an element of the positive constitutional morality of the PFI.

2   Public-private partnerships in the United States of America

1.   Introduction

Throughout the previous chapter, we examined the systems of accountability which have been developed for PFI in the UK and the use of public money within it, from the perspective of the relevant criteria and constitutional principles. As was revealed in terms of this research, the government has made little use of legislation in the promotion of PPPs in the UK; the result of this is that the NAO and the PAC – which have been envisioned as organs of auditing scrutiny – perform a normative role using the mechanism of VfM. Furthermore, the limited use of legislation has a negative impact on the constitutional accountability of PPPs. In this chapter, we will turn our attention to the USA. Our purpose will be to examine, through a similar prism of scrutiny, the role of the criteria in the systems of accountability developed for PPPs in the USA.

As has been the case in the UK, PPPs have been used extensively in the USA, with sectors such as those of transport, transit, and urban regeneration dominating the scene. Other sectors also feature significantly, such as those of water treatment and also of defence. An important difference between the UK and the USA can be seen in the role of the legislature in the promotion of PPPs. For the UK, we have seen that the promotion of PPPs is mainly a matter for the executive, which will usually use its common law powers to participate in PPPs and commit public money. By contrast, in the USA, the promotion of PPPs is mostly a matter for the legislature. It is the legislative power which will enact the legislation and which will make PPPs possible. This characteristic of the US Constitution is not limited to the federal level, but also embraces state PPPs. PPPs at all levels are normally conducted after authorisation to contract awarded by the legislature, which provides accountability mechanisms and criteria by means of legislation.

The enactment of a substantial amount of legislation on PPPs has produced a large number of criteria upon which the evaluation of PPPs is based. Each law sets its own criteria for evaluation of PPPs and this diversity of criteria does not contribute to effective accountability. As we will argue later on, the appropriate framework to solve these problems would be to allow discussion about them on the grounds of the constitutional requirement of due process, and the duty of the executive to systematise the criteria of accountability provided by the legislation. The reason why we will support this case is that the resulting picture of public accountability which derives from the co-existence of so many criteria of evaluation for PPPs – criteria as diverse as effectiveness, public interest, propriety and reasonableness, to name but a few – is vague. Vagueness is one of the grounds of the procedural aspect of due process, which is established with the Fifth Amendment of the US Constitution.

A solid point of departure towards the establishment of this argument is the analysis of the characteristics and scope of the integration of PPPs in the Economic Constitution of the USA.

2. The integration of PPPs to the Economic Constitution in the USA

In order to provide the characteristics of the integration of PPPs to the USA Economic Constitution, we first need a very basic sketch of the structure of control in economic matters at federal levels. The reason for this is that PPPs are economic structures, and they are, therefore, substantially exposed to the basic mechanisms of economic accountability.

2.1. *The Economic Constitution in the USA – the basic structure*

The system of accountability over economic matters and matters of economic policy in the US Economic Constitution is based on a substantial role played by the Congress. The basic skeletal framework of the Economic Constitution of the USA is provided in Art I, §§ 8 and 9 of the US Constitution. According to § 8 of Art I:

> The Congress shall have Power To lay and collect Taxes, Duties, Imposts and Excises, to pay the Debts and provide for the common Defense and general Welfare of the USA (. . .). To borrow Money on the credit of the USA.

The same section provides the Congress with the widely-acknowledged power of regulating the commerce among the states. It is charged:

> To regulate Commerce with foreign Nations, and among the several States, and with the Indian Tribes.[1]

The Constitution provides these economic powers to the Congress, as well as the ability to 'make all Laws which shall be necessary and proper for carrying

---

1 U.S. Const. Art. I, § 8.

into Execution the foregoing Powers, and all other Powers vested by this Constitution in the Government of the USA, or in any Department or Officer thereof'.[2]

The above prescriptions are completed by the economic provisions of Art I, § 9, which lays the constitutional requirements of the use of public money by the Executive:

> No Money shall be drawn from the Treasury, but in Consequence of Appropriations made by Law; and a regular Statement and Account of the Receipts and Expenditures of all public Money shall be published from time to time.

These provisions essentially outline the economic powers of the raising and disposing of funds to the Congress. The Congress has, by the power vested in it through the Constitution, the power to collect money by imposing taxes, to borrow them, to regulate the commerce between the states, and to make any law which is required in order for these powers to be exercised. The Executive has the power to draw money from these, but only based on law, and only by informing the Congress and the public about how these monies were spent through regular statements. A similar duty of oversight of the executive is drawn by the requirement of Article II, § 3, which requires the President to give information to the Congress 'about the state of the union' and to 'recommend to their consideration such measures as he shall judge necessary and expedient'.

The powers established in Art I, § 8, including the economic powers which we have mentioned, are theoretically a numerus clausus of powers, which – in constitutional theory – means that the Congress has no other powers except those enumerated in this section. However, the Supreme Court has broadly interpreted the provision of Art I, § 8, which we saw earlier, and which permits Congress to enact any laws which are necessary and proper for the execution of these powers.[3] These powers can be combined so that the Congress legislates on subjects qualitatively different from those subjects explicitly provided. In this way, for instance, in the case of *McCulloch v Maryland*, 17 U.S. (4 Wheat.) 316 [1819], which is considered a landmark case, the Court accepted that under the 'necessary and proper' clause, Congress had the power to charter a federal bank that performed all the functions that state-chartered banks could perform, competing directly with them. The authorities that the Court used to substantiate the constitutional exercise of this non-enumerated economic power by the Congress, were the clauses providing for the taxation and spending economic

---

2 Ibid.
3 Robert Allen Sedler, *Constitutional Law in the United States* (2nd edn, Kluwer Law International 2014) 42–6.

powers of the Congress, the power to raise and support armies, and the economic power to regulate interstate commerce.

In this way, Congress enjoys very important and wide-ranging powers in terms of the Economic Constitution of the USA. The Executive, which has the power to draw money, can only do so based on appropriations made by law, and it has the constitutional duty to inform both Congress and the public over its use of these funds. As we will see, the omnipotence of the Congress to enact legislation regulating economic life finds a rich field of expression in the use of PPPs in the USA. There are laws behind most of the PPPs at federal level, and also behind nearly every form of federal contribution to PPPs at state level. This particular contribution is generally wide, especially in the areas of transport and water provision. Furthermore, this culture of the legal substantiation of expenses, which derives from the rich powers of the Congress, has significantly affected the culture related to PPPs inside the states, irrespective of federal contribution to these projects. There is a rich seam of legislation across the states, which either focus on PPPs in general or which authorise specific projects.

2.2. Conclusions with respect to the focus and methodology of research in this chapter

Having provided this very basic account of the Economic Constitution in the USA, we may carry forward an important conclusion which will guide us in the next sections of the present chapter. This conclusion is that Congress possesses important powers for the regulation of the economic activity of the USA, both at federal and state levels.

It is important to note that the system in the USA is presidential, and it therefore lacks the Parliamentary tradition which exists in the UK. Nevertheless, this does not mean that the executive is not accountable to the legislature in the USA, but rather that this accountability is manifest in different form. The Congress has the ability of oversight towards the spending of the executive in PPPs, and based on the results of this oversight, the Congress may or may not approve the expenditure requested by the executive. In addition, it may choose whether or not to enact legislation desired by the executive, or to expose the executive to political consequences, such as exposure to the public. In this way, although the term 'oversight' is notionally different from the term 'accountability', in the USA 'oversight' leads to accountability because of the important powers of the Congress. As we discussed in the Introduction, accountability, according to Bovens, is defined as the process through which an actor has to explain to a forum his actions and may face consequences.[4] This definition is fulfilled with the USA oversight, because if the explanations that the executive

---

4 See our Introduction pp. xxx–xxx [orig. 10–14].

provide the Congress for its spending of public money in PPPs are not satisfactory in terms of this oversight, then the Congress may bring significant consequences to the executive, such as the non-approval of the respective budgets, the non-enactment of legislation desired by the executive, and various political consequences.

In that sense, when we refer to 'criteria of accountability' in the USA, we refer to these criteria that the law provides as relevant to the exercise of legislative oversight. As we will see, these criteria can be those which are prescribed as necessary in the presentation of documents to the legislature, criteria which will inform the evaluation of bids, and criteria which are deemed necessary for the contracting activity of government. The reason for this is that all these types of criteria will inform the oversight and can lead, in cases where the legislature is not satisfied, to several kinds of negative consequences for the government. In this way, if the legislature is not satisfied that, for instance, the government promoted effectiveness in its contracting activity, the legislature may disapprove budgets dedicated to a specific PPP. In the same way, if the legislature concludes that one of the criteria of evaluation of bids has not been fulfilled, then it might not approve a specific project when presented for legislative review. For these reasons, in relation to the present chapter, we will refer to criteria of accountability as criteria which, by impacting the result of the oversight, can lead – as Bovens detailed – to the occurrence of negative consequences to the contracting government.

The difference between the two systems also affects the role of the committees. In the UK, we chose to focus on the work of the PAC and other committees in Parliament in order to explore the prescriptions established for the PPPs, and which determine the basic parameters of the accountability for PPPs to the legislature. In the USA, there is neither an equivalent to the PAC, nor any other committee which has overall responsibility in the holding to account of the executive over PPPs. Instead it is through the enactment of legislation that the Congress, as well as the state legislatures, hold the government accountable over PPPs, because the enactment of this legislation depends upon the results of the oversight exercised by the legislature. Furthermore, this legislation determines the basic normative prescriptions of PPPs, rather than providing this through the work of the committees, as is the case in the UK parliamentary system. For these reasons, a substantial point of focus for the USA system of accountability over PPPs depends upon the content and the enactment of this legislation, which materialises the wide powers of the legislature in the USA.

The closest mechanism to the UK system of the examination in parliamentary committees is that of the Congressional Hearings. The main purpose of these hearings is to provide information to specialised committees of the Congress on how to proceed with the enactment of legislation.

With respect to this basic tendency, in which hearings serve as mechanisms of acquiring information, a first example would be the hearing entitled 'Overview of Public-Private Partnerships in Highway and Transit Projects'. The Committee on Transportation and Infrastructure receives information in order to 'explore how the TIFIA program[5] is working, and what changes we may need to make in the next authorization bill which we hopefully can complete later this year'. Similarly, in the hearing entitled 'Reducing Childhood Obesity: Public-Private Partnerships to Improve Nutrition and Increase Physical Activity in Children', the Committee received testimonies with the purpose of improving and discussing the proposed 'Childhood Obesity Reduction Bill'.[6] In a similar way, the hearing under the title 'The Use of PPPs as a Management Tool for Federal Real Property' considers the characteristics of a proposed Federal Asset Management bill, which would provide authorisation for the use of PPPs in real property by the General Services Administration (GSA).[7] Similarly, in the hearing entitled 'Redeveloping Federal Property through PPPs', the committee received testimonies related to the Federal Triangle South in Washington 'as a case study for redeveloping underutilized Federal properties through PPPs'.[8] Legislation, both already enacted,[9] and proposed,[10] has also been an important point of reference in a discussion aiming to assess whether PPPs are indeed a viable option. In the same spirit, the agency in question is asked directly whether there is anything that the Congress can do legislatively to accelerate the evaluations of the agency with respect to the advancement of a PPP.[11]

Other hearings, however, despite the fact that they maintain the focus on the acquisition of information, also contain an aspect requiring a clear request for explanation from a witness which originates from the executive. An example of a congressional hearing which demonstrates this trend is 'The DHS Infrastructure Protection Division; Public-Private Partnerships to Secure Critical Infrastructure', in which a subject central to the discussion is whether the Home Department has adequately fulfilled its missions of the Homeland Security Act of 2002[12]

---

5 TIFIA stands for the 'Transportation Infrastructure Finance and Innovation Act', which is an important piece of PPP legislation which we will see in time.

6 Committee on Health, Education, Labor, and Pensions of the United States Senate, *Hearing on Reducing Childhood Obesity: Public-Private Partnerships to Improve Nutrition and Increase Physical Activity in Children* (108th Congress, 2004) 8.

7 Subcommittee on Technology and Procurement Policy of the Committee on Government Reform of the House of Representatives, *Hearing on the Use of Public-Private Partnerships as a Management Tool for Federal Real Property* (107th Congress, 2001) 6, 14, 15, 38.

8 Subcommittee on Economic Development, Public Buildings, and Energy Management of the Committee on Transportation and Infrastructure of the House of Representatives, *Hearing on Federal Triangle South: Redeveloping Underutilized Federal Property through Public-Private Partnerships* (113th Congress, 2013) V.

9 Ibid VII and 50.

10 Ibid VII and 4.

11 Ibid 17.

12 Subcommittee on Infrastructure and Border Security, and Subcommittee on Cybersecurity, Science and Research and Development of the Select Committee on Homeland Security of the House of Representatives, *Hearing on the DHS Infrastructure Protection Division; Public-Private Partnerships to Secure Critical Infrastructures* (108th Congress, 2014) 32.

which created the Department.[13] It also required evaluation of whether further steps are necessary, including the enactment of further legislation,[14] and the provision of additional funding.[15] A further example is the hearing entitled 'Public-Private Partnerships: Innovative Financing and Protecting the Public Interest'. In this specific hearing, the committee examined whether PPPs are a viable way to fill the funding gap for transport infrastructure which would soon be expected for the fulfilment of future transportation bills.[16] While the focus on the committee is again towards future legislation,[17] the difference with other reports is that the committee challenges the representative of the Federal Department of Transportation on the steps which have been taken to protect the public interest. Persistent points of interest for the committee are concerns over possible 'sweetheart deals' with private companies,[18] the probabilities of achieving alignment between public and private interests,[19] advances of the executive to augment or update the federal investment,[20] and the properties of model PPP-enabling legislation for the states prepared by the department.[21] Even in this case however, in which the representative of the government is asked questions which challenge the steps it has taken, the report offers a strong factual and descriptive background, intended to fully inform the committee.

The reports take a descriptive, rather than a prescriptive approach towards the criteria of evaluation and accountability for PPPs when they examine the possible legislative options. This creates a clear difference between the role of the PAC and the other committees which we saw in the UK. Crucially, none of the USA reports contains a distinct section which offers suggestions to the government, probably because this would be a breach of the separation of powers doctrine which is strict in the US Constitutional model. The criteria which they use are quite diverse and include those of public (or best) interest,[22] (fair) value,[23]

---

13 Ibid.

14 Ibid 29.

15 Ibid 2, 21.

16 Subcommittee on Highways and Transit of the Committee on Transportation and Infrastructure of the House of Representatives, *Hearing on Public-Private Partnerships: Innovative Financing and Protecting the Public Interest* (110th Congress, 2007) 1.

17 Ibid 75.

18 Ibid 19.

19 Ibid 6.

20 Ibid 10.

21 Ibid 10–11.

22 Ibid 14.

23 Subcommittee on Economic Development, Public Buildings, and Energy Management of the Committee on Transportation and Infrastructure of the House of Representatives, *Hearing on Federal Triangle South: Redeveloping Underutilized Federal Property through Public-Private Partnerships* 10, 30; Subcommittee on Technology and Procurement Policy of the Committee on Government Reform of the House of Representatives, *Hearing on the Use of Public-Private Partnerships as a Management Tool for Federal Real Property* 2.

efficiency,[24] effectiveness,[25] and others, dependent on which one bets fits the specific piece of legislation they examine or they try to discuss. In none of them do we find either a definition or something which remotely resembles a definition of these notions.

For these reasons, we considered it an appropriate research decision to focus on the provisions of legislation for PPPs in the USA, rather than on congressional hearings as we did in the UK. Legislation in the USA is the main mechanism employed by Congress to prescribe criteria of accountability for PPPs, rather than the workings of the committees of the legislature as was the case in the UK. Further to that, it is through the enactment of legislation itself that Congress, as a forum of accountability, expresses its concerns around, or encouragement of, government action in PPPs.

The final point which needs to be highlighted with respect to our decision to focus on legislation instead of Congressional hearings refers to the main argument which we seek to establish in this chapter. In the UK chapter, we argued that the basic cause of the problem of accountability in the UK is that the PAC and the NAO establish normative prescriptions with respect to the main criterion of accountability, in other words, the criterion of VfM. In the USA, our argument is critically different. We will argue that the problem of accountability lies not so much with the way that congressional committees perceive the criteria, but rather, largely on the limited co-ordination of these criteria into consistent, uniform meanings by a central co-ordinating mechanism.

2.3. PPPs in the USA and their scope

The previous sub-section outlining the Economic Constitution in the USA has shown that Congress plays an important role in the area of economic regulation and accountability. The instrument through which this role is materialised with respect to PPPs is the production of legislation. This provides accountability mechanisms and criteria and is frequently the means by which projects are authorised. Before we discuss the characteristics of this legislation, it is important to provide for the use and conception of PPPs in the USA.

---

24 Subcommittee on Highways and Transit of the Committee on Transportation and Infrastructure of the House of Representatives, *Hearing on Public-Private Partnerships: State and User Perspectives* (110th Congress, 2007) 29.
25 Ibid; Panel on Public-Private Partnerships of the Committee on Transportation and Infrastructure of the House of Representatives, *Overview of Public-Private Partnerships in Highway and Transit Projects* (113th Congress, 2014) 18; Committee on Health, Education, Labor, and Pensions of the United States Senate, *Hearing on Reducing Childhood Obesity: Public-Private Partnerships to Improve Nutrition and Increase Physical Activity in Children* 20.

A good definition for PPPs in the USA originates from the Government Accountability Office (GAO), which is the equivalent body to the UK's NAO and is headed by the Comptroller General of the USA. According to the GAO:

> Under a public-private partnership, sometimes referred to as a public-private venture, a contractual arrangement is formed between public and private-sector partners. These arrangements typically involve a government agency contracting with a private partner to renovate, construct, operate, maintain, and/or manage a facility or system, in whole or in part, that provides a public service. Under these arrangements, the agency may retain ownership of the public facility or system, but the private party generally invests its own capital to design and develop the properties. Typically, each partner shares in income resulting from the partnership. Such a venture, although a contractual arrangement, differs from typical service contracting in that the private-sector partner usually makes a substantial cash, at-risk, equity investment in the project, and the public sector gains access to new revenue or service delivery capacity without having to pay the private-sector partner.[26]

The definition provided by the GAO is also followed in other sources, such as the Department of Transport,[27] the National Council for PPPs,[28] and across the Congress.[29] The definition itself shares important similarities with the UK definition for PFI. As is the case in the UK definition, PPPs in the USA are contracts; these contracts involve the renovation, construction, operation, maintenance and/or management of a facility which provides a public service. We should note, however, that the GAO definition refers not only to facilities, but also to systems, which can be the object of a US PPP contract. The term 'system' in this context, signals an important difference between the object of PPPs in the two legal systems; this is that, in the USA, PPPs are conceived in broader terms, and are not simply referring to projects which are tied to a facility. They also include a broader collection of arrangements between the public and the private sector, such as agreements for urban regeneration and development.

---

26 United States General Accounting Office, *Public-Private Partnerships – Terms Related to Building and Facility Partnerships* (Glossary, GAO/GGD-99-71, 1999) 13–14.

27 Department of Transportation – Federal Highway Administration, 'Glossary' <http://www.fhwa.dot.gov/ipd/glossary/> accessed 10 September 2017.

28 The National Council of Public-Private Partnerships, 'Glossary of Terms' <http://www.ncppp.org/ppp-basics/glossary-of-terms/> accessed 10 September 2017.

29 Subcommittee on Highways and Transit of the Committee on Transportation and Infrastructure of the House of Representatives, *Hearing on Public-Private Partnerships: Innovative Financing and Protecting the Public Interest* vi.

Anthony Wall illustrates such agreements[30] by reference to the Baltimore development renaissance strategy, adopted throughout the 1970s, 1980s and 2000s. In this case, the problem which the public sector needed to resolve was job losses in the manufacturing sector coupled with a growing trend for suburbanisation, both of which were contributing causes to a falling population. In the context of the renaissance strategy which was adopted, financial incentives were offered to the private sector so that it invested in the area around the port. This led to $800 million of private investment in the decade between 1976 and 1986, almost half of which went to town centre projects, such as the harbour. A convention centre was also built, which increased the customers for local hotels. These, in turn, also received incentives such as below market-rate loans to build around the harbour. Further to these, luxury housing was built, as well as office space and new hotels. It is crucial to draw attention to the fact that, in projects like this, which are considered to be PPPs, the subject is not the building or even the operation of a facility as such, but a broader plan through which the public and the private sector collaborate to achieve social goals, such as reducing unemployment, and raising living standards, to name but two. In such cases, the government exercises its influence over the economy by offering incentives to the private sector which, it predicts, will behave in a specific way, leading to the achievement of the said social goals. This model is quite far removed from the contract and facility-based approach which is stressed in the definition of the PFI in the UK.

In this way, in the USA, PPPs refer not only to facilities as such but also to projects, which are better defined as 'systems', and which include broader social goals which are to be achieved through arrangements between the public and the private sector. For B. Guy Peters,[31] this is an important context from which to isolate the five points which characterise a PPP: the partnership must involve two or more actors, out of which one must be a public entity, each one of these two actors must be able to bargain on his behalf, the partnership should involve a long-lasting relationship, each actor should be able to contribute goods, whether they be material or symbolic, to the relationship, and all actors must have a joint responsibility for the results of the partnership. As is clear to see, Peters describes PPPs in broader terms, focusing on the idea of contributions by the partners, contributions which are broadly defined and which – if deemed appropriate – can exist merely in a symbolic way.

Although the difference which we highlighted between the conception of PPPs in the UK and the USA is existent, it would not be accurate to exaggerate. The

---

30 Anthony Wall, *Public-Private Partnerships in the USA: Lessons to be learned for the United Kingdom* (Routledge 2012) 98–9.

31 B. Guy Peters, '"With a little help from our friends": Public-Private Partnerships as Institutions and Instruments' in Jon Pierre (ed), *Partnerships in Urban Governance: European and American Experience* (St Martin's Press 1998) 11–33.

reason being that, as is the case with the UK's PFI projects, those in the USA usually appear more or less linked with the provision of infrastructure. Taking the year 2000 as our starting point, we will now examine some examples[32] of PPPs related to the construction of infrastructure.

In the area of defence, the Lackland Air Force Base Housing in Texas was procured by means of PPP. The project was agreed between the US Air Force as public partner and the Landmark Organisation Inc. as private contractor, with a starting point in 2001, a project duration of 50 years and an overall value of $42.6m.

Another example of a PPP, this time from the broader area of water provision and management, water-treatment, and desalination projects, is that of the Southwest Water Treatment Plant in San Juan Capistrano in California which was agreed between the Capistrano Valley Water District, as public partner, and ECO Resources, as private contractor. The starting point for this treatment plant was in 2003, the project duration set at 20 years and its value was $25 m. Similarly, the Lake Pleasant Water Treatment Plant in Arizona is a PPP project, agreed between the City of Phoenix, as public partner, and American Water, as private contractor. Again, the starting point was in 2003, the project duration set at 15 years, and its value was $336 m. A further example is the Santa Paula Water Recycling Facility which was agreed between the City of Santa Paula, as public partner, and the Santa Paula Water, LLC, as private contractor. The starting point was in 2008, its duration 30 years and its value $60 m. An additional important water-related PPP project, dealing with desalination, is the Taunton River Desalination Plant, which was agreed between the Massachusetts Municipal Authority, as public partner, and the InimaUSA Corp. for Aquaria Water as private contractor. The starting point was in 2006, the project duration 20 years and its value $60 m. Water desalination is also the object of the Carlsbad Desalination Project which was agreed between the City of Carlsbad, as public partner and the Poseidon Resources Corporation, as private contractor. The starting point was in 2008, its duration 30 years with two additional 30-year terms and its value $300m. A final example in the area of water treatment refers to the Huntington Beach Water Desalination Facility which was a PPP project signed between the City of Huntington Beach, as public partner and the Poseidon Resources Corporation, as private contractor. The starting point was in 2009, its duration 30 years and its value was $250 m.

Apart from water, a further area of PPP investment is that of Transport, which always attracts very expensive projects and important federal capital input.

---

32 Anthony E. Boardman and Aidan R. Vining, 'P3s in North America: Renting the Money (in Canada), selling the roads (in the USA)' in Graham A. Hodge, Carsten Greve and Anthony E. Boardman (eds), *International Handbook on Public-Private Partnerships* (Edward Elgar Publishing 2010) 383–7.

A prime illustrative example, for our purposes, is the Chicago Skyway PPP project, agreed between the Illinois Toll Highway Authority, as public partner and the Skyway Concession Company, as private contractor. The starting point was in 2004, its duration set at 99 years and its value $1.83 bn. Similarly, another significant transport project was the Indiana Toll Road, agreed between the Indiana Finance Authority, as public partner and the ITR Concession Company LLLC: Cintra and the Macquire Infrastructure Group as private contractors. The starting point was in 2006, the project duration set at 75 years and its value was $3.8 bn. The I-495 Capital Beltway High Occupancy Toll Lanes in Virginia also belong to the family of PPP transport-projects. It was signed between the Virginia Department of Transportation, as public partner, and the Fluor-Transurban, as private contractor. The starting point was in 2008, the project duration 80 years and its value was $1.9 bn. A further example of a PPP project in this sector is the Port of Miami Tunnel project, agreed between the Florida Department of Transportation, as public partner and the Miami Access Tunnel, as private contractor. The starting point was in 2008, its duration 31 years and its value $914 m. Similarly, and again located in Florida, we find the Interstate 595 Express PPP project agreed between the Florida Department of Transportation, as public partner and the ACS Infrastructure Development, as private contractor. The starting point was in 2008, its duration 35 years and its value 1.79 bn. Finally, among the PPPs in the transport sector we find the State Highway 130 which is a PPP project agreed between the Texas Department of Transportation, as public partner and the SH 130 Concession Company, LLC, as private contractor. The starting point was in 2008, its duration 50 years and its value was $1.3 bn.

We also find PPPs in the energy sector. A good example of an energy project would be the PPP contract for District Energy Systems in Nashville, which was forged between the City of Nashville, as public partner and the Constellation Energy Projects & Services Group, Inc. as private contractor. The starting point was in 2003, its duration 15 years and its value was $46 m. A further example in the same sector would be the Lakeland Electrical PPP project, agreed between the Florida Municipal Power Agency, as public partner and SunEdison, as private contractor. The starting point was in 2009, its duration 20 years and its value was undisclosed.

There are several preliminary observations which can be made with respect to PPP activity in the USA based on the projects to which we have referred. The first is that, as in the UK, USA PPPs also absorb significant amounts of capital, which can cost millions of dollars and even extend to billions. In addition, another point which we can observe relates to contract duration. While, in the UK, 30 years seems to be the rule by which PFI projects define their maximum duration, in the USA this does not seem to be the case. Once again, US projects are long-term, but, sometimes, they significantly exceed the 30 years' trend and extend to between 50- and 99-year periods. These two observations are significant for our purpose in this section, which is to define the basic characteristics of the integration of PPPs to the Economic Constitution of the USA.

Further to these comparative points, which place the PPPs in the USA on a more or less similar footing to the PFI in the UK, there is one substantial difference: this difference is based upon the use of legislation as an instrument of the promotion of PPPs. Congress has important powers of economic regulation in terms of the Economic Constitution in the USA and this has led to the production of more legislation on PPPs at the federal level, as well as to the promotion of a constitutional culture across the states in which PPPs have to be based on state legislation.

2.4.   *The widespread use of legislation in PPPs*

The general picture across the USA is that, behind every PPP project, irrespective of whether this project is at state or federal level, there is, in almost all cases, primary legislation shaping it. This legislation typically provides for future authorisations by the legislature, maximum duration of the projects, and reporting requirements of the executive to the legislature. Further to that, it provides criteria and mechanisms of accountability. This overall picture is in contrast with the one in the UK, where, as we saw, the main principle is that of contracting by virtue of the inherent powers of the Crown. Contrary to that, in the USA, legislation is typically used to authorise the executive to proceed into PPP agreements.

It is an important feature worth highlighting that the PPPs which we will see in relation to this point regarding legislation originate both from federal and state levels. We want to assert that the reason for this is that the promotion of PPPs based on legislation, rather than on the inherent capacity of the government to contract, is a matter of Economic Constitution which covers the whole of the USA, and not just the federal government – which is the primary focus of our book. Furthermore, in most of the states' PPP activities, the federal government offers a substantial level of economic contribution, which is again rooted in the central role of the federal legislature, namely, the Congress.

A very good illustration of the role of the legislature with respect to authorising and providing accountability mechanisms for PPPs is the Indiana Turnpike project. The project is an example of the Buy-Build-Operate model (BBO). In terms of the BBO PPP model, the transaction takes the form of a contract of asset sale, which also provides for the obligation by the private contractor to rehabilitate or expand the existing facility. The public authority sells the asset to the private contractor, and the latter makes improvements which are necessary for the operation of the facility. It is worth us providing a point of comparison at this point: in the UK, this BBO type would not qualify as a PFI. Instead, it would be considered a type of privatisation.[33] Following this pattern, the Indiana Turnpike was purchased from the State of Indiana by a consortium of companies which undertook the obligation to operate, maintain and develop

---

33 United States General Accounting Office, 4.

the highways for 75 years. This PPP was based on the House Enrolled Act No. 1008, which is codified in the Eighth Title of the Indiana Code.

Indiana Code (IC) § 8-15.5.-1-2 (2015) provides full authority for the executive to enter into PPPs. With respect to accountability, the legislature is provided with all powers of authorisation in PPPs; in this way, the law provides that any decision involving a PPP which will entail tolls has to receive authorisation by the legislature, including, specifically, 'any part of Interstate Highway 69'. It is very clearly provided that:

> (e) The authority may enter into a public-private agreement for a facility project if the general assembly, by statute, authorize the authority to enter into a public-private agreement for the facility project.[34]

In terms of consistent payments by the public authority to the private contractor, again they have to be authorised, according to IC § 8-15.5-10-3, by a statute. The law also delineates a definition for PPPs:

> Sec. 8. 'Public-private agreement' means an agreement under this article between a private entity and the authority under which the private entity, acting on behalf of the authority (and, where applicable, a governmental entity) as lessee, licensee, or franchisee, will plan, design, acquire, construct, reconstruct, equip, improve, extend, expand, lease, operate, repair, manage, maintain, or finance a project.[35]

As a criterion on which accountability will be based, the law provides the one of the 'public interest', setting that 'the authority may enter into a public-private agreement with multiple private entities (. . .), if the authority determines in writing that it is in the public interest to do so'.[36] The fact that the criterion of the 'public interest' is the basic standard for contracting is also implicit in IC § 8-15.5-1-3, where the legislature provides that its rationale for enacting these provisions is the service of the public interest. 'Reasonableness' is also provided as a criterion based upon which the years of the duration of the contract should be evaluated, as well as being a criterion for the determination of the terms of contracts.[37] With respect to maintaining the condition of the facility and ensuring the standard of the operation, the law gives an indication as to its parameters of expectation when describing the standards of debt which it considers appropriate: the income has to be sufficient to keep 'the project in sound physical and financial condition to render adequate and efficient service'.[38]

---

34 IC § 8-15.5-1-2 (2015).
35 IC § 8-15.5-2-8.
36 IC § 8-15.5-5-5.
37 IC § 8-15.5-10-2.
38 IC § 8-15.5-7-4.

In this way, the Indiana Turnpike PPP project was based in law which provides for accountability. The law provided the main standards or criteria designed to determine the accountability of the actors of the project: the department must be held accountable, based on whether or not the project was in the public interest, whether the terms which were agreed were considered reasonable, and on whether the financial structure can ensure that the project is maintained in a condition which can safeguard 'adequate and appropriate service'. These criteria of accountability operate as part of the richly varied raft of mechanisms of public accountability that the law provides, which include the need for legislation authorising almost everything throughout the PPP project, safeguarding the involvement of the legislature at a significant level. The law was also very detailed in providing definition for PPPs and in determining which of its aspects can be contracted out.

If we try to focus a little more on the criteria that the law provides, such as those of the public interest, the reasonableness of the terms, or the adequacy of the provided service, we notice that these criteria mostly lack a concrete and specific meaning. They are criteria which will be relevant in the oversight of the legislature when it approves the project, but, apart from providing these criteria, the law does not really describe what they stand for. Further to that, we may notice that these criteria that the law provides are criteria for which, if we were to try to capture their meanings, we would have to focus on the literature provided by the discipline of public administration. We will expand in detail on these distinctions later. However, if we were to describe this kind of criteria using a specific term, we would describe them as 'administrative', due to the sources that have to be consulted in order to determine their meaning in the absence of legislative definition.

A second project which illustrates the role of legislation in PPPs in the USA is the 91 Express Lanes in California. The project belongs to the Build-Operate-Transfer (BOT) model. According to this model, the public authority provides the specifications for a facility, which is then built by the private party. Subsequently, that private party operates the facility for a specified period of time under a franchise agreement or other contract with the agency. Finally, it transfers the facility to the agency at the end of the term provided by the contract. Given that, in most cases, the private contractor will be responsible for the financing of the facility, the term of the contract must be adequate for the contractor to realise a profit for its investment. At the end of the franchise period, the public authority has the right to take over the operation of the facility, contract the operations to the original contractor or assign the operation to a new contractor.[39] In this way, following the BOT model, the 91 Express Lanes was developed through a partnership between the California Department of Transportation (Caltrans) and the California Private Transportation Company (CPTC) on land

39 United States General Accounting Office 3.

leased by the State of California. On completion, the CPTC, which developed and built the road, transferred the project's ownership to Caltrans with the agreement to lease the facility back from the agency for 35 years.[40] As in the previous case, the legislation upon which the PPP was based made specific mention of the type of PPP.

By virtue of the California Assembly Bill 680, section 1, which was enacted by the state legislature in 1989:

> (c) One important alternative is privately funded Build-Operate-Transfer (BOT) projects whereby private entities obtain exclusive development agreements to build, with private funds, all or a portion of public transportation projects for the citizens of California.[41]

The current version of this legislation, in California Streets and Highway Code (SHC), also provides for the main criteria on which an award will be based. These are those of 'lowest bid' and 'best value':

> (2) When evaluating a proposal submitted by the contracting entity or lessee, the department or the regional transportation agency may award a contract on the basis of the lowest bid or best value.[42]

Legislation provides additional criteria, by analysing 'best value' in the cases of specific components:

> (a)(1) 'Best value' means a value determined by objective criteria, including, but not limited to, price, features, functions, life-cycle costs, and other criteria deemed appropriate by the department or the regional transportation agency.[43]

The law, in SHC § 143(c)(5) (West 2015) and SHC § 143(c)(2) also provides necessary review via the legislature, which, additionally, is to be accompanied by public hearing. In terms of ongoing monitoring, the department is required by SHC § 143(h)(2) to regularly inspect the facility and require the contracting entity to maintain the facility to the appropriate standards. There is also provision for the return for investment which the contractor will make, based on tolls collected. Such returns need to be deemed reasonable.

---

40 Department of Transportation – Federal Highway Administration, 'Excellence in Highway Design: Category 8-Public/Private Participation' (2003) <http://www.fhwa.dot.gov/eihd/91exp.cfm> accessed 10 September 2017.
41 'Assembly Bill No. 680' (1989) <http://www.dot.ca.gov/hq/paffairs/about/toll/ab680.htm> accessed 10 September 2017.
42 SHC § 143 (2) (West 2015). See also SHC § 143 (g)(1)(C).
43 SHC § 143 (a)(1).

The enabling legislation which was considered necessary for the validity of the PPP contract, provided the model of the agreement for BOT in a very direct way. Further to this, the legislation which exists around the project provides the properties on which the evaluation of the bids will be based, as well as a means of monitoring by the department with overall responsibility for the projects. The California legislation builds extensively on the criterion of best value, which serves as a point of reference for the project during the contractor selection process. Apart from a point of reference for the awarding of the project contract, legislation also serves as an instrument of accountability in the public sector. The department will have to explain the project against the legislature and also explain its view that the project represents 'best value', or that it was selected based on the 'lowest bid', and that the costs are 'reasonable'. Similarly, based on these concepts, the department will hold the different individuals involved in the project accountable for whether or not their negotiations with the private contractor achieved these results.

In this way, in this piece of legislation, which has provided the basis for the Californian PPP project for the 91 Express Lanes, is similar to the earlier arrangement. Behind this specific PPP project was legislation, which provided the mechanisms for awarding the project, and ongoing monitoring and accountability. If we focus on these criteria of accountability, we notice a number of similarities and a number of differences with the previous piece of enabling legislation.

To begin with, both pieces of legislation refer to the criterion of 'reasonableness', which we defined as a criterion which is administrative. Furthermore, as was the case with the previous illustration, the criterion is provided by the law, but it is not defined. The criteria of 'best value' and 'lowest bid', however, are criteria which are defined. For the criterion of 'best value', the legislation provides its components in detail. The criterion of 'lowest bid' is also defined, not by the legislation itself but by its own concrete meaning: it refers to the single bid which has the lowest mathematical value. In this way, these criteria contrast with the criteria provided in the previous piece of legislation because they are defined, either from the legislation itself or by their own content.

A further difference is that the criteria of 'best value' and 'lowest bid' are of a different nature than criteria such as those of 'public interest' and 'reasonableness': this is because they originate from the province of economics, rather than the province of public administration. In this way, when we inquire about the components of the criterion of 'best value' as the law provides these components, we will have to focus on the theoretical approaches of the disciplines of economics and finance, rather than the approaches of the discipline of public administration. As we did earlier,[44] when we defined the administrative criteria,

---

44 See p. xxx [orig. 115]

it would be appropriate to define the criteria which draw their meanings from the disciplines of economics, as financial criteria.

A further example of a PPP project based on legislation, this time from the federal government, is that of the PPP contract between the US Air Force and the Landmark Organisation Inc., for the creation of an Air Force Base in Lackland, Texas.[45] The contract had a value of $42.6 m and a duration of 50 years, with 2001 as a starting date. Under its terms, the private contractor provided 420 new housing units, by replacing 272 existing units and adding 148 new ones.[46] The type of economic organisation of the project followed the Design-Build-Operate (DBO) pattern, in which the private party – typically a real estate developer – is responsible for the financing of the construction or development of a public facility. In exchange, he receives the right to build residential housing, commercial stores or industrial facilities at the site. He may also operate the facility under the oversight of the government, and has the right to use the facility to secure income from user fees.[47] In the specific project at Lackland, the Government leased the land to the private contractor and undertook the guarantee for a loan against the risks of base closure, downsizing and deployment. The private contractor owned the units and undertook their operation and maintenance for the 50-year term of the contract.[48]

As in previously-detailed cases, the PPP contract was based on legislation, namely the National Defense Authorisation Act for Fiscal Year 1996.[49] The Act amended Chapter 169 of title 10 of the U.S. Code and, in § 2872, it provided that:

> the Secretary concerned may exercise any authority or any combination of authorities provided under this subchapter in order to provide for the acquisition or construction by private persons of the following: (1) Family housing units on or near military installations within the USA and its territories and possessions. (2) Military unaccompanied housing units on or near such military installations.[50]

---

45 Subcommittee on Technology and Procurement Policy of the Committee on Government Reform of the House of Representatives, *Hearing on the Use of Public-Private Partnerships as a Management Tool for Federal Real Property* 45.

46 'Military Housing Privatization Initiative: Hearings Before the Subcommittee on Military Installations and Facilities of the House Committee on Armed Services, 106th Congress (statement of Randall A. Yim, Deputy Under Secretary of Defence, Installations' (2000) <http://www.defenselink.mil/acq/installation/hrso> accessed 8 November 2015.

47 United States General Accounting Office 5.

48 Hearing, supra note 430; see also 'AFB Solicitation No. F41689-96-R0025' (2000) <http://www.afcee.brooks.af.mil/dc/dch/hpdata/hpdata.asp> accessed 8 November 2015.

49 National Defense Authorization Act of 1996, Pub. L. No. 104–6, 110 Stat. 186 (1996).

50 National Defense Authorization Act § 2872. Corresponds to current 10 U.S.C. § 2872 (2012).

And, in § 2874:

> (a) The Secretary concerned may enter into contracts for the lease of military family housing units or military unaccompanied housing units to be constructed under this subchapter. (b) A contract under this section may be for any period that the Secretary concerned determines appropriate and may provide for the owner of the leased property to operate and maintain the property.[51]

Apart from this authorisation, the Act provided further details on the accountability structures. Specifically, it provided that the authorisation to participate in the described PPP contracts will expire 5 years after the enactment of the National Defence Authorization Act of 1996.[52] Furthermore, the Secretary of State will have to 'transmit to the appropriate committees of Congress' annual reports, together with:

> (2) A methodology for evaluating the extent and effectiveness of the use of the authorities under this subchapter during such preceding fiscal year.
> (3) A description of the objectives of the Department of Defense for providing military family housing and military unaccompanied housing for members of the armed forces.[53]

The concept of effectiveness in the accountability process is similarly stressed in § 2884, which provided for the final report to be submitted at the expiration of the authorisation. This report 'shall assess the effectiveness of such authority in providing for the construction and improvement of military family housing and military unaccompanied housing'.[54]

The legislation on which the PPP project of Air Force Base in Lackland is based provides for important aspects of the project, as was the case in other pieces of legislation which we have seen. First of all, it authorises the Minister to contract, consistent with the pattern with which we are becoming familiar, in which PPPs are usually based on legislative authorisation and provision. In addition, this piece of legislation delineates the functions which can be assigned to the private sector and the financial instrument which is to be used as well as the content of the terms

---

51 National Defense Authorization Act § 2874. Corresponds to current 10 U.S.C. § 2874.
52 National Defense Authorization Act § 2885.
53 National Defense Authorization Act § 2884. Corresponds to current 10 U.S.C. § 2884.
54 Ibid. Please note that the current version of the relevant sections (10 U.S.C. § 2871–2885) refers to effectiveness as a measure of accountability of the Secretary of State to the Congress: 'Each Secretary concerned shall prescribe regulations to effectively oversee and manage military housing privatization projects carried out under this subchapter during the course of the construction or renovation of the housing units' (§ 2885). The rest of the provisions establish technical rules for measuring the effectiveness of the programme, such as the debt coverage ratio and occupancy rates (Ibid).

of this lease. The maximum term of these agreements is provided and there is also provision for accountability arrangements. Such accountability arrangements involve the award of a central role to Congress, which is intended to oversee the programme and decide whether it should be continued. The central concept of this accountability, as indicated by the law, is the criterion of 'effectiveness' based on which Congress determines the extent to which the programme has been carried out according to its direction when enacting the specific piece of legislation.

If we focus on the criterion of 'effectiveness' which is provided for the accountability over the project, we notice a familiar pattern; this is that the law provides the criterion, but does not provide how this criterion is to be construed. Consequently, when Congress enquires as to whether the specific criterion that the law provides has been fulfilled, this question will be problematic; this is because there will not be a definition of the criterion or a description of the relevant factors which have to be taken into account within the text of the law. With respect to its nature, we note that the criterion of effectiveness more closely resembles criteria such as that of 'best value' than criteria such as that of 'public interest', and thus draws its meanings from the disciplines of economics and finance. In this sense, it would be more accurate if we were to consider it a financial criterion.

A final example which we will provide, again from the federal government, is the one of the VA Medical Center Mixed-Use Development Complex at the VA Medical Center in Durham, North Carolina. It is a project which follows the Enhanced Use Leasing type (EUL), which is specifically for the use of the Department of Veterans' Affairs. The purpose of these PPPs is to enable the Department of Veterans' Affairs to lease its property long-term, either to the private sector or to other public authorities for use which is unrelated to the Department's activities. The funds which the Department receives from these transactions are used to enhance its own programmes or activities.[55] The specific PPP contract detailed here was signed between the Department of Veterans' Affairs and the LCOR North Carolina LLC. The project involved the provision of three acres of property for development by the private sector, and LCOR committed to construct a 19,000-square-foot clinic facility at the existing hospital, accompanied by 40,000 square feet of research space.

This EUL project also has a statutory footing, specifically the 38 U.S.C. § 8161 et seq (2012), which authorises the Secretary of State to participate in these agreements:

> The Secretary may in accordance with this subchapter enter into leases with respect to real property that is under the jurisdiction or control of the Secretary. Any such lease under this subchapter may be referred to as an 'enhanced-use lease'.[56]

---

55 United States General Accounting Office 6–7.
56 38 U.S.C. § 8162 (2012).

Further to this, 38 U.S.C. §§ 8161 to 8169 provide the complete details of how this PPP operates. The law,[57] in § 8162, provides for the maximum term of these PPPs, which is 75 years; once again this exemplifies a much longer period than the PFI in the UK, and serves to highlight the comparative difference which we noted earlier.

In terms of accountability arrangements, the Secretary can only enter into them after receiving certification by the OMB,[58] which, as we will see, is an organ belonging to the executive. There are also several stages of accountability arrangements to Congress. The first of these stages relates to the feedback and overview which is given to the Congressional Veterans' Affairs Committees, and which relates to the public hearing exercises. According to the law,[59] the Secretary of State must organise a public hearing before he enters into an EUL contract. In these hearings, the views which will be taken into account are those of the veterans' service organisations and 'other interested parties'. The hearing itself is a mechanism of public participation. However, before the hearing, Congress has to be informed in detail about its properties[60]; in cases where the Secretary of State decides to proceed with the PPP, once again, Congress has to be notified. This notification, however, is more than the mere provision of information, it is also a structure of accountability, because the Secretary has to explain 'the background of, rationale for, and economic factors in support of, the proposed lease' as well as the way that the project will contribute 'in a cost-effective manner' to the mission of the department.[61] This counts as an accountability mechanism, rather than just a simple provision of information, due to the fact that the Secretary has to explain to the forum of the Congressional committee, and he may face consequences in any given situation when his explanations are not satisfactory, such as the non-appropriation of the necessary expenses. Further to these mechanisms, and yet staying with the subject of accountability mechanisms to Congress, the Secretary of State is required to submit a report to Congress at least once every year, which details 'identifying the actions taken by the Secretary to implement and administer enhanced-use leases'.[62] Similarly, as part of the annual budget submission of the President to the Congress, the Secretary has to submit 'a detailed report of the consideration received' for the EUL, and an overview explaining how the Secretary is utilising this consideration to support veterans.[63]

There are several criteria on which the accountability of the Secretary of State will be based, and these take place at several stages. At the top of his list, any

57 Ibid.
58 38 U.S.C. § 8162(b)(6).
59 38 U.S.C. § 8163(a).
60 38 U.S.C. § 8163(b).
61 Ibid.
62 38 U.S.C. § 8168(a).
63 38 U.S.C. § 8168(b).

consideration that the Secretary of State agrees in carrying out the programme, has to be of 'fair value'.[64] Next on the list we would expect to find the criterion of 'best interest of the Department' and then the criterion of being in the 'best interest of the USA' will form the basis of the decisions of dispositions of EUL properties either throughout or after the expiration of the programme.[65] Based on these concepts, which are provided directly by law, the Secretary of State may be held accountable on issues such as whether the consideration provided in the agreement is of 'fair value', or whether disposal of properties is considered to be in the best interests of the USA and the department. Other criteria which may inform the accountability process are indirectly provided by the law: for instance, the law provides that the Secretary, in his notice for hearing, will have to provide 'a summary of cost-benefit analysis' of the project, and whether the programme is 'inconsistent with the mission of the department', together with a description of 'how the proposed lease would affect the services to the veterans'. Despite the fact that these last criteria are not provided directly as criteria of accountability, they may inform the accountability process, given that the law considers them essential properties for informing the decision to proceed with the contract which is the object of the accountability relationship.

If we examine the criteria which the law provides and which are relevant in the accountability processes, we notice that they are not defined by the legislation. In this sense, legislation refers to the criteria of 'fair value' and 'best interest', without providing details of how these criteria are to be construed. In order to establish their meaning, we would need to follow slightly different pathways. For the criterion of 'fair value', we would have to inquire into sources originating from the discipline of economics, given that the notion of 'value' is a financial one. On the other hand, the criterion of 'best interest', sharing a resemblance with the criterion of 'public interest' which we saw earlier, would have to qualify as an administrative, rather than a financial criterion. The reason behind this is that, in order to establish the concept of the 'best interest', we would have to inquire into the discipline of public administration, which would be more relevant to it than the discipline of economics.

There are many more such examples beyond these four which we cannot fully analyse here due to space constraints. Amongst them are the Dulles Greenway extension of the Dulles Toll Road in the State of Virginia, a project belonging to the Build-Own-Operate (BOO) type,[66] and which was based on legislation, namely the Virginia Highway Corporation Act of 1988. The tunnel for the Port of Miami, a project of the Design-Build-Finance-Operate (DBFO) model,[67] was also based on legislation, namely the Florida Statute 334.30 (2015),

---

64 38 U.S.C. § 8162(b)(3)(A) and 38 U.S.C. § 8164(b).
65 38 U.S.C. § 8164.
66 United States General Accounting Office 3.
67 Wall 3.

which also provides for legislative approval for every project. Another one is the Texas Corridor PPP, which is a project of the Design-Build Operate type (DBO),[68] which was enabled by an amendment of the Constitution in 2001[69] and section 227.011 of the Texas Transportation Code (2003) and did not proceed when the legislature, finally, dropped its support for the project (moratorium on the project was placed with section 223.210 of the Texas Transportation Code (2007)). The Fulton County Water Waste PPP project was a further project for the provision of services by a private contractor which was based on legislation, namely § 36-60-15.1 of the Georgia Code (2015). Also, Indiana's Gary International Airport, a PPP project of the Developer Financing model, was similarly based on legislation, namely the provisions of § 8-22-3-11(20) (2015) of the Indiana Code which directly authorised the project. Finally, the Anton-Anderson Memorial Tunnel, a PPP project of the Build-Own-Operate (BOO)[70] model was authorised based on several legislative packages[71] which have now developed to the provisions of Alaska Statutes § 36.30 (2015).

All these pieces of legislation have a number of common characteristics which we have analysed in our previous examples, including the authorisation of PPP activity or authorisation of the specific projects themselves and provision of criteria of evaluation and accountability. As we have seen, there is a fair degree of diversity within such criteria. Furthermore, they are not usually defined by the law, and they tend to follow two distinct patterns: either they are predominantly financial in nature or they more comfortably align with criteria of public administration. Criteria of the first category, such as those of effectiveness, have to be approached from the disciplines of economics and finance, in order for the user of these criteria to establish a meaning for them; criteria of the second category, such as those of 'public interest', have to be approached from the perspective of public administration, which, together with the relevant administrative practice, will inform the user on how they can be meaningfully construed. This distinction, as we have already mentioned, is one which we are merely briefly introducing here; we will return to it in detail in a later part of the chapter.

2.5. *Federal involvement*

Throughout the previous section we visited a number of examples of indicative types of PPPs in the USA together with the legislation which enabled these projects, and provided for their accountability arrangements. Many of the PPPs

---

68 United States General Accounting Office 5.
69 Texas Const. Art III, § 49-k.
70 United States General Accounting Office 5.
71 U.S. Department of Transportation – Federal Highway Administration, *Case Studies of Transportation Public-Private Partnerships in the United States* (Final Report – Work Order 05-002, 2007) 3–11.

which we have analysed are drawn from the state level. We have provided these examples together with federal illustrations in order to demonstrate that there is no difference in the techniques used in federal and state legislation. This, though, might give the impression that PPPs in the USA are a matter of states' business. However, as we continue our account of the role of legislation in the accountability for PPPs, we will see that the federal government also has important powers enabling states-related PPPs financing with public money. The respective legislation provides for PPP financing programmes, and for the federal public money to be awarded to them as well as for mechanisms and criteria of accountability.

2.5.1. *Means and instruments of federal involvement*

Existing critical literature in this field has already commented upon the fact that,[72] unlike many countries, including the UK, the USA has no single federal agency with oversight or overall responsibility for PPP policy. The federal government, however, promotes PPPs using a large number of instruments and initiatives which demonstrate a statutory footing.

Among the most important of these instruments and initiatives is the programme of federal promotion, the Transportation Infrastructure Finance and Innovation Act (TIFIA), which was enacted in 1998 during the second term of Bill Clinton's administration as part of the Transportation Equity Act for the Twenty-first Century (TEA-21). TIFIA provides long-term financing to highway and transit projects in the USA at all levels of governance, as long as they have dedicated revenue sources, such as is the case in PPPs. According to the US Department of the Treasury, TIFIA:

> focuses on attracting substantial private and other non-federal co-investment by providing supplemental and subordinate capital, and plays a significant role in transport PPP investment. In many cases, the lower cost of capital and flexible terms offered by TIFIA are critical factors in determining whether a PPP is a viable and cost-effective option for a project.[73]

From 2008 to 2013, TIFIA assistance amounted to about 23 per cent of the total PPP project value, and 35 per cent of PPP debt.[74] Eligible applicants for TIFIA federal assistance include state and local governments, transit agencies, railway companies and private entities. The terms of the TIFIA programme are

---

72 Arthur L. Smith, 'PPP Financing in the USA' in Akintola Akintoye and Matthias Beck (eds), *Policy, Finance & Management for Public-Private Partnerships* (Wiley-Blackwell 2009) 199–200.

73 U.S. Department of the Treasury – Office of Economic Policy, *Expanding our Nation's Infrastructure through Innovative Financing* (2014) 9.

74 Ibid.

provided by law, in sections 601–610 of title 23 of the U.S.C. (2012). TIFIA is especially focused to PPP transport projects and it provides, in its § 602, that 'A State, local government, public authority, public-private partnership, or any other legal entity undertaking the project and authorized by the Secretary shall submit a project application that is acceptable to the Secretary'.[75]

Projects which can receive federal help have to fulfil the criteria of creditworthiness,[76] and have a substantial economic value which is exemplified by law with specific amounts for each kind of project.[77] The means of repayment of the federal credit instruments of TIFIA should be 'tolls, user fees, payments owing to the obligor under a public-private partnership or other dedicated revenue sources that also secure or fund the project obligations'.[78] The form of assistance to be selected is, according to the law, a decision to be made via the discretionary authority of the Secretary of State.[79]

One type of federal funding to PPPs is the contribution in the form of secured loans.[80] These secured loans can be used 'to finance eligible project costs', 'to refinance interim construction financing of eligible project costs', 'to refinance existing Federal credit instruments for rural infrastructure projects' or 'to refinance long-term project obligations or Federal credit instruments, if the refinancing provides additional funding capacity for the completion, enhancement, or expansion' of the projects.[81] A substantial advantage for these loans is that they have a very slow maturity date, which can be anything up to 35 years,[82] and they are to be repaid with tolls, user fees, payments under a PPP, and – in rural projects – with any other revenue stream available to a State infrastructure bank.[83] Their maximum amount can be up to 49 per cent of reasonably-anticipated costs.[84]

Further to the secured loans, an additional means of federal assistance to PPP transport projects is through loan guarantees. These loan guarantees can be used instead of a secured loan, in cases where the Secretary of State perceives that the budgetary cost between the two instruments are the same.[85] The terms of this federal assistance is the same as those of secured loans, with the exception of the interest rate, which can be negotiated between the obligor and the lender, with the consent of the Secretary.[86]

75 23 U.S.C. § 602 (2012).
76 23 U.S.C. § 602(a)(2).
77 23 U.S.C. § 602(5).
78 23 U.S.C. § 602(6).
79 23 U.S.C. § 602 (9).
80 23 U.S.C. § 603(a)(1).
81 Ibid.
82 23 U.S.C. § 603(a)(3).
83 23 U.S.C. § 603(b)(3).
84 23 U.S.C. § 603(b)(2).
85 23 U.S.C. § 603(e).
86 Ibid.

The final instrument of federal involvement in PPPs which is provided by TIFIA is the lines of credit.[87] The instrument of a line of credit is similar to the previous two, with the exception that, under this form, the federal government attaches the provision of direct loans to certain events, or upon the arrival of specific dates.[88] A further difference is that the total amount of a line of credit cannot exceed the 33 per cent of the 'reasonably anticipated eligible project costs.[89] However, it is possible to receive a line of credit in addition to federal assistance provided by the other instruments, just as long as the total combined amount does not exceed 49 per cent of the anticipated costs of the project. The means of repayment of the lines of credit are also similar to the previous two instruments; they also include tolls, user fees, payments under a PPP and other dedicated revenue sources.[90]

TIFIA – like some other statutes – also provides its own accountability procedures. The authority for spending and borrowing is awarded to the Secretary on a fiscal-year basis by Congress,[91] and he will be obliged to report to that same Congress every 2 years:

> On June 1, 2012, and every 2 years thereafter, the Secretary shall submit to Congress a report summarizing the financial performance of the projects that are receiving, or have received, assistance under the TIFIA program, including a recommendation as to whether the objectives of the TIFIA program are best served by— (1) continuing the program under the authority of the Secretary; (2) establishing a Federal corporation or federally sponsored enterprise to administer the program; or (3) phasing out the program and relying on the capital markets to fund the types of infrastructure investments assisted by the TIFIA program without Federal participation.[92]

The reporting requirements of the Secretary, on the basis of which the Congress will decide whether to provide authority for public money to be spent on transportation PPPs, don't stop there; the Secretary is obliged to submit separate reports to the Committee on Transportation and Infrastructure, to the House of Representatives and also to the Committee on Environment and Public Works of the Senate. Further to this, given the fact that many infrastructure projects are run by the states, the act prescribes the relationship between TIFIA and state law. It clarifies that the credit assistance by the federal government does not mean that the receiver can bypass any state permit which is required, any

---

87 23 U.S.C. § 604(a).
88 Ibid.
89 23 U.S.C. § 604(b).
90 23 U.S.C. § 604(b)(5).
91 23 U.S.C. § 608.
92 23 U.S.C. § 609.

limit that states impose in their infrastructure projects, and – more generally – any law (including regulations) which is applicable to the construction or operation of the project.[93]

The criteria of 'creditworthiness', and of 'substantial economic value' which have to be fulfilled for PPPs which are to receive federal assistance are criteria of accountability. The Secretary will have to substantiate in his report that the projects which he has selected are creditworthy and of substantial economic value; in cases where the Congress does not share his views, the Secretary may have a negative consequence conferred upon him: this might be both serious and far-reaching, such as that his request for funding for the next fiscal year might not be approved. A further consequence that the Congress might decide to confer is that the programme must be continued, but by the authority of a different body, such as a Federal corporation or federally sponsored enterprise.

Legislation defines the criterion of 'substantial economic value', by directly providing in USC § 602 (5) economic values for every type of project which is to receive federal assistance. The meaning of the criterion of 'creditworthiness', however, is exposed to a fair degree of subjectivity. The law does not define it, and it does not provide prescriptions on how it is to be approached. Both criteria are predominantly economic in their nature. This means that, resembling other criteria – such as that of best value – they are basically dependent upon the discipline of economics for their defining features, rather than the discipline of public administration.

A further federal instrument, in addition to TIFIA, which assists PPPs by facilitating the provision of public money for them in the areas of water and waste management is the Water Infrastructure Finance and Innovation Act (WIFIA) of 2014, which is contained in the Water Resources Reform and Development Act of 2014. In December 2014, based on this Act, Congress provided \$2.2 m to the Environmental Protection Agency for the purposes of the WIFIA programme to cover needs such as the hiring of qualified staff, developing guidance and application materials and developing the credit model.[94] For the provision of actual federal financial assistance to water projects, the Act provided the Secretary of State and the Administrator of the Environmental Protection Agency with more than a doubling of financial resources over a period of 5 years, rising from \$20 m for 2015, \$25 m for 2016, \$35 m for 2017, and \$45 m for 2018 to 50 m for 2019.

The Act provides for federal assistance to be provided for eligible projects after applications have been made. A wide range of water related projects are

---

93 23 U.S.C. § 606.

94 US Environmental Protection Agency, 'Learn About the Water Infrastructure Finance and Innovation Act Program' (2003) <https://www.epa.gov/wifia/learn-about-water-infrastructure-finance-and-innovation-act-program> accessed 4 July 2016.

authorised for assistance under the Act, including 'any project for flood damage reduction, hurricane and storm damage reduction, environmental restoration, coastal or inland harbor navigation improvement, or inland and intracoastal waterways navigation improvement that the Secretary determines is technically sound, economically justified, and environmentally acceptable', 'a project for enhanced energy efficiency in the operation of a public water system or a publicly owned treatment works', 'a project for repair, rehabilitation, or replacement of a treatment works, community water system, or aging water distribution or waste collection facility (including a facility that serves a population or community of an Indian reservation', 'a brackish or sea water desalination project, a managed aquifer recharge project, or a water recycling project'.[95]

There are several criteria that the Act establishes for the selection of projects which shall receive federal help, and these also serve as criteria of accountability in the holding of the Secretary to account for his decisions to award federal assistance to projects.[96] The first criterion is that of creditworthiness,[97] for which the Secretary or Administrator must consider factors such as the terms, conditions and financial structure, the dedicated revenue sources, and the financial assumptions on which the project is based, as well as the 'financial soundness and credit history of the obligor'.[98] Further to that, in establishing the creditworthiness of the obligor, the Secretary of State and the Administrator have to take into account the security features of the project and the ratings of the rating agencies. The second criterion which will have an impact on the decision to assist a project is its cost, which – as was the case with the TIFIA – needs to be substantial. It is provided to those projects costing at least $20 m[99] (unless it is a small community water infrastructure project, for which the threshold is $5 m). A further criterion is the ability of the project to secure dedicated revenue sources,[100] which essentially refers to the economic sustainability of the project. Other criteria are the extent to which the project involves private financing,[101] whether the assistance could speed up the commencement of the project[102] whether the approaches that it takes are innovative,[103] the amount of budget authority required,[104] whether it is designed to serve regions with

95 33 U.S.C.A. § 3905. Please note that we cite the United States Code Annotated (U.S.C.A.) because the provisions of WIFIA, which came in force in 2014 are not included in the latest official edition of the United States Code which was published in 2012.
96 33 U.S.C.A. § 3913(a)(1)(C).
97 33 U.S.C.A. § 3907.
98 33 U.S.C.A. § 3907 (a)(1)(B).
99 33 U.S.C.A. § 3907(a)(2).
100 33 U.S.C.A. § 3907(a)(3).
101 33 U.S.C.A. § 3907 (b)(2)(B).
102 33 U.S.C.A. § 3907 (b)(2)(C).
103 33 U.S.C.A. § 3907 (b)(2)(D).
104 33 U.S.C.A. § 3907 (b)(2)(E).

significant water resource challenges,[105] whether it addresses municipal, state or regional priorities,[106] and the readiness of the project to proceed to development,[107] among others. All these criteria – and more – which are provided in the detailed provisions of the Act are to be used for the selection of the projects which will receive federal assistance, as well as functioning as criteria for holding the Secretary or the Administrator to account with respect to how well he selected the project.[108]

In terms of the form of the federal assistance, as was the case with the TIFIA, the first instrument is that of secured loans.[109] In a further parallel with TIFIA, the amount of a secured loan cannot exceed the 49 per cent of 'reasonably anticipated eligible project costs',[110] and if the secured loan does not receive an investment-grade rating, the loan cannot exceed the amount of the senior obligations of the project. If the WIFIA federal assistance is provided together with other federal assistance, the total cannot be more than 80 per cent of the total project cost.[111] The maturity date of the loan is to be determined as either 35 years after the date of completion or, if the useful life of the project is less than 35 years, the useful life of the project.[112]

Similar to TIFIA, the Act also provides the instrument of loan guarantees[113]:

> The Secretary or the Administrator, as applicable, may provide a loan guarantee to a lender in lieu of making a secured loan under this section, if the Secretary or the Administrator, as applicable, determines that the budgetary cost of the loan guarantee is substantially the same as that of a secured loan.

The accountability process of all WIFIA projects is similar to those of TIFIA[114]:

> As soon as practicable after each fiscal year for which amounts are made available to carry out this chapter, the Secretary and the Administrator shall publish on a dedicated, publicly accessible Internet site—(1) each application received for assistance under this chapter; and (2) a list of the projects selected for assistance under this chapter, including—(A) a description of each project; (B) the amount of financial assistance provided for each project;

105 33 U.S.C.A. § 3907 (b)(2)(H).
106 33 U.S.C.A. § 3907 (b)(2)(I).
107 33 U.S.C.A. § 3907 (b)(2)(J).
108 33 U.S.C.A. § 3913 (a)(1)(C).
109 33 U.S.C.A. § 3908 (a)(2).
110 33 U.S.C.A. § 3908 (b)(2).
111 33 U.S.C.A. § 3908 (b)(9).
112 33 U.S.C.A. § 3908 (a)(5).
113 33 U.S.C.A. § 3908 (e).
114 33 U.S.C.A. § 3913 (a).

and (C) the basis for the selection of each project with respect to the requirements of this chapter.

Completing the accountability requirements of the Act, the Comptroller General of the USA is requested to submit his own reports 4 years after the enactment of WIFIA (in other words, in this instance, on June 10, 2014).[115] The bodies to receive it are the Committee on Environment and Public Works of the Senate and the Committee on Transportation and Infrastructure of the House of Representatives. His report must refer to the applications received for federal help under WIFIA, the selected projects, the type and amount of federal assistance, the financial performance of the projects, the benefits and impacts of the implementation of WIFIA and an evaluation of the feasibility of attracting non-federal public or private financing as a result of having WIFIA. The report must also include recommendations on whether the objectives of the chapter are better served by continuing the authority of the Secretary or Administrator under WIFIA, or whether it would be better either to establish a government corporation instead, or to terminate their authority altogether and rely on capital markets. He is also authorised to propose changes 'to improve the efficiency and effectiveness of this chapter in providing financing for water infrastructure projects, taking into consideration the recommendations'.[116]

It is worth our drawing attention to the fact that this last provision is one of the most fundamental differences between TIFIA and WIFIA. For TIFIA, the tasks which are prescribed for the Comptroller General in WIFIA are prescribed for the Secretary. In other words, the WIFIA is more advanced and sophisticated in terms of checks and balances, because it provides that the Comptroller will report to Congress on the overall viability of the programme, evaluating the work of the Secretary. By contrast, in TIFIA, the Secretary must report an evaluation of his own work to Congress. The difference here is important. As we explained earlier, the criteria of accountability which are provided by the Act include the complete list of the criteria of the selection of eligible projects, and it is a given that the Secretary will have to justify whether the selected projects complied with the requirements of the project selection. To these we need to add the ones of efficiency and effectiveness which are provided for the report of the C&AG of the USA.

A further point to be observed refers to the criteria on which the accountability of the Secretary will be based. The Secretary will have to convince, through his report that he has selected the appropriate projects for federal help, based on the ample criteria that the law provides, such as those of 'creditworthiness', 'substantial cost', and the 'ability of the project to secure dedicated revenue sources'. Further

---

115 33 U.S.C.A. § 3913 (b).
116 Ibid.

to that the Comptroller will report on whether the Secretary satisfies the criteria of effectiveness and efficiency. If the Secretary does not convince that he has satisfied all these criteria, he risks negative consequences originating from the opinions of the Congress, as the forum of accountability, over his performance. Such consequences can range from the non-approval of financing for selected projects to the replacement of the authority of the Secretary over these projects by a different organ. These criteria that the Secretary will have to satisfy in his selection of PPPs are distanced from concrete and specific meaning. With the exception of the criterion of 'substantial cost', which is defined with specific amounts, the law does not provide a specific definition for these criteria. Furthermore, we notice that the criteria that the law provides are mostly financial; this is because if we were to closely scrutinise their construction, in order to do so effectively, we would have to focus on literature provided by the discipline of finance.

A further instrument of the federal financing of PPPs is Private Activity Bonds (PAB). Through legislation, the federal government permits the state and local governments to issue bonds which are exempt from federal tax. The instrument of PABs, is a form of federal promotion and finance for PPP infrastructure because the federal government agrees to forfeit the tax which would normally be owed to it. PABs are available for projects which belong to a wide range of areas, such as 'airports, docks and wharves, mass commuting facilities, facilities for the furnishing of water, sewage facilities, solid waste disposal facilities, qualified residential rental projects, facilities for the local furnishing of electric energy or gas, local district heating or cooling facilities, qualified hazardous waste facilities, high-speed intercity rail facilities, environmental enhancements of hydroelectric generating facilities, qualified public educational facilities, qualified green building and sustainable design projects, or qualified highway or surface freight transfer facilities'.[117]

The relevant sections of the Internal Revenue Code are sections 141–7 of title 26 of the U.S. Code (2012) and – as it was the case with the other instruments of federal promotion which we explored earlier – they constitute primary legislation. These sections provide specific requirements for PPPs which are to be financed with PABs as well as specific accountability arrangements. Through this, § 142 (b) provides that if a special exempt bond is to be used for the construction of airports, docks and wharves, mass commuting facilities and environmental enhancements of hydroelectric generating facilities, this will only be possible if the property is owned by a governmental unit. This signifies that, for these facilities to receive support, only the lease type of PPP contracts can be used, because only they preserve the ownership of the public authority on the asset. Furthermore, an important requirement for tax exempt financing is established by defining tax exempt status as one which does not exceed 120 per cent of the economic life of the facility.[118]

---

117 26 U.S.C. § 142(a) (2012).
118 26 U.S.C. § 147(b).

For water projects, which are not covered by the prescription above and which amount to a substantial and broad area of PPP involvement, inclusion in the tax exempt status is possible if the water is to be made available to the public and either the facility is operated by a public unit or 'the rates for the furnishing or sale of the water have been established or approved by a State or political subdivision thereof, by an agency or instrumentality of the USA, or by a public service or public utility commission or other similar body of any State or political subdivision thereof'.[119] In this way, the law accepts the provision of federal help to PPPs for water, given that, in these projects, the public authority authorises the operation of the water facility by a private contractor.

The law also authorises the provision of this instrument of federal assistance for PPPs related to education. For the PPP contract to be eligible for Private Activity Bond financing this PPP agreement:

> A public-private partnership agreement is described in this paragraph if it is an agreement—(A) under which the corporation agrees—(i) to do 1 or more of the following: construct, rehabilitate, refurbish, or equip a school facility, and (ii) at the end of the term of the agreement, to transfer the school facility to such agency for no additional consideration, and (B) the term of which does not exceed the term of the issue to be used to provide the school facility.[120]

With respect to accountability arrangements, the law prescribes that, for a PAB to be issued, there should be public approval.[121] This public approval consists of the approval of the governmental unit which either issued the bond or on behalf of which the bond was issued, and its reach extends as far as the inclusion of each governmental unit which has jurisdiction over the area involved. The approval by the governmental unit will be considered as having been given if it is given either by an elected representative of the governmental unit 'after public hearing following reasonable public notice' or by voter referendum.[122]

In this way, the law essentially provides that if federal assistance is to be provided for projects in the states or the localities, this has to be done in a democratic way, involving a referendum, and an approval of the legislature, or the elected official.[123] This is particularly important because it creates an incentive for the states to provide authorisations of projects in terms of their respective legislatures, a tendency which, as we have already seen, is widespread.

---

119 26 U.S.C. § 142(e).
120 26 U.S.C. § 142(k).
121 26 U.S.C. § 147(f)(1).
122 26 U.S.C. § 147(f)(2)(B).
123 26 U.S.C. § 147(f)(2)(E)(i).

With respect to the accountability arrangements from the perspective of the federal government which provides the financial assistance, it is important to notice an important difference to the regime established by the TIFIA and the WIFIA. In those Acts, a Secretary of State was invested with the discretion to decide when to provide financing, and this Secretary was accountable towards Congress for his decisions either to support or not to support specific projects, by means of reports in which he has to explain his decisions. The regime established by the PABs is different: Congress prescribes, through law, both eligibility criteria, and the tests which need to be passed by a project for it to receive financing. Beyond these features for selection, all qualifying projects receive their funding, without the discretionary authority of a Secretary who is generally responsible for all projects which receive assistance in this way.

The two aforementioned preliminary tests which the projects need to pass are, first, a 'usage' test which requires that more than 10 per cent of the proceeds of the issue are to be used for any private business use, and, second, a security test.[124] The security test requires that the payment on the principal of, or the interest on, more than 10 per cent of the proceeds are secured by private means. After a project passes these two tests, then it has to belong to one of the qualified private activities, as defined in detail by the law, in order to receive financing through tax-exempt bonds. Finally, Congress sets yearly caps for each separate activity, their distribution among states and their maximum amounts.[125]

In this way Congress has complete control over the award of federal assistance in the shape of these tax-exempt bonds: it details the activities which qualify, and it provides the technical parameters of their determination. The Internal Revenue Service (IRS), which is a department of the Treasury, will only need to verify that the technical prescriptions of the law are fulfilled for each application which it receives, and thus has no discretion over the awarding of federal assistance. For its own accountability over the performance of its duties, including the awarding of tax-exempt bonds, the law provides for the responsibility of the Treasury Inspector General of Tax Administration, which is to perform economy, effectiveness and efficiency audits on the performance of the IRS:

> § 2. Purpose and establishment of Offices of Inspector General; departments and agencies involved: In order to create independent and objective units—
> (1) to conduct and supervise audits and investigations relating to the programs and operations of the establishments listed in section 12 (2);
> (2) to provide leadership and coordination and recommend policies for activities designed (A) to promote economy, efficiency, and effectiveness in the administration of, and (B) to prevent and detect fraud and abuse in, such programs and operations; and, such as the Treasury Inspector General

---

124 26 U.S.C. § 141.
125 26 U.S.C. § 146.

of Tax Administration, which reports to Congress on the performance of the duties of the Internal Revenue Service.[126]

By virtue of this provision, for example, the Treasury Inspector General of Tax Administration performed his 2009 report to Congress on the use of PABs. The report analyses the structures which the IRS has established to monitor compliance with the caps established by Congress of the projects which have received tax-exempt bonds.[127]

As we may notice with respect to the criteria of economy, effectiveness and efficiency, which the law provides, each is exposed to fair degree of subjectivity, without the law providing any definition around how they are to be construed. Beyond this, it is of significance and importance that the nature of these criteria is financial. This means that, in order to understand what they require and how they have to be construed, the relevant bodies will have to seek to understand specific aspects of the discipline of finance which develops such concepts.

With the examination of the PABs and their accountability arrangements, we have provided a fairly detailed account of the PPP activity in the USA from the perspective of the federal government. With respect to this perspective, as we have seen, the federal government participates in PPPs both directly but also indirectly, by contributing federal public money to PPPs across the USA. In both cases the basis of its participation is legislation, which provides detailed basic characteristics of this participation and accountability criteria and arrangements.

2.5.2. The absence of a central co-ordinating authority and the role of the Government Accountability Office

There have been a large number of programmes which materialise the involvement of the federal government to PPPs, and which depend upon both the support of local or state PPPs, and the direct participation of the federal government in such transactions. These we have detailed in the previous section. These instruments, consistent with the rule of the Economic Constitution which we distinguish in the present section, are almost always based on legislation which provides for authorisation as well as criteria and mechanisms of accountability.

A characteristic of the federal involvement to PPPs, however, and one which has already been shown by the relevant literature, is that this participation lacks

---

126 5 U.S.C. § 2. The provision applies to the Treasury Inspector General of Tax Administration by virtue of 5 U.S.C. § 8(D)(h).

127 Treasury Inspector General for Tax Administration, *Future Tax Revenues are at Risk because certain Tax-Exempt Bonds may exceed Annual Dollar Limits without Detection* (2009-10-097).

a central control and accountability mechanism.[128] More specifically, from the point of view of the executive, there is no body comparable to the PUK (PUK), which would take ultimate responsibility for the promotion and co-ordination of PPPs; similarly, from the viewpoint of the legislature, there is no body equivalent to the PAC with responsibility for Congressional oversight across the whole of the PPP programme. This has been succinctly summarised by Arthur L. Smith:

> Discussion of PPP financing in the US is further complicated by the fragmented nature of the US PPP market. Unlike many countries (e.g., the UK, Ireland, the Czech Republic etc.), the US has no single federal agency with oversight of PPP policy and issues. Authority to undertake PPPs is typically granted to agencies by the Congress on an agency-specific basis, or even function-specific or project-specific basis. There is no standard approach to federal PPPs for infrastructure analogous to, for example, the UK's PFI (PFI). (. . .) On the positive side, this fragmented environment makes the US a virtual 'PPP laboratory' in which a number of varied approaches to PPP structure and finance have been attempted, with varying degrees of success, providing valuable lessons learned. Less positively, this fragmentation makes the US a more complex investment environment. In addition, although hundreds of PPPs are created in the US each year, the lack of a central agency to track and report these transactions makes it more difficult to demonstrate the full extent of PPP activity.[129]

Similarly, as the GAO has highlighted:

> Some countries have further protected the public interest in transit projects that use alternative approaches by establishing quasi-governmental entities to assist project sponsors in implementing these arrangements. Entities such as PUK, (. . .) are often fee-for-service and associated with Treasury Departments on the provincial and national levels. These quasi-governmental entities all develop guidance such as standardize contracts and provide technical assistance to support transit projects that use alternative approaches.[130]

---

128 The limited co-ordination in the contracting activity of government in the USA has been discussed in terms of a series of interviews I conducted with Professor Duncan Kennedy, Carter Professor of General Jurisprudence at Harvard University (Cambridge, Massachusetts, United States, September 2013–December 2014). The interviews confirmed, rather than provided, the factual part related to the subject of limited co-ordination.
129 Smith 200.
130 United States General Accountability Office, *Public Transportation – Federal Project Approval Process Remains a Barrier to Greater Private Sector Role and DOT Could*

Under the same framework, there is no committee in the US Congress which has responsibility for the overall accountability of PPPs, such as that responsibility which is recognised for the PAC in the UK. The PAC authors numerous reports on PPPs every year, and it has the chance, as we showed, to systematise the criteria of accountability for the PPPs, such as that of VfM, into specific normative prescriptions which are applied across the complete PPP spectrum. Such a committee does not exist in the Congress. In this way, in the USA, there are two factors which – in combination – have a negative impact on the co-ordination of all the criteria and mechanisms of accountability that the numerous laws at all levels, federal, state and local, provide. These two factors are that first, there is no central agency with authority over the whole of the PPP programme, and, second, there is no committee with overall responsibility over government's accountability for PPPs.

Apart from the negative impact on the co-ordination of the various mechanisms and criteria that the different pieces of legislation provide, this situation has a negative impact on the co-ordinating powers of the Government Accountability Office (GAO).

The GAO is an institution which might be viewed as the organ which is most analogous to the NAO in the UK. The General Accountability Office, headed by the Comptroller General of the USA,[131] was first established under the name 'General Accounting Office'[132] with the Budget and Accounting Act of 1921,[133] the same Act which first established the Office of Management and Budget (OMB).[134] Since its foundation, the General Accounting Office has been defined as an agency independent from the Executive[135] in the legislative branch of the federal government, and has been headed by the Comptroller General of the USA,[136] who is appointed by the President with the advice of the Senate.[137] It is commonly referred to as the 'investigative arm of Congress'.[138] It examines

Enhance Efforts to Assist Project Sponsors (Report to Congressional Committees, GAO-10-19, 2009) 37.

131 31 U.S.C. § 702(b) (2012).
132 United States Government Accountability Office, *About GAO* (2014) 2; United States General Accounting Office, *GAO's Congressional Protocols* (GAO/OCG-00-2, 2000) 6–16.
133 Budget and Accounting Act 1921, codified as amended in scattered sections of Title 31 U.S.C.
134 31 U.S.C. § 207 (under the name 'Bureau of the Budget').
135 31 U.S.C. § 301. Current legislation uses the term 'instrumentality' to describe it (31 U.S.C. § 702(a)). It is clear, however, (31 U.S.C. § 701) that the term 'agency' includes the term 'instrumentality'. This interpretation also complies with the provision of the 31 U.S.C. § 704, which provides that all laws generally related to the administration of an agency apply to the Comptroller General.
136 31 U.S.C. § 702(b).
137 31 U.S.C. § 703(a)(1).
138 Frederick M. Kaiser, *CRS Report for Congress: GAO: Government Accountability Office and General Accounting Office* (Congressional Research Service, RL30349, 2008) 4.

how public money is spent and provides advice to both Congress and agencies, as well as the President, when requested,[139] on various subjects related to the handling of public money, including how they can improve their constitutional role towards public money and how they can improve their performance in terms of this role.[140]

It is worth us highlighting that the role of the GAO with respect to PPPs is not as intense as the UK equivalent. The GAO has produced a relatively small number of reports which examine PPPs, and there can be no comparison to the sheer number of reports produced on the subject by the NAO, which is 'by far the biggest producer of reports on PPPs'[141] compared to the USA. Further to this, the reports of the GAO tend to describe the findings of the office to Congress, rather than prescribing interpretations of the criteria of accountability or delineating policies and outcomes which need to be achieved according to the opinion of the Comptroller.

It is, perhaps, unsurprising, therefore, that we find that the Comptroller authored several of his reports without putting forward any recommendations or suggestions. One of them, entitled 'PPPs: Key Elements of Federal Building and Facility Partnerships', sought to identify the common characteristics of successful PPPs. By examining six case studies,[142] the Comptroller distinguished five key characteristics. These were the use of PPPs as a means to respond to fiscal and community pressures, the statutory basis of the respective projects which provided for the ability of the agencies to use the resulting revenues to achieve their goals, the adoption of the necessary organisational structures, and the importance given to

Roger R. Trask, *United States General Accounting Office: History Program: GAO History 1921–1991* (OP-3-HP, 1991); Darrell Hevenor Smith, *The General Accounting Office: Its History, Activities, and Organization* (Johns Hopkins University Press 1927), esp. 66ff; Harvey C. Mansfield, *The Comptroller General: A Study of the Law and Practice of Financial Administration* (Yale University Press 1939), esp. 247ff; Thomas D. Morgan, 'The General Accounting Office: One Hope for Congress to Regain Parity of Power with the President' (1972–1973) 51 North Carolina Law Review 1279, esp. 1280–3; Frederick C. Mosher, *The GAO: The Quest for Accountability in American Government* (Westview Press 1979), esp. 18ff, 220; Joseph Pois, *Watchdog on the Potomac: A Study of the Comptroller General of the United States* (University Press of America 1979), esp. 105–10.

139 31 U.S.C. § 719(e).

140 31 U.S.C. § 712.

141 Ineke Boers and others, 'Public-Private Partnerships: International Audit Findings' in Piet De Vries and Etienne B. Yehoue (eds), *The Routledge Companion to Public–Private Partnerships* (Routledge 2013) 453.

142 United States General Accounting Office, *Public-Private Partnerships: Key Elements of Federal Building and Facility Parterships* (Report to the Hon Stephen Horn Committee on Government Reform House of Representatives GAO/GGD-99-23, 1999) 7. These case studies were the ones of Fort Mason Foundation and the Thoreau Center agreed by the Department of the Interior, the Veteran Affairs Regional Office and the Cold Spring Medical Facility in Indiana by the Department of Veteran Affairs, the Grand Central Station Post Office and the Rincon Center Post Office by the U.S. Postal Service.

careful planning before the project[143] and the support of the local stakeholders. Similarly highly descriptive, yet lacking recommendations or suggestions, is the report entitled 'Water Infrastructure: Information on Financing, Capital Planning, and Privatization'. This report established that the revenues from user charges exceeded the cost of service provision in water and waste water utilities by 39 per cent and 33 per cent respectively[144] and it described additional sources of finance for the facilities.[145] The report described the perceived link between a lack of planning on the part of many authorities and the deterioration of their finance sources, and distinguished how the outcomes of the responses of private contractors related to the factors which would make them likely to invest. A third report which is, once again, highly descriptive, is entitled 'Depot Maintenance: Status of the Public-Private Partnership for Repair of the Dual-Mode Transmitter in the F-16 Fire-Control Radar'. The said report referred to a public-private partnership between the Air Logistics Complex of the Department of Defense (DOD) and a private contractor for the repair of certain transmitters in the F16 airplanes which comprised some foreign military sales.[146] The GAO reviewed the PPP agreement, the DOD policy and guidance on PPPs and other previous reports of relevant agencies. The report determined that the partnership had not – since its establishment in 2011 – undertaken any such repair activity and that, therefore, there were no cost savings to report. Similarly, it determined that there had not been any benefit resulting from the sale to foreign customers, and the factors which led to this result included the loyalty of those customers to their existing repair contractors, and the lengthy processes which exist for procurement in other countries.[147]

Certain other reports also share this prevailing theme of intensely descriptive content, but they also provide recommendations and suggestions. Unfortunately, however, the small size of the cohort of relevant reports makes it impossible to distinguish and generalise upon its patterns. One report from this rarefied group which includes recommendations is entitled 'PPPs: Pilot Program Needed to Demonstrate the Actual Benefits of Using Partnerships'. In this report, which was originally ordered by four members of Congress, the Comptroller was asked to assist it to identify the benefits to the federal government of entering into PPPs on federal real estate.[148] The Comptroller described the different benefits[149]

---

143 Ibid 14.
144 Ibid 6.
145 Ibid 23.
146 United States Government Accountability Office, *Depot Maintenance: Status of the Public-Private Partnerships for Repair of the Dual-Mode Transmitter in the F-16 Fire-Control Radar* (Briefing to the Senate Armed Services Committee, GAO-15-249R, 2015) 1.
147 Ibid 12.
148 United States General Accounting Office, *Public-Private Partnerships: Pilot Program Needed to Demonstrate the Actual Benefits of Using Partnerships* (Report to Congressional Requests, GAO-01-906, 2001) 1.
149 Ibid 5.

of the use of PPPs, and recommended the launching of a pilot programme to determine how these benefits ought to materialise in practice. Similarly, another very recent report containing recommendations and suggestions is entitled 'Depot Maintenance: Persistent Deficiencies Limit Accuracy and Usefulness of DOD's Funding Allocation Data Reported to Congress'. This report aimed to examine whether the US Department of Defense complied with the provisions of 10 U.S.C. § 2466 (2012), which required them to use no more than 50 per cent of annual depot maintenance finding for work performed by private sector contractors. After intense criticism of the data submitted by the department which 'was inaccurate, containing data errors, omissions, and inconsistencies',[150] the GAO described the causes of these problems.[151] Based on these causes, it recommended enhanced reporting requirements for the Department of Defense containing additional elements such as how it intends to make good these problems. A question from Congress was also put to them, suggesting that it would consider requiring them to make good the problems.[152]

One reason that there is this intensely descriptive, rather than prescriptive, dimension to the reports of the GAO is, arguably, because there is already sufficient analytic legislation which covers the normative needs of the system. From these analyses, we notice that the major role that the GAO performs with respect to PPPs is to inform Congress, rather than to co-ordinate the criteria and the mechanisms of accountability that the various pieces of legislation provide. It is a body which participates in a number of the many mechanisms of accountability that the various pieces of legislation provide, rather than being a body with either an ordained mission or actual function of co-ordinating the different mechanisms into a unified system of evaluation and accountability. This latter role would potentially be able to be performed if it was serving a body such as the UK PAC, which has undertaken the co-ordination of accountability in PPPs, holding accountable an agency with responsibility over the whole of the promotion of the PPP programme. However, as we have stressed, these co-ordinating mechanisms are absent in the Economic Constitution of the USA.

3.   Accountability and legislation

The previous section of this chapter has shown that the production of legislation providing means and criteria for accountability around PPPs is a characteristic of the US Economic Constitution which is coupled with the lack of a co-ordinating mechanism. The rich presence of legislation should theoretically mean

---

150 United States Government Accountability Office, *Depot Maintenance: Persistent Deficiencies Limit Accuracy and Usefulness of DOD's Funding Allocation Data Reported to Congress* (Report to Congressional Committees, GAO-06-88, 2005) 9.
151 Ibid 15–17.
152 Ibid 22.

increased constitutional accountability. With the requirement of legislation behind every PPP project, the legislature has the ability to question the promotion of PPPs by the executive and the consequent expenditure of public money in them. If not satisfied, it can stop enacting legislation or directly change the ways that PPPs are used.

The problem, however, in this system is that, while these laws on PPPs exist, the criteria of accountability which they provide are exposed to a substantial degree of subjectivity. We have evidenced many of these criteria through our examination of examples earlier in this chapter, and explored features including those of 'public interest', 'efficiency', 'effectiveness', 'advantageous' character of the project, 'economy' and others, which – as we will see in detail in the next section – do not have a consistent meaning. Apart from the vagueness of each of the criteria which the legislation uses as a basis of accountability, the second problem is that legislation has been used too extensively: behind every PPP project, there are various pieces of legislation which will be invoked, each one providing for its own mechanisms of accountability and for its own criteria of evaluation. By means of illustration, in one specific project related to water, the first piece of legislation to be applied will be the state legislation on the project, providing mechanisms and criteria of accountability; the second piece of legislation will be the federal legislation on environmental review, again, providing for its own criteria; the third piece of legislation, would be that related to federal contribution to the project by means of WIFIA provisions. Finally, in cases where the federal government decides to contribute to the project by means of PABs, there will also be legislation related to the PABs which will be applicable, together with its mechanisms and criteria of accountability. In this way, the criteria of accountability provided by the legislation are exposed to a fair degree of subjectivity, but the issue is further complicated by the highly complex system, involving the parallel application of many criteria. As we described earlier, the USA lacks a central mechanism such as the PAC in the UK, or a specialised federal agency dedicated to PPP, such as the PUK. Because of this gap, there is limited co-ordination of all these parallel mechanisms of the criteria of accountability.

These two problems hinder the accountability for PPPs. Congress is required to oversee the executive in its financial expenditure by virtue of the Constitution. This oversight cannot operate effectively if the criteria on which the executive will be held to account are subjective and if there is limited co-ordination of these criteria, and on how they will work with each other in the parallel application of legislation. This is the reason why, in spite of a great deal of PPP legislation, the USA does not benefit from better accountability arrangements.

Our claim that the systems around the accountability of PPPs in the USA are less than efficacious is not novel. There is a sizeable body of literature which discusses accountability in PPPs and each commentator provides solutions based on different frameworks of analysis. It is from the discussion of this literature that we will begin our exploration of the problems and their potential solutions.

3.1.   Existing frameworks of analysis

In the USA, a considerable body of legislation dedicated to PPPs exists and yet, despite the provision of both criteria and mechanisms of accountability, PPPs are exposed to challenges of accountability. The most relevant existing literature which discusses these challenges can be distinguished as viewing the problem from two perspectives, those of Public Administration and Constitutional Law. While the commentators agree that there are concerns over the accountability of PPPs, they do not attribute these concerns to the vagueness of the criteria of evaluation or to overuse of legislation for PPPs employing many parallel systems of accountability, as we do in this book.

The first framework of analysis includes arguments of Administrative Science and Public Management. According to the literature developed in this category, the issues of oversight and accountability in public contracting need to be resolved with administrative reforms which operate in a number of different directions, related to the managerial relationships in the bureaucracy. In this way, according to John D. Donahue, whose argument represents this category of analysis, the problem of accountability in modern government contracting stems from the fact that activities which, in keeping with their complexity, should be directly attended to by the government, have instead been outsourced.[153] According to Donahue, the solution to this problem could be found via a tripartite criterion which should be used – in his opinion – in deciding whether or not activities should be contracted. The three relevant aspects, for Donahue, are specificity, ease of evaluation, and competition.[154] In this way, if an activity is specific enough, easy to evaluate and can gather offers from as many different competitors as possible, this activity would be suitable for outsourcing.

As we see, Donahue attributes the basic reason for the problem of accountability to the complexity of the task which is outsourced by the government. Our analysis differs from his due to the fact that the basic problem for us is less the complexity of the activity but rather the complexity of the accountability arrangements which are developed in terms of the outsourcing. In this sense, the water project which we illustrated earlier is not a complicated government activity: the government needs to employ a company to sanitise the water. The problem in the accountability of such a PPP derives from the complexity of the legal framework which has been developed for this accountability, spanning criteria which are vague and numerous, and which are provided by many poorly co-ordinated laws which establish many parallel mechanisms of accountability.

For Miriam Seifter, the problem of PPP accountability rests with the broad decision-making power given to the private sector, the pitting of their interests

---

153 John D. Donahue, 'The Transformation of Government Work – Causes, Consequences and Distortions' in Martha Minow and Judy Freeman (eds), *Government by Contract: Outsourcing and American Democracy* (Harvard University Press 2009) 42.
154 Ibid 44.

against those of the government and the existence of procedures which make it difficult to pinpoint the wrongdoers.[155] According to her, part of the solution would be to increase overview and scrutiny.[156] Our argument is closer to that of Seifter than it is to Donahue, because our research also shares the starting point of the problems of overseeing the PPP activities of the government; however, the problem as we perceive it does not lie in the quantity of overview which, according to Seifter, is too little and needs to be increased. The problem for us lies in the quality of the existing overview, which suffers because of criteria and systems of accountability which are exposed to a considerable degree of subjectivity and complexity.

A further framework which is employed in the wider discussion around accountability issues of PPPs is that of Constitutional Law. Commentators who approach the problem from this dimension employ analyses of Constitutional Law around the subject of accountability in PPPs, and one of the most important claims which such commentators make focuses on the constitutional value of due process. As we will see, the analysis attempted in this chapter is close to the arguments made in the Constitutional Law literature.

One of the most representative writers in the framework of Constitutional Law of PPPs is Gillian Metzger. Metzger begins her contribution by producing an overview of the current application of Constitutional Law in PPPs, and she notes that it has frequently been employed in a way which pushes for less rather than more scrutiny.[157] As a solution, she proposes a reformulated version of due process. More specifically, she determines that significant gaps exist in the present understanding of the due process doctrine, in its application to address issues of the lack of accountability and transparency. In order to address these gaps, it is likely that a change of the doctrine would be most welcome: such modification should signify the duty of the government to oversee and supervise private contractors. This would result in important benefits, not only in accountability and transparency, but also in addressing – to some extent – the present weaknesses of the private delegation doctrine, which underscores the importance of government supervision.[158]

Metzger's views are closely linked to the argument which we are supporting in this chapter. Her theoretical framework constructs a due process requirement for the government to supervise. Our argument, here, traces the problems of accountability in PPPs to the fact that the criteria and mechanisms of

---

155 Miriam Seifter, 'Rent-a-Regulator – Design and Innovation in Environmental Decision Making' in Martha Minow and Judy Freeman (eds), *Government by Contract: Outsourcing and American Democracy* (Harvard University Press 2009) 108.
156 Ibid.
157 Gillian Metzger, 'Private Delegations, Due Process, and the Duty to Supervise' in Martha Minow and Judy Freeman (eds), *Government by Contract: Outsourcing and American Democracy* (Harvard University Press 2009) 291.
158 Ibid 307–8.

accountability are exposed to a significant degree of complexity and subjectivity. In this way, the due process requirement of the government to supervise is hindered by the problems in the criteria and mechanisms of accountability. In order to illustrate this point, we need to return, briefly, to our example of the water PPP project. Here, a contractor, an officer, a minister and the legislature are all interconnected through links of accountability. They each face a complicated system of criteria on which this accountability is based, and each one of the criteria is exposed to subjectivity and uncertainty. When each of them is asked the question 'Over which criterion will you supervise and hold accountable the other parts of the link?', the answer that each will give will be subjective, because each will use his own interpretations of the criteria of accountability that the law requires, such as those of effectiveness and efficiency. In this way, the complexity and ambiguity of the systems of accountability and supervision hinder the quality of accountability and supervision which will be exercised. For this reason, as we will show, the due process requirement of the government to supervise, which Metzger sees as the root of the problems of accountability, should be exemplified into a due process requirement of the government to systematise and co-ordinate the criteria of accountability for PPPs.

A second commentator who approaches the problem of accountability on PPPs from the framework of Constitutional Law is Paul Verkuil. Verkuil argues that the non-delegation doctrine requires that transfers of power from public to private parties must be accompanied by procedural standards, but that, in some cases, the doctrine should require that such transfers should not occur at all.[159] If the function which is to be outsourced to private contractors involves policymaking, it cannot be transferred and it should be performed by government officials[160]; policymaking is reserved for the political branches of government by the Constitution.[161] Similarly, the overview function should not be delegated, as this compromises trust, diminishes the public role and raises constitutional concerns. In privatisation settings there is transfer of policy-making to the private sector, and while this policy-making does not extend to the creation of laws, due process would require that the decision maker should be a public actor. For this reason, according to Verkuil, when the grant of power has a public dimension, this grant of power 'can be viewed as "publicised" for due process purposes'.[162] For Verkuil, due process could be invoked in privatisation settings in order to substantiate the argument that the activities of the private contractor should be susceptible to constitutional constraints, and in order to substantiate the notion that, in certain contexts, the relevant delegations are prohibited.

159 Paul Verkuil, 'Outsourcing and the Duty to Govern' in Martha Minow and Judy Freeman (eds), *Government by Contract: Outsourcing and American Democracy* (Harvard University Press 2009) 310.
160 Ibid 313.
161 Ibid 314.
162 Ibid.

A striking aspect of Verkuil's theory focuses more upon the prohibition of delegation of certain functions to the private sector than Metzger's, which tries to distinguish how these contracted-out relationships should operate. In this way, our theory is closer to Metzger's ideas, because – like her – we focus on the operation of contracted-out relationships in PPPs, rather than on the constitutional constraints which exist prohibiting this outsourcing. However, Verkuil, like Metzger, accepts the possibility that due process has to be applied in government contracting. For him, due process will require that a certain function is exercised by a public official when this function is essentially a public function. This characteristic brings our framework close to his, because we will also focus on the application of due process in public contracting. However, from this application, we construct a responsibility for the government to systematise and co-ordinate the criteria and the mechanisms of accountability, rather than a governmental responsibility to keep certain functions as public. In this last respect the focus of Verkuil and the focus of our current chapter is different.

The argument which we try to establish in this book complements and specialises many of the theories supported by the aforementioned literature. For us, the problem of overview, monitoring and accountability is that the criteria and the mechanisms upon which these relationships are based are exposed to a considerable degree of complexity and subjectivity. This hinders the quality of the scrutiny, monitoring and accountability, and a systematisation of these mechanisms and criteria could contribute to the improvement of this quality. This systematisation is, in our opinion, rooted in a duty of due process of the government which, as Metzger argues, is required to supervise government contracting. In this way, the due process duty to supervise can be understood, in PPPs, as a duty to systematise the mechanisms and the criteria of accountability.

Having provided a sketch of the positioning of our research in the context of the existing literature, we may now proceed to detail the finer aspects of our argument. The first area to explore is the idea that the criteria which we saw the legislation provide for PPPs are exposed to a considerable degree of complexity and subjectivity.

3.2. Criteria of evaluation and accountability provided by legislation

We saw in the previous section of this chapter that a characteristic of the promotion of PPPs in the USA is the enactment of a significant amount of legislation, both at federal and state level. This has resulted in the creation and co-existence of many criteria of accountability, which are used as a point of reference in the respective mechanisms of accountability employed for PPPs. In this section we will see the criteria in a more systematic way, and we will develop how each one of them is exposed to subjectivity. A further purpose of this section is to see how certain criteria of accountability, apart from serving as criteria of accountability, also serve in some cases as principles which direct the regulation of PPPs. This is a factor which further aggravates the consequences of their exposure to subjectivity.

3.2.1. Basic distinctions

Some of the predominant criteria which are used in terms of accountability over PPPs in the USA, as they are provided by the different pieces of relevant legislation, are those upon which we will focus, and include best (or public) interest, economy, efficiency, effectiveness, cost reduction, best value, safety, quality, and performance. These criteria – many of which we have already encountered in our previous discussion of PPP legislation – serve as points of reference in the accountability mechanisms and they are crucial for PPPs at both federal and state levels. In order to effectively analyse these criteria, it would be useful to differentiate them into two categories, financial and administrative. We have already introduced this distinction, yet in this part we will focus on it in more detail, using it as a framework of analysing the criteria of accountability and their exposure to subjectivity.

The first category for criteria of accountability could be characterised as predominantly financial. The most common financial criteria are those of economy, efficiency, effectiveness, cost reduction and best value. The reason why they are characterised as financial is that they draw their notional understandings from the fields of economics and finance. In this way, when, for example, a contracting officer is prescribed by law to select a contractor based on the criterion of 'economy', and he needs to know precisely how he could be held accountable for his choice, the answer will be provided by the existing literature in the field of finance defining how 'economy' is perceived. In this way, the determination of the content of each financial criterion depends on the ways that experts in the field of finance perceive them and impart their views in the relevant literature.

The second category of criteria which are used in evaluation and accountability is that of administrative criteria. Such criteria would be those of public (or best) interest, uniformity, consistency, safety, quality, and performance. These criteria are characterised as administrative because they draw their understanding from their use in the context of administrative operation. In this way, when a contracting officer is prescribed to select a contractor based on 'performance', and he needs to know the detail around what he might be held accountable for, he will have to consult the practice of the organisation in order to determine what understanding this practice attributes to the term 'performance'. In this way, the determination of the content of each one of the administrative criteria is made predominantly by administrative and bureaucratic structures, and is informed by the way that the experts in these structures perceive them.

A further distinction which can be made in terms of the criteria of evaluation refers to the use of techniques. Some of the criteria use techniques to determine their application, while others do not, and are, instead, approached in a more theoretical way. The reason why this distinction of the criteria between technical and non-technical is interesting is because the use of a technique is a factor which limits – to a certain extent – the exposure to subjectivity of the specific technical criteria. As we will see, however, this limitation of subjectivity is, at best, partial.

When we refer to subjectivity of the criteria of evaluation and accountability, we mean that each one of the criteria has multiple perceptions in their respective fields. So, one team of experts which could be called to apply them is likely to provide a different understanding in the accountability process compared to another team. Consequently, we will argue, they cannot serve as a stable point of reference in the accountability process, and their use could potentially raise concerns of due process.

3.2.2. *Financial criteria*

The first category of financial criteria contains those which are predominantly shaped by economists and financial managers, and so, for this reason, we have named them financial. These are the criteria of economy, efficiency, effectiveness, cost reduction and best value.

The first criterion of the financial category, which is used extensively as a point of reference in accountability relationships, is that of economy. We have already seen[163] that the criterion of economy is one of the criteria on which the audit for the performance of the IRS is based,[164] including the awarding of tax-exempt bonds to PPPs. Apart from the uses of 'economy' which we have already seen, at the federal level, the Office of Federal Procurement in the OMB is prescribed to 'promote economy, efficiency and effectiveness in the procurement of property and services by the executive branch of the Federal Government'.[165] The criterion of economy is also stressed as a principle for the designing of the simplified acquisition procedures of the federal acquisition regulation, whose goal is 'to promote efficiency and economy in contracting and avoid unnecessary burdens for agencies and contractors'.[166] The promotion of economy is also used as the goal while pursuing acquisitions under the simplified procedures.[167]

The evaluation of the criterion of economy is part of the investigation into whether or not the resources are used following the principles of economy and efficiency delineated in the subsequent regulations and provisions of government

---

163 See p. xxx [orig. 133]
164 5 U.S.C. § 2 (2012) and 5 U.S.C. § 8(D)(h).
165 41 U.S.C. § 1101.
166 41 U.S.C. § 3305. Similar prescription, again based on economy and efficiency, is prescribed as a principle for the simplified acquisition procedures provided by the Federal Acquisition Regulations, in 41 U.S.C. § 1901.
167 41 U.S.C. § 1901(a).

guidelines.[168] This cyclical feature heavily depends on the methodological tools used each time. These include the timeliness of the processes, unit costs, defect or error rates, accuracy, and adherence to specific schedules which are provided. Nevertheless, the timeliness and adequacy which are critical measures of these methodological tools strongly depend on regulations, which may simply not be there. It mostly falls to the evaluators themselves to judge whether these characteristics are there or not.[169] The criterion of economy, however, is a technical criterion because it uses the mathematical techniques of quantitative analysis, and, to a certain extent, this single factor limits and mitigates its ambiguity.

The second predominantly financial criterion is that of efficiency. Together with economy, it is one of the values that the OMB is prescribed to promote.[170] Efficiency is also one of the factors which will determine the way that the head of each executive agency will establish and operate acquisition programmes, which have to 'be designed to maximize efficiency'.[171] The criterion of efficiency coupled with that of economy is also used as a principle for the design of the Federal Acquisition Regulation with respect to the simplified acquisition procedures.[172]

The criterion of efficiency is vulnerable to similar concerns around subjectivity to that of economy and it is defined as contracting with the view of achieving the most output for the least reasonable cost.[173] The methodologies used are similar to those used for the criterion of economy, while reasonableness, as part of the definition, adds an additional layer of ambiguity, given that the political and administrative goals which are associated with government contracting can shape the reasonableness of these evaluations in many different ways. Again, even these can depend on the variable opinions of the specific set of experts who carry out the evaluations. However, the criterion of efficiency is also classified as a technical criterion, and, using similar techniques to the criterion of economy, is a factor which operates and which, to a certain extent, limits ambiguity.

The third of the financial criteria is that of effectiveness. Together with economy and efficiency, it is a criterion that the OMB is prescribed to promote.[174] Furthermore, the concept of effectiveness is crucial to the understanding of standards of federal procurement policy, which are defined as 'the criteria for determining the effectiveness of the procurement system by measuring the performance of the various elements of the system'.[175] Effectiveness is also

---

168 Kathryn E. Newcomer, 'Evaluating Public Programs' in James L. Perry (ed), *Handbook of Public Administration* (2nd edn, Jossey-Bass 1996) 565.
169 Ibid.
170 41 U.S.C. § 1101.
171 41 U.S.C. § 1704(c)(2)(C).
172 41 U.S.C § 3305 and 41 U.S.C. § 1901.
173 Ibid.
174 41 U.S.C. § 1101.
175 41 U.S.C. § 114.

important in the determination of the functions of the Administrator, who is the head of the Office of Federal Procurement Policy,[176] which provides overall direction of procurement policy and leadership in the development of procurement systems of the executive agencies.[177] One of his functions is to establish 'criteria and procedures to ensure the effective and timely solicitation of the viewpoints of interested parties in the development of procurement policies, regulations, procedures and forms'.[178] The concept is also used as a point of reference for the establishment and maintenance of 'procedures and processes for analysing the functions of a program, project, system, product, item of equipment, building, facility, service, or supply of the agency'.[179]

Effectiveness is a criterion which is exposed to ambiguity because the legislation around it is fairly unclear. This is the case whether it is an effectiveness related purely to costs or to sets of different economic or political goals, like stewardship and programme design, to name but two examples. An additional layer of ambiguity exists because of the fact that each one of the types of the concept of effectiveness is also largely lacking in definition and uncertain. For example, with respect to the cost-related type of effectiveness, which is meant to be the most technocratic, the associated examination relates the costs of a given programme activity to measures of specific (intended or unintended) programme outcomes. When these cost effectiveness studies take place with respect to a transactional activity of a corporation, the outcomes are considerably easier to define than at a federal level which affects a complicated economy with multiple dependencies in national and international fields. Furthermore, even if this difficulty of measuring the possible outcomes is somehow resolved, there is a second one, related to the high dependence of the measurement to the programme objectives, which mostly lack the necessary clarity.[180] Meanwhile, alongside both of these potential areas of difficulty, the criterion of effectiveness is also highly technical, which is a factor which – to some extent – mitigates its inherent ambiguity.

The same considerations are also true in other conceptualisations of effectiveness, like stewardship. The understanding of effectiveness around stewardship relates to the responsibility of public organisations, as it is shared between them, for acquiring resources and using them appropriately.[181] However, the acquisition of resources, and the propriety of their disposition are – once again – abstract notions and it is unclear precisely how any of these terms is used. Questions can be asked around some of these issues: Is the acquisition the transfer of

---

176 41 U.S.C. § 1102.
177 41 U.S.C. § 1121.
178 41 U.S.C. § 1122(a)(7).
179 41 U.S.C. § 1711.
180 Newcomer 566.
181 James L. Perry, 'Effective Enterprises, Effective Administrators' in James L. Perry (ed), *Handbook of Public Administration* (2nd edn, Jossey-Bass 1996) 737.

property, or does it mean any change in the legal rights or economic interests associated with the asset? Does the term 'appropriate use' only cover the economic use or does it extend to considerations of policy and regulation? The persistence and importance of these unresolved questions, as well as the discretion of the evaluation teams to use any of the associated understandings of these highly abstract notions and definitions, makes the criterion of effectiveness highly ambiguous and uncertain. The stewardship type of effectiveness remains, of course, a technical criterion, which is a factor that limits the associated ambiguity to some degree.

The fourth criterion is that of cost reduction. The Administrator of the Federal Procurement Office has to develop 'standard contract forms and contract language in order to reduce the Federal Government's cost of procuring property and services and the private sector's cost of doing business with the Federal Government'.[182] Similarly, the officers who deal with procurement in each executive agency are accountable to the head of their agency for their efforts to 'achieve cost savings'.[183]

With respect to cost reduction, the public finance calculation of the measure of cost is highly dependent on considerations of discounted value of the assets and cash flows of their expected use. However, these considerations are not straightforward for government contracting, especially when it significantly extends over time, since they depend on variables – such as the discount rate – that are time sensitive. It is important to note that the expected use of the asset does not merely cover the relevant consumers of the planned public services who are going to use the asset, but that it is also a measurement of their expected quantity, frequency of use and of the possible amounts that they would be willing to pay. The arbitrary character of these considerations share the clouding of the relevant calculations by the evaluation teams with our earlier examples.[184] The criterion of cost reduction is another technical one which, once again, helps with stabilisation, limiting, to some extent, the ambiguity of the notion.

The fifth criterion which can be characterised as financial is that of 'best value'. We have already seen the criterion previously, in its variation of 'substantial economic value', when examining TIFIA. Further to that the criterion of best value is determined as one[185] of the aims that Chief Acquisition Officers should have in establishing policies, procedures and practices for the agency.[186] The fact that the law uses the criterion of best value as a means of describing the aims of the Chief Acquisition Officers signifies that it is considered one of the values

---

182 41 U.S.C. § 1122(a)(8).
183 41 U.S.C. § 1706.
184 Harvey S. Rosen, *Public Finance* (3rd edn, Irwin 1992) 262–3.
185 The other aim is the one of 'lowest cost'.
186 41 U.S.C. § 1702(b)(3)(B).

which have to be promoted in contracting, or, in other words, as a pathway to achieving acceptable contractual performance. In this sense, the criterion is implied as a criterion of accountability for PPPs, rather than provided directly as such.

The criterion of best value is highly ambiguous in the US because it lacks an extensive systematic formula comparable to the one that was developed during the Thatcher years in the UK, and from which the modern notion of VfM has evolved.[187] In addition, a substantial factor which contributes to the ambiguity of the criterion is that the concept of 'value' in the U.S.A. has been used as a general notion in the transformation between conventional and modern management throughout the last three decades. Value as an understanding relative to the perceptions of the company managers, potential company customers, and prospective buyers of its shares began to be understood beyond the traditional microeconomic analysis: value is now defined in this context as something 'held in high esteem or appreciation', as 'having worth', and as something which is 'valid and sound'.[188] It is perceived as a 'measurement of relative worth', as 'the estimate in which something is held related to principles or standards of what is valuable in life', and 'the quality of a thing considered in respect of its power and validity for a specified purpose or effect'.[189]

It is clear that such an expansive understanding of value is contributing significantly to the ambiguity of the criterion of best value in government contracting, especially when coupled with the absence of associated holistic technical methods. The criterion of best value is the only one in the category of financial criteria which is predominantly non-technical, making its use by the law as an evaluation criterion for public contracts highly unstable.

Concluding the part of our argument related to financial criteria, we may summarise our analysis by emphasising that all of these criteria are exposed to subjectivity which, in almost all cases, however, is being limited to a certain extent due to the fact that many of them are technical. Despite the mitigation of ambiguity due to technical construction, however, as we have analytically exposed in the examination of each one of them, the notional parts which compose them are disputed in the discipline of finance; many varying views are supported. This factor makes them substantially unstable and subjective with regard to interpretation and understanding in terms of the evaluation of public contracts by the economic participants, such as customers and contract managers. Due to this ambiguity, the evaluation teams who apply the financial criteria in terms of specific projects enjoy substantial freedom in the determination of the notional content of each one of them.

---

187 To the best of our knowledge, none of the leading treatises in public finances in the USA provides a definition of the concept of 'best value'.
188 Eleanor Bloxham, *Economic Value Management: Applications and Techniques* (Wiley 2003) 5.
189 Ibid.

3.2.3. Administrative criteria

The second category of criteria which we have distinguished is predominantly shaped by administrators and bureaucrats, and for this reason they are described as Administrative. These are the criteria of uniformity, public (or best) interest, safety, quality, and performance, and each one of them is exposed to a considerable level of ambiguity.

The first criterion of the administrative category is that of 'best' or 'public interest'. The criterion of best interest of the federal government or of the procuring agency is used in many points of the federal system of accountability for PPPs. The law provides an almost unlimited authority to the contracting officers to follow procedures other than that of the sealed-bid type, when this will promote, under the determination of the head of the agency, the best interest of the Federal Government.[190] Furthermore, multi-year contracts such as PPPs are only permitted when 'a multi-year contract will serve the best interests of the Federal Government by encouraging full and open competition or promoting economy in administration, performance, and operation of the agency's programs'. In a similar way, the principle for the design of regulations applicable to procurement contracts for services or properties, is that these regulations provide criteria to determine whether the contract would not be in the 'best interests of the Federal Government'.[191]

The criterion of public interest has appeared in two important GAO reports, and although neither of which defined it, both used it to substantiate their conclusions. The first one of these reports is entitled 'Highway PPPs: More Rigorous Up-front Analysis Could Better Secure Potential Benefits and Protect the Public Interest'. The report discussed the observation that, throughout the implementation of PPPs, the various actors which exist use a variety of mechanisms to establish the public interest behind the PPPs, such as asset performance measures, financial mechanisms, accountability and flexibility structures, workforce oriented initiatives, financial analyses and bidding processes.[192] However, there is limited use, as the Comptroller has noted, of 'systematic, formal processes and approaches to the identification and assessment of public interest issues in the USA'.[193] The report recommended to Congress that the Secretary of Transportation should consult with the key stakeholders representing national interests in order 'to develop and submit objective criteria for identifying national public interests in highway PPPs'.[194] These criteria, according to the report, 'should

---

190　41 U.S.C. § 3901.
191　41 U.S.C. § 4103(d)(4)(B).
192　United States Government Accountability Office, *Highway Public-Private Partnerships: More Rigorous Up-front Analysis Could Better Secure Potential Benefits and Protect the Public Interest* (Report to Congressional Requests, GAO-08-44, 2008).
193　Ibid 56.
194　Ibid 73.

be crafted to allow the department to play a targeted role in ensuring that national interests are considered in highway PPPs, as appropriate'.[195] The Executive is directed by the Comptroller to recommend that the Secretary of Transportation 'directs the Federal Highway Administrator to clarify federal-aid highway regulations on the methodology for determining excess toll revenue, including the reasonable rate of return to private investors in highway PPPs that involve federal investment'.[196]

The second report which used the concept of public interest is that entitled 'Federal-Aid Highways: Increased Reliance on Contractors Can Pose Oversight Challenges for Federal and State Officials'. The report noted that the State Departments of Transportation (DOTs) have increased the use of contracting-out of highway activities, and this has been accompanied by increased reliance on consultants and contractors over the project quality.[197] Despite this fact, the Comptroller noted that none of the State DOTs which it examined formally assess costs and benefits before the decision to contract out.[198] The report recommended that the Secretary of Transportation direct the Administrator of the Federal Highway Administration (FHWA) to work with FHWA division offices in order to:

(1) give appropriate consideration to the identified areas of risk related to the increased use of consultants and contractors as division offices work to target their oversight activities and (2) develop and implement performance measures to better assess the effectiveness of state DOTs' controls related to the use of consultants and contractors to better ensure that the public interest is protected.[199]

As is very evident, these two reports use the concept of public interest without providing information on either how they define it or on how they perceive it. They *do* both provide that the public interest is a goal, however, neither specifies what this goal is, or how it can be achieved.

The second one of the administrative criteria is that of uniformity. The criterion of uniformity is set as an aim for the design of the accounting standards which govern 'measurement, assignment, and allocation of costs to contracts with the Federal Government'[200] by the Cost Accounting Standards Board. The

---

195 Ibid.
196 Ibid 74.
197 United States Government Accountability Office, *Federal Highways: Increased Reliance on Contractors Can Pose Oversight Challenges for Federal and State Officials* (Report to the Chairman, Committee on Transportation and Infrastructure, House of Representatives, GAO-08-198, 2008) 12.
198 Ibid. p. 29.
199 Ibid p. 43.
200 41 U.S.C. § 1502(a)(1) (2012).

criterion of uniformity is also provided as a goal for the implementation of 'systems, technologies, procedures and processes'[201] in agencies which aim to utilise the benefits of electronic commerce in procurement. There are also cases in which uniformity is set by the law as a value which needs to be avoided, rather than pursued. In this way, the law prohibits regulations which will define the concepts of 'significantly more important' and 'significantly less important' as specific numeric values that would be applied uniformly in all solicitations of government contracts.[202] Further to this, the Federal Acquisition Regulation should contain guidance which will promote a uniform approach in procurement across government in Design-Build selection procedures.[203]

The idea of uniformity has been a dominant theme in the regulation of the American Public Administration and one which expands in a variety of different and unrelated wider issues including those of the issuance of coins,[204] administrative adjudication,[205] taxation,[206,207]; and the administration of elections,[208] amongst others. The reason underlying this persistence of the idea of uniformity across the American public sector can easily be attributed to the needs of a multilevel federal system of governance to establish a level of consistency. However, the use of the concept in such a variety of issues has involved a substantial notional broadening of the idea of uniformity, and there is not a set understanding, common to all the areas, that is being used. In short, then, and perhaps rather ironically, the concept of uniformity is a moveable feast. This fact makes the use of the concept of uniformity subjective as a criterion of evaluation in federal contracting, because it is not clear, and it does not offer a common understanding of the criterion, on which specific aspects of the transactional activity of the government should be promoted, setting aside the case-by-case transactional behaviour. This matter consequently arbitrarily defaults to the contract teams to decide upon.

201 41 U.S.C. § 2301.

202 41 U.S.C § 3306(c)(2).

203 41 U.S.C. § 3309(e)(3).

204 Thomas Jefferson, *Report to the House of Representatives: Plan for Establishing Uniformity in the Coinage, Weights, and Measures of the United States* (1st Congress, 1790).

205 This matter is related to the much-disputed issue of the relationship between Congress and the bureaucracy. According to some of the critical literature, Congress promoted uniformity in the procedures of the agencies, in an effort to control a part of their operation which had become autonomous. See, Daniel F. Solomon, 'Fundamental Fairness, Judicial Efficiency and Uniformity: Revisiting the Administrative Procedure Act' (2013) 33 Journal of the National Association of Administrative Law Judiciary 52, 100–11.

206 Robert J. Freeman and others, *Governmental and Nonprofit Accounting: Theory and Practice* (International edn, Pearson Prentice Hall 2009) 824, 829–32.

207 According to art. I, § 8 of the US Constitution, 'all Duties, Imposts and Excises shall be uniform throughout the USA'.

208 Richard Rose, 'Elections and Electoral Systems: Choices and Alternatives' in Vernon Bogdanor and David Butler (eds), *Democracy and Elections: Electoral Systems and Their Political Consequences* (1983) 22.

The third administrative criterion is that of safety. The improvement of safety is prescribed as the aim of the procedures and processes that the executive agencies have to adopt with respect to projects of 'value engineering'.[209] The criterion of safety is also one of the criteria which have to be taken into account in designing procedures for supplies in exclusion of a particular source.[210]

The notion of safety is substantially ambiguous in its conceptualisation in the bureaucracy. The reason behind this is that safety is understood in a negative sense, as an effort to eliminate or limit risk,[211] and the concept of risk is an extremely broad notion. For this reason, there are various understandings and interpretations of the notion of safety across the administration, and these mirror the way that risk is conceived. They are similarly diverse, and include safety as avoidance of the risk of being liable, safety in relation to press releases, and safety around the risk of the bad reputation of the agency, to name but three examples.[212] Such diverse options point us to the fact that the concept of safety cannot be considered as a stable criterion of evaluation in government contracting, given that it has no common uniform interpretation and that it is unclear exactly to which conceptualisation of risk the public authority must direct its efforts to promote safety when negotiating or concluding the public contract.

The fourth administrative criterion is that of quality. As was the case with safety, it is also prescribed as one of the aims of 'value engineering'.[213] The quality of the goods and services to be provided by the government contract is one of the factors which are prescribed to be crucial in the evaluation process of executive agencies,[214] together with the factors of cost and price.[215] The criterion of quality also has a decisive role in the procurement of complicated advisory services, given that the law empowers the head of the executive agency to determine, in the solicitation, that only one contract will be awarded if a single bidder is capable of offering the services at 'the level of quality required'.[216]

The criterion of quality is a technical criterion. Quality is basically promoted through the technical assessments. As with other technical criteria on which we elaborated earlier, quality is exemplified via a number of tests, including those of customer satisfaction, employee involvement and development, continuous learning and improvement, prevention over inspection, supplier partnerships,

209 41 U.S.C. § 1711.
210 41 U.S.C. § 3303.
211 John D. Donahue, *Making Washington Work: Tales of Innovation in the Federal Government* (Brookings Institution Press 1999) 24, 114–15.
212 Charles Wise, 'Understanding your Liability as Public Administrator' in James L. Perry (ed), *Handbook of Public Administration* (2nd edn, Jossey-Bass 1996) 713.
213 41 U.S.C. § 1711.
214 41 U.S.C. § 3306(c)(1)(A).
215 41 U.S.C. § 3306(c)(1)(B).
216 41 U.S.C. § 4105(f)(2)(A). See also 41 U.S.C. § 4106(C)(2).

senior executive leadership, information and analysis and many others.[217] The reason why this criterion can be considered ambiguous is rooted in its enforcement mechanism, the Malcolm Baldrige National Quality Award, which uses criteria that overlap and which 'lead to confusion and conceptual overload'.[218] Although the associated ambiguity is limited, to a certain degree, because the criterion is technical, a lack of clarity in the assessment tools makes this criterion too unstable for use as a means of evaluation and accountability.

The fifth criterion of the administrative category is that of performance and this is one which is stressed in many areas of commentary. A satisfactory 'performance record' is important for the determination of a responsible contractor with a historically-sound track-record,[219] and can, thereby, participate in full and open competition around government procurement.[220] To aid this tracking process, the Administrator of General Services is prescribed to maintain records of the performance of certain groups of government contractors.[221] At the same time, performance, which is broadly understood to be a range of acceptable characteristics or minimum acceptable standards, is one of the types of specifications which are required in the solicitation of bids for government projects.[222] The criterion of performance is also one of those based on which the authorities are prescribed by law to make payments to contractors of property and services.[223]

The criterion of performance is yet another technical criterion. As has been distinguished,[224] there are eight aspects of the performance measurement. These are, the evaluation of agency performance, control over the agency, the determination of how much resource will be budgeted to each agency, the motivation of the agency to be more efficient, the promotion of governmental reliability across the society, the recognition of success, learning from mistakes, and, lastly, the measurement of continuous improvement. Ambiguity around the performance measures is rooted in an extremely multi-centred system which defines performance standards and techniques: The National Academy of Public Administration, the American Society for Public Administration, the Federal Accounting Standards Advisory Board, the Government Accounting Standards Board and the Government Finance Officers Association, as well as various other supervisory organs, are all bodies which set standards of performance. In addition, standards are periodically released by the GAO, and new standards are set after every new

---

217 Van Wart 269.
218 Ibid.
219 41 U.S.C. § 113.
220 41 U.S.C. § 107.
221 41 U.S.C. § 2313(a).
222 41 U.S.C. § 3306(a)(3).
223 41 U.S.C. § 4502(a).
224 Robert D. Behn, 'Why Measure Performance? Different Purposes Require Different Measures' (2003) 63 Public Administration Review 586, 587–93.

President comes into office. The result is a performance landscape full of different measures which have no simple relationship between each other, and it falls, once again, to the evaluation teams or their superiors in the hierarchy to decide which system of performance measurement will be used. Although ambiguity is potentially limited to an extent due to the technicality of the criterion of performance, this technicality does not manage to stabilise a criterion so heavily exposed to different systems of measurement, qualification and understanding.

In this way, as was the case with the financial criteria of evaluation, we have established, through our analysis of the administrative criteria, that they are exposed to a considerable degree of subjectivity. There is uncertainty in the construction of each one of them. This uncertainty is rooted in the fact of their broad construction in both theory and practice as well as in the plethora of definitions which coexist and the associated lack of unanimity on a relatively stable notional framework of reference or analysis. As we have seen in our elaboration of each one of the criteria earlier,[225] the fact that some of them are technical mitigates this ambiguity, at least to some extent, without, however, managing to fully stabilise them.[226] The reasons behind this include the variety of methodologies and standard setting techniques which have been developed and which coexist, leading to different results, interpretations and understandings, as well as the lack of agreement on a common enforcement mechanism. As a result of these, the burden of determining the Administrative criteria falls to the specific evaluation teams which will use them in terms of their assessment of government contracts; these teams, due to the substantial ambiguity of these criteria, possess substantial liberty in the determination of their notional content.

3.3. *The criteria of accountability as a matter exposed to subjectivity*

As we saw earlier, the criteria which are used in terms of public accountability for PPPs and other government contracts, are exposed to a considerable degree of subjectivity. This subjectivity hinders the public accountability process because

---

225 See here, pp xxx–xxx [orig. 146–151](Financial Criteria); xxx–xxx [orig. 151–156] (Administrative Criteria).

226 Some indicative examples include: United States Government Accountability Office, *DCAA Audits: Widespread Problems with Audit Quality Require Significant Reform* (Report to the Committee on Homeland Security and Governmental Affairs of the US Senate, GAO-09-468, 2009); United States Government Accountability Office, *Federal Highways: Increased Reliance on Contractors Can Pose Oversight Challenges for Federal and State Officials*; United States Government Accountability Office, *Highway Public-Private Partnerships: More Rigorous Up-front Analysis Could Better Secure Potential Benefits and Protect the Public Interest* 14–17, 42–6, 46–62, 76, 81.

it is an obstacle to the qualification of the actions of the supervised organ by the scrutinising body which holds this organ accountable.

Congress is supposed to exercise oversight over the activities of the executive, by means of the provisions of the US Constitution which we were introduced to in the first section of the present chapter. This overview is to be carried out based on the criteria of accountability which we have previously analysed. However, when these criteria are exposed to subjectivity, there can be no certainty over which of their meanings the accountability process will employ. The executive might have used one conception of any of them, while Congress might use another.

In the same way, the relationships of accountability inside the bureaucracy are hindered, and for similar reasons. When a contracting officer has to explain his decision to use a contract to his bureaucratic superiors, he will have to provide this explanation based on the criteria of accountability which we outlined earlier. The potential for the subjective interpretation of these criteria hinders the accountability process because his perception could place his interpretations at any point on a spectrum of possibilities, and this could significantly differ from the point on that same spectrum chosen by the bureaucratic superior who will hold him accountable.

The exposure of the criteria to a wide degree of subjectivity is, in this way, non-compliant to the requirements of public accountability and oversight. It hinders the ability of Congress to oversee, as is provided by the Constitution, as well as the effectiveness of accountability inside the bureaucracy itself. The question which arises in the face of this problem is what the law can do in order to improve the stability of the criteria of accountability. We will now turn our attention to this issue.

4.   Due process in public contracting

In the previous section we saw that the criteria of accountability which are provided by the various pieces of legislation for PPPs are exposed to a significant degree of subjectivity and complexity. This, as we noted, hinders the accountability process and the requirement of oversight which is a constitutional necessity, established in the provisions of the Constitution which provide for the economic powers of Congress.

In this way, the subjectivity and the complexity of the criteria of accountability are factors which distance the US system of promotion of PPPs from the prescriptions of the Economic Constitution. In view of this reality, the important question is whether or not the government has a constitutional duty to correct it. Whether, in other words, the government has a duty to provide an element of co-ordination and systematisation of the various criteria of accountability which are provided by the law. A question which accompanies the previous one in case of an affirmative answer would be the following: if there is a duty for the government to systematise and co-ordinate, then how is this duty to be exercised?

Before approaching these questions, it is necessary that we elaborate on what we mean by 'government' when we refer to the government's duty to systematise. To a significant degree, the duty of systematisation which we try to construe refers to the executive power of the federal government. Federal executive, as we will show, has to be recognised with a constitutional duty to systematise and co-ordinate the various criteria of accountability which are provided by the numerous laws on PPPs. To a lesser degree, for some cases in which the criteria of accountability are linked with criminal provisions, this duty of systematisation falls on the shoulders of the federal legislature. In this way, when we refer to the duty of the federal government to systematise and co-ordinate, we mean, in the main, the executive power, and, to a lesser degree, the legislative power of the federal government.

We have consciously selected to construe the basic duty of systematisation as a duty which belongs predominantly to the executive rather than the legislature, largely because of the suitability of the executive to co-ordinate. The executive possesses a level of expertise on PPPs which derives from its contact with contractors and its key involvement in advertising PPP projects and being responsible for the selection of an appropriate contractor. It has the ability, in its hierarchical structure, to issue guidelines which could be in the position to promote specific interpretations of the criteria and advance the task of their systematisation. The Congress, on the other hand, with its complicated structure and multimember composition would be a slower organ to promote the systematisation, while its basic instrument to do so would be the lengthy process of the enactment of legislation. For these reasons, we selected to focus our argument on a model of systematisation which is based on the predominant role of the executive, while reserving a co-ordinating role for the legislature only for such cases where legislative intervention is required.

A first basis for the duty of the executive and the legislature to systematise can be found in the provision of the Constitution which establish the responsibilities of the holders of these offices towards the Constitution. The President has a constitutional duty to uphold the US Constitution,[227] while the members of the Congress have a constitutional duty to support the US Constitution.[228] Consequently, if the exposure to the criteria to subjectivity distances the promotion of PPPs from the provisions of the US Constitution, because it hinders the oversight of Congress which is established by the Constitution, then the executive and the legislature are constitutionally required to correct this. However, apart from this general duty to systematise the criteria, we will support

---

227 This duty derives from the Vesting Clause, Take Care Clause, and the Presidential Oath of Office, which are the clauses of Art II of the Constitution which 'together suggest the president's broader obligations to uphold the Constitution'. Scott C. James, 'The Evolution of Presidency: Between the Promise and the Fear' in Joel D. Aberbach and Mark A. Peterson (eds), *The Executive Branch* (Oxford University Press 2005) 6.
228 U.S. Const. Art. II.

that there is a second basis for both the executive and the legislature, which is rooted in an additional institution of the Constitution. This institution is that of due process.

As we have seen earlier, critical literature has used the institution of due process in order to construct positive duties for the government. For Gillian Metzger, for instance, the institution of due process needs to be reformed in its application to government contracts, and this reform should involve the recognition of a positive duty of the government to oversee private contractors. Similarly, for Paul Verkuil, the reformulation of the doctrine of due process should involve the recognition of a positive duty of the government to keep certain core government activities public. For Metzger, the particular value of due process which requires the government to take corrective action is the principle of the prohibition of arbitrary action, while for Verkuil, the respective value of due process is the principle of accountable policy decision-making.

One of the reasons which motivates these critical commentators to substantiate their proposals for reform of the institution of due process is its core function in the operation of the Constitution in the USA. Due process was established for the federal government by the Fifth Amendment in 1795,[229] which provides that '[no person shall be] deprived of life, liberty or property, without Due Process of law'. Similarly, due process was also established by the Fourteenth Amendment of 1868[230] also towards state government, 'nor shall any State deprive any person of life, liberty, or property, without Due Process of law'. The slight differences of wording between the two provisions have been uniformly considered as insignificant, and the two articles are considered by both theory[231] and practice[232] as containing the same norm for federal and state government respectively. In other words, due process is a value of the US Constitution which enjoys a recognition which is both well established and catholic in the sense that it covers both the federal and the state governments.

Rooted in the recognition of due process is the prohibition of vagueness of laws, which will now be our primary point of focus. According to the Supreme Court[233] a statute is void for vagueness whenever 'men of common intelligence must necessarily guess at its meaning and differ as to its application'. The doctrine is applied predominantly in Constitutional Law and Administrative Law as well as in Criminal Law and Criminal Procedure.[234] It is, therefore, a principle which enjoys holistic recognition in the American legal system, as well as specific recognition and application in the field of Constitutional and Administrative Law.

---

229 U.S. Const. Amend. V.
230 U.S. Const. Amend. XIV.
231 Frank Easterbook, 'Substance and Due Process' (1982) Supreme Court Review 85, 102.
232 *Hurtado v. People of State of California* 4, S.Ct. 292 (1884).
233 *Connally v. General Const. Co.* 46, S.Ct. 126, 127 [1926].
234 Daniel Hall, *Criminal Law and Procedure* (6th edn, Delmar 2012) 284.

In this way, vagueness of law is prohibited in American Constitutional Law, and this prohibition of vagueness is rooted in the core institution of due process. In the present section, we will be attempting to construe a positive duty of government to systematise the criteria of evaluation based on this concept, specifically, the prohibition of vagueness. Both Metzger and Verkuil have attempted to construe a reformed due process doctrine: for Metzger this reformed doctrine should impose a positive duty to the government to supervise private contractors, rooted in the value of due process which prohibits arbitrary action. For Verkuil, this reformed doctrine should impose a positive duty to the government to keep certain functions public, rooted in the value of accountable decision-making. For us, this reformed due process doctrine should also impose a positive duty upon the government to systematise the criteria of accountability, rooted in the value of certainty of law and prohibition of vagueness.

On a very basic level, the definition that the Supreme Court gives for vagueness seems to fit the subjectivity of the criteria of accountability for PPPs. We saw earlier that the Supreme Court defines that a statute is void if vague; this determination of vagueness means when men of common intelligence must necessarily guess at a statute's meaning and differ as to its application. This holds for the criteria of accountability for PPPs: for each one of them, men of common intelligence – and even qualified experts as we have observed – must necessarily guess at their meaning and differ as to their application. A man of common intelligence, even an auditor, has to hypothesise on the meaning of criteria such as effectiveness, efficiency and public interest, to name but a few of the problematic criteria we have explored, and will thus differ in the way that he will apply it, in comparison with other men of common intelligence, or practitioners.

In order to advance our argument from this starting point, however, we have to see the ways in which the courts have applied 'vagueness' in settings of public contracting, such as PPPs, while discussing the constitutionality of legislation and other normative instruments.

4.1. *The vagueness doctrine in government contracting*

As we saw in the previous sub-section, the question which we need to address is whether the doctrine of the prohibition of vagueness is applicable to government contracts. The first case which points to an affirmative answer is that of the *Turner v. Chicago Housing Authority*.[235] In this case, the issue at stake was a government contract of tenancy. The contract was between the Chicago Housing Authority, which was an Illinois municipal corporation, which receives funding under the USA Housing Act of 1937 and which provides and manages subsidised housing. The plaintiffs were leaseholders whose tenancies were

---

235 *Turner v. Chicago Housing Authority* 760 F.Supp. 1299 [1991].

terminated because of the misconduct of non-residents who came to visit them, with the misconduct taking place outside their apartments. Part of the tenancy agreement included the following:

> The Tenant shall . . . (k) conduct himself and cause other persons who are on the premises with his consent to conduct themselves in a manner which will not disturb his neighbor's peaceful enjoyment of their accommodations and will be conducive to maintaining the development in a decent, safe and sanitary condition.[236]

The plaintiffs argued that this part of the lease should not be enforceable because it is vague. The defendant municipal corporation argued that the constitutional doctrine of vagueness cannot apply to a contract, but is only applicable to statutes and regulations. Despite the fact that the court did not accept that the lease contract was vague, it accepted the applications of the doctrine of vagueness to government contracts, but less strictly:

> In any event, since the lease provision is neither unconstitutionally vague nor unconstitutionally overbroad, it will be assumed, without deciding, that those doctrines apply to the lease provision. However, the vagueness doctrine does not apply equally to all circumstances. It applies less strictly to enactments concerned with economic regulation and those involving only civil penalties (. . .). Thus, to the extent the doctrine should be applied to a government contract, it applies less strictly. On the other hand, it applies more strictly to the extent it impinges on constitutionally protected rights such as First Amendment rights.[237]

The *Turner* case, therefore, provides a scope for the application of vagueness doctrine. The doctrine applies primarily to statutes and regulations, and these are the primary point of reference. It also applies to government contracts, but less strictly; its most strict application is reserved for cases where a fundamental right, protected under the Constitution, is at stake. Such rights are those of the First Amendment, such as, for example, the rights of peaceful assembly, freedom of speech, and the establishment and free exercise of religion, amongst others.

In the context of contracts, however, the question which naturally arises is around the parameters, or standards, of this less strict application. An important, illuminating case with respect to this question is the *Trojan Technologies, Inc. v. Commonwealth of Pennsylvania*.[238] In this case, a Canadian corporation which

236 Ibid 1303.
237 Ibid 1308.
238 *Trojan Technologies, Inc. v. Commonwealth of Pennsylvania* 916 F.2d 903 (1990).

was engaged in the manufacture of equipment used in waste water and sewage treatment facilities brought a suit challenging the constitutionality of the Pennsylvania Steel Products Procurement Act 1978. The Act provides that suppliers contracting with a public agency in connection with a public works project to provide products must use steel which is American-made.[239] The appellant contended that the range of products which are covered by the requirement was too broad. The Act prescribed that violation of these requirements would signify the return of the payments by the contractor and the prohibition of bidding in public agency contracts for 5 years.[240]

In order to establish vagueness, the court used the following criterion:

> a statute should be struck as vague if (1) it fails to give a person of ordinary intelligence a reasonable opportunity to know what is prohibited, or (2) it fails to provide explicit standards to the enforcing officer, in this case Pennsylvania's Attorney General.[241]

The questioned remained, however, what were the standards of strictness that would be used to establish that the criterion had been fulfilled? The appellants claimed that, as strict standards were necessary, because the sanctions that the statute in question imposed (in other words, both the return of payments and exclusion from bidding) were severe. However, due to the fact that the difference aimed at a 'civil statute',[242] rather than one providing for criminal sanctions, the court reasoned that a less strict review was necessary, declaring that 'we know of no case in which a civil statute has been subjected to strict vagueness review'.[243] As justification for the reasoning, the court cited the case of *Village of Hoffman Estates v. Flipside, Hoffman Estates Inc*,[244] which stated that 'economic regulation is subject to a less strict vagueness test because its subject matter is often more narrow, and because businesses, which face economic demands to plan behaviour carefully, can be expected to consult relevant legislation in advance of action'.[245] Further to that, the court in *Trojan* reasoned that the sanctions of the statute in question were not as severe as the appellants contended: even if the statute served to exclude them from bidding in agency contracts, they were still able to bid in non-government contracts in the state, or in government contracts in other states.[246]

---

239 73 P.S. § 1884 (1978).
240 73 P.S. § 1885(b).
241 *Trojan* 914.
242 Ibid.
243 Ibid.
244 *Village of Hoffman Estates v. Flipside, Hoffman Estates Inc* 102 S.Ct. 1186 (1982).
245 Ibid 1193–4.
246 *Trojan* 914.

In establishing vagueness, therefore, the court used the less strict standard of review. In this context of the less strict review, the court rejected the claim of the appellants that the definition of 'steel products' was vague. It explained that:

> Inability to satisfy a clear but demanding standard is different from inability in the first instance to determine what the standard is.[247]

The material from *Trojan* provides us with important details for the margins of vagueness which would be considered acceptable for statutes establishing criteria for PPPs. In the first instance, the criterion which can be used is that a statute is vague if it fails to provide a person of ordinary intelligence a reasonable opportunity to know what is prohibited or if it fails to provide explicit standards to the enforcing officer on its application. This being the criterion, however, its application will be less strict in statutes of economic regulation, such as in those statutes which provide criteria for accountability for PPPs. This less strict application will be based on taking into account the nature of the legislation, rather than upon how economically severe its outcomes are. In this context, taking into account the commercial practice, its meaning will be differentiated according to whether the criteria of accountability are difficult to understand or difficult to prove.

Not all PPP statutes, however, are statutes of purely economic regulation. As we will see, there are PPP statutes which provide for criminal sanctions linked to the criteria of accountability. For this reason, it is important to see how the courts have construed the stricter application of the doctrine of vagueness in government contracting.

A good case which illustrates the stricter application of the doctrine is the *Rayco Construction Company, Inc. v. Vorsanger*.[248] In this case, an Oklahoma contractor, who had submitted a low bid to construct a building on the campus of the University of Arkansas, brought action attacking the constitutional validity of the Act 264 of 1961.[249] The Act is an Arkansas statute which gives a 3 per cent bidding preference on public contracts to bids which fall within the terms of the statute. The terms which, according to the Act, are relevant in determining whether the bidding preference will be given in public contracts, and which have been criticised for unconstitutional vagueness, are the satisfactory performance of prior contracts, and the payment of state and county taxes for 2 years prior on plant or equipment required for the performance of the contract. At the same time, the Act provided for criminal punishment of either agency officials

---

247 Ibid 915.
248 *Rayco Construction Company, Inc. v. Vorsanger* 397 F.Supp. 1105 (1975).
249 Arkansas Act 264 of 1961, Ark.Stats.Ann. § 14–622 et seq (1961). Hereinafter Arkansas Act 264.

or the contractors which violate its terms, stating that it will pursue anyone who 'is guilty of a misdemeanour and punishable for each offense by a fine of not less than $50.00 nor more than $1,000.00 or by imprisonment for not more than six months, or both'.[250] It is worth highlighting that the exact criminal act is not specified by the criminal provision; instead, this provides, more generally, for the criminal liability of officials or contractors 'violating the provisions of the Act'.[251] The court addressed the claim of the vagueness of the Act with the following statement:

> Taking up, first, the question of due process, we assume for purposes of discussion that a State may by statute and without violating the Equal Protection Clause of the 14th Amendment give a certain category of bidders on public contracts a preference over bidders not included within that category, provided that the State has a legitimate and substantial interest in granting the preference and that the criteria to be employed in determining what bidders are entitled to the preference are reasonable and non-discriminatory.
>
> We think, however, that if a State, like Arkansas adopts a preference statute and sets out determining criteria and where the statute provides further that both bidders and contracting officers who violate its terms may be punished criminally, due process requires that the criteria set out in the statute be sufficiently definite and concrete to enable bidders to compute their bids intelligently, to enable contracting officers to grant or withhold preferences fairly and intelligently, and to enable both bidders and contracting officers to avoid criminal violations of the statute.[252]

In this way, the court establishes a standard for the test that it applies to vagueness, which is that the criteria 'should be sufficiently definite and concrete'.[253] But how is the notion of sufficiency lent parameters? It must be sufficient enough to enable bidders to compute their bids intelligently, to enable officers to select fairly and intelligently and to enable both of them to avoid criminal violations.

This case record proceeds by elaborating on the court's distinctly disparaging view on the criteria of the specific case:

> The criteria set out in Section 1 of Act 264 are not defined in the Act; they do not define themselves, and they are so vague as to be almost meaningless.[254]

---

250 Arkansas Act 264 § 4.
251 Ibid.
252 *Rayco* 1110.
253 Ibid.
254 Ibid.

The points that are accepted as invoking the constitutional prohibition of vagueness are the following three: the first is that satisfactory performance of prior public contracts is not defined,[255] the second is that ownership of plant and equipment, which points to PPPs and – according to the court – 'completely ignores the fact that much contracting is done today by contractors who lease or rent, rather than own, the instrumentalities by means of which their contracts are performed'.[256] The third point is that the Act does not define the term 'state and county taxes'.[257]

From this case we notice the properties of a stricter application of the doctrine of vagueness in government contract settings, such as PPPs, when criminal prosecution is linked to the relevant legal provisions. The principle is that the criteria have to be sufficiently clear and concrete. For them to be sufficiently clear and concrete, they have to be in a position to enable (not to give a reasonable opportunity, as in *Trojan*, but actually to *enable*) the bidders to compute their bids intelligently, to enable officers to select fairly and intelligently and to enable both bidders and contracting officers to avoid criminal violations. These have to be defined in the Act. If they are not defined in the Act, the criteria have to have obvious meaning, in other words, they must be able to define themselves. In all cases, the criteria should not be so vague that they are rendered meaningless.

This has an important bearing upon our main argument about due process and the criteria of evaluation in PPPs, because the due process requirements will be stricter in cases where the relevant Acts also refer to the possibility of criminal charges. In addition, we note that the measure which is provided for the establishment of the vagueness in these cases is that the criteria should enable the bidders to calculate their PPP bids intelligently, to enable the contracting officers to choose fairly, and also to enable those who may face criminal charges to avoid them. The content of the criteria has to be defined by the law, or else they have to stand alone as self-evident, and they must not – in any case – be so vague as to be meaningless. These prescriptions comfortably fit with our prior analysis on the criteria. They are not defined by their respective Acts, the Acts merely provide which the criteria are, but they do not define these criteria. The criteria are most certainly not responsible for defining themselves because this serves to invite many theories which provide for what each criterion means. They are in many cases, especially in the field of non-technical criteria such as those of public interest and fairness, which *are* so vague as to be meaningless. They do not enable the bidders to calculate their bids intelligently because the law does not inform the bidders on which

255 Ibid.
256 Ibid.
257 Ibid.

version of every criterion their bids will be evaluated. Similarly, and for the same reason, they do not enable the officers to choose fairly, because the law does not clearly provide them with the meaning of the criteria which they will use in their choice. Finally, as we will evidence in the next section, they do not facilitate the people who are likely to face criminal charges with the ability to avoid them.

One exemplary case of a PPP statute which includes criminal provisions which are connected to the criteria of evaluation is that of Title 32 of the Code of the State of Georgia.[258] According to Ga. Code Ann., § 32-2-80:

> Upon approval by the department, the commissioner shall select the respondent for project implementation based upon contract terms that are the most satisfactory and advantageous to the state and to the department based upon a thorough assessment of value and the ability of the final project's characteristics to meet state strategic goals and investment policies as provided for by paragraphs (1) through (10) of subsection (a) of Code Section 32-2-41.1.

Our eyes are immediately drawn to some of the criteria of evaluation which are used here, namely those of 'value' and 'ability (. . .) to meet state strategic goals and investment policies', while, for the reader's guidance, the section points to Ga. Code Ann., § 32-2-41.1, which provides numerous other criteria, such as:

> (1) Growth in private-sector employment, development of work force, and improved access to jobs; (2) Reduction in traffic congestion; (3) Improved efficiency and reliability of commutes in major metropolitan areas; (4) Efficiency of freight, cargo, and goods movement; (5) Coordination of transportation investment with development patterns in major metropolitan areas; (6) Market driven travel demand management; (7) Optimized capital asset management; (8) Reduction in accidents resulting in injury and loss of life; (9) Border-to-border and interregional connectivity; and (10) Support for local connectivity to the state-wide transportation network.

Among the criteria provided, we notice the concept of efficiency, together with others no less ill-defined, such as 'reliability', and 'optimised capital asset management', to highlight but two examples. As we have already analysed, the criteria of 'value' and 'efficiency' are both exposed to a substantial degree of

---

258 The statute (Ga. Code Ann., § 32 (2015)) is considered PPP-enabling legislation: Kevin Pula, *Public-Private Partnerships for Transportation – Categorisation and Analysis of State Statutes* (National Conference of State Legislatures, January 2016). The relevant sections are Ga. Code Ann., § 32-2-41(b)(6) and §§ 32-2-78-80.

vagueness, especially given that neither is technical. Despite this vagueness, however, the provision simultaneously incriminates anyone who offends it. According to Ga. Code Ann., § 32-1-10:

> (a) Any person who violates any of the provisions of this title for which no specific penalty is provided, whether or not such act or omission is expressly declared elsewhere in this title to be unlawful, or who violates any of the rules and regulations issued under authority of and in accord with the provisions of this title shall be guilty of a misdemeanour.

It is evident, from the language used, that the criminal provision does not distinguish between persons belonging to the public authority, and who will make the PPP contract, and bidders or contractors. It prescribes, instead, that 'any person' will be held guilty of misdemeanour if he 'violates any of the provisions of the title'.

The first person who is, without doubt, in a position to violate the provision of Ga. Code Ann., § 32-2-80 which provides for the assessment of bids, is the commissioner, who 'shall select the respondent for project implementation based upon contract terms that are the most satisfactory and advantageous (. . .) as provided for by paragraphs (1) through (10) of subsection (a) of Code Section 32-2-41.1'. The liability of the commissioner is detailed through reference to the ambiguous criteria of evaluation, and, therefore, it may be argued that it is exposed to vagueness. The statute does not define the criminal act, nor does it provide a reasonable person, acting – in this case – as the commissioner, with the ability to know if he is acting in violation of the section. In other words, if the commissioner assesses the project based on a set of techniques for the definition and the elaboration of the criteria of evaluation, the state will always be able to accuse him of accepting a different definition, and thus as having 'violated' the provision of the title which determines the criteria of evaluation. This obviously leaves the commissioner vulnerable.

Although the provision of criteria of evaluation for PPPs in way which is linked with criminal sanctions is generally rare in the USA, the Title 32 of the Code of the State of Georgia is not the only example. A further example is § 54-1-119 of the Tennessee Code Annotated (2015), which provides for criteria of accountability for PPPs, and in its §54-1-203 provides for criminal sanctions to the ones 'performing any prohibited act', without distinguishing between contracting officers and contractors. This 'prohibited act' remains undefined. It is determined by reference to the criteria, such as the 'innovative' character of the project which are both vague and ill-defined. A public official who decides to make a contract with a PPP contractor having concluded that the contract is 'innovative', might be considered to be doing a 'prohibited act', in the scenario in which a different technique of the establishment of the criterion of 'innovative' is employed. It has to be noted that beyond these illustrations which focus on contracting officers, the problem of criminalising the contracting process exists for contractors too. Literature has highlighted the possibility of contractors being held liable for honest mistakes in pricing and the techniques employed to reach the offer price, as required by a criterion of evaluation.[259] The particular federal provisions which are applied in that respect are the ones of 18 U.S.C. section 1001 (False Statements), section 371 of 18 U.S.C. (Conspiracy), 18 U.S.C. section 287 (False Claims), and the notorious blanket provision of section 2 of 18 U.S.C. (Aiding and Abetting). The inappropriate application of these statutes to criminalise honest mistakes could be very much limited from stable criteria which specifically provide specifically which techniques are to be employed and which data must be taken into account in the evaluation of a contract.

We have deduced from all the cases which we have seen which establish the two viewpoints on the evaluation of vagueness based on a strict or less strict application, that this differentiation depends upon the clarity and self-evidencing qualities of the provision to all parties involved. However, the courts will also take into account other factors, such as the behaviour of the parties in the government contract. An example of this trend is the *Cleveland* case.[260] In this case, an unsuccessful bidder on a public contract to build a facility at State university challenged the constitutionality of § 9.312 of the Ohio Revised Code (R.C.), which establishes the requirements for bidders of public contracts. According to this law, a government contract is to be awarded to the lowest responsive and responsible bidder:

> The factors that the state agency or political subdivision shall consider in determining whether a bidder on the contract is responsible include the experience of the bidder, his financial condition, his conduct and performance on previous contracts, his facilities, his management skills, and his ability to execute the contract properly.[261]

The court reasoned that these provisions are not unconstitutionally vague. The criterion which the court used was that:

> a person of ordinary intelligence can understand the criteria being evaluated in determining responsibility, namely, the bidder's experience, financial condition, conduct and performance of previous contracts, facilities, management skills, and ability to execute the contract properly.[262]

259 Steven D. Overly, 'Government Contractors, Beware: Civil and Criminal Penalties Abound for Defective Pricing' (1987) 20 Loyola of Los Angeles Law Review 597, 613–31 and 640–1.
260 *Cleveland Construction, Inc., v. Ohio Department of Administrative Services, General Services Administration* 121 Ohio App.3d 372 (1997).
261 R.C. § 9.312 (1995).
262 *Cleveland* 392.

In establishing this judgement, the court took into account the behaviour of the complaining bidder as well as that of the other bidders for the project. If, according to the court, the contractor had not understood the criteria, he could have contacted the State Department of Administrative Agencies specifically to enquire about their meaning. He did not do that, nor was any further evidence presented showing that any other bidder had had difficulty understanding the criteria.[263] In this way, the court followed a slightly different pathway than the courts in *Rayco* and *Trojan*. In both of the latter cases, the courts discussed whether the provisions were able to be materially understood by a contractor, a bidder or an officer, as the court constructed this person in an abstract way. In this particular case, the court proceeded one step further: it attempted to construe from the behaviour of the specific bidders whether the prescription of the provision was indeed clear to them.

The *Cleveland* case thus deserves its place among the corpus of important cases which have discussed the properties of the doctrine of the prohibition of vagueness in the field of government contracts, such as the PPPs. The value of these cases is that they have provided us with the principles by which the courts define the conception of vagueness in government contracts, the limits of that doctrine, and the extent of its application. The *Turner* case illustrated the principle that the prohibition of vagueness has certainly been applied to enactments of economic regulation, however, this has been effected less strictly than in other cases where fundamental rights are at stake. This less strict application has been discussed in *Trojan*, where we saw that the court used a definition of vagueness which focused on the perception of the reasonable person, and on the provision of guiding standards by the legislation. The properties of the stricter application, on the other hand, were examined by *Rayco*, where the court used a criterion for the definition of vagueness which required higher standards for the legislation in question: this legislation had to be very detailed, providing the highest and strictest levels of certainty to its interpreters. The *Cleveland* case, in its turn, illustrated the importance of taking into account the individual actions of the persons involved, which would then shed light on the application of the doctrine in less strict contexts.

4.2.   *The application of the constitutional prohibition of vagueness in PPPs*

We have analysed the important cases which deal with the doctrine of vagueness in the field of government contracting. These cases provide the basic principles of the operation of the doctrine when the legislation in question focuses on government contracts, such as PPPs. The issue which we will now examine is how these principles can be implemented in the construction of a

263 Ibid.

reformulated due process duty of the executive and the legislature to systematise the criteria of accountability.

Our starting point will be how the criteria of accountability for PPPs fits with the standards provided by these cases. According to *Trojan*, a statute will be void as vague if either: (a) it fails to give a person of ordinary intelligence a reasonable opportunity to know what is prohibited, or, (b) it fails to provide explicit standards to the enforcing officer. It is a criterion which encompasses most of the legislation which exists for PPPs, at both federal and state levels. These pieces of legislation provide criteria of accountability, such as effectiveness, public interest, and value, amongst others, without providing a person of ordinary intelligence a reasonable opportunity to know what these terms mean. Similarly, the legislation in question does not provide explicit standards to the enforcing officers so that they can interpret the provision. In this way, by means of illustration, when the legislation in question provides that a PPP contract should be signed by the contracting officer when it satisfies the public interest, or when it achieves best value, the legislation does not provide precisely what is meant by these terms. When a superior bureaucratic organ, or the legislature exercising its rights of oversight, questions whether the contracting officer made the contract whilst safeguarding these values, there will be nothing to turn to in the legislation which exemplifies what these terms mean.

A further standard which is provided, and which, moreover, is more demanding since it has been applied in cases for which there were criminal provisions provided by the legislation, is the standard set in the *Rayco* case. In cases of legislation on PPPs which connect the criteria of accountability with criminal sanctions, this standard provides a variety of requirements for the validity of the legislation, which exceed the requirements for *Trojan*. The criteria of accountability for PPPs, as they are provided by the legislation, should be such that they enable the people involved to perceive their meaning in the highest level of detail; this level of detail should be so sophisticated that it enables bidders to calculate intelligently, for contracting officers to choose fairly, and for everyone to avoid criminal liability. Borrowing from the principle of *Rayco*, these criteria of accountability should be defined by the law, or else possess stand-alone comprehensibility, and they should never be so vague as to be meaningless. As we highlighted earlier, these prescriptions are quite some distance from the current reality of the criteria of accountability. Most criteria are not definite enough to permit bidders and contracting officers to understand their content. The laws themselves do not define the criteria, and the latter most certainly do not define themselves, given that they are exposed to a variety of possible meanings and interpretations.

A distinction which we made was between criteria which are technical, such as effectiveness, and criteria which are not, such as public interest. The existence of a technique, in most financial criteria, is a factor which potentially limits the ambiguity of the technical criteria to a certain extent. The reason is that a technique provides a level of certainty and consistency over the accountability process, because the people involved have an opportunity to predict its outcomes.

These techniques, however, do not completely insulate a criterion from subjectivity, because – as we have shown – techniques can be applied in many different ways. However, they are a stabilising factor in the criteria of accountability. Furthermore, the existence of such techniques limits, to a certain extent, the level of discretion that the government has in shaping the criteria in question. This is because these techniques are established with input from both the administration and the relevant scientific disciplines – such as statistics – with the latter to some degree controlling the discretion of the administration. We deduce from this that, although the duty of systematisation of the criteria of accountability is to be exercised in both technical and non-technical criteria, it should, arguably, be exercised in a more intensive way in the non-technical ones, which are mostly administrative, and more vulnerable to the twin features of subjectivity and administrative discretion.

Having established these basic principles, we may now explore the possibilities of this broader duty to systemise more thoroughly. The basic distinction which is our starting point is that between criminal and non-criminal contexts. In cases in which there are no criminal sanctions, vagueness is more likely to be tolerated, as the case-law has indicated, than in cases where these criminal sanctions exist. According to the standard of *Trojan* and *Cleveland*, the guide in the systematisation of these criteria should be whether a reasonable person has an acceptable opportunity of understanding what is meant by each criterion and whether there can be a standard which can point to a direction of interpretation. Further characteristics which are to be taken into account include the commercial practice, according to *Cleveland*, and the means which are available to the citizen to make inquiries to the administration on the content of these criteria. These characteristics of the standards of *Trojan* and *Cleveland* point towards several directions that the executive can take in order to proceed in the systematisation process for criteria which are not linked with criminal sanctions. Avenues should be created in the exercise of this duty of the executive to systematise, permitting the citizens to shape an understanding of how the executive intends or perceives these criteria. Similarly, the executive has to be consistent in its prescriptions of the criteria of accountability and provide relevant guidance.

The need for systematisation of the criteria of accountability, therefore, in cases where these criteria are not connected with criminal sanctions, can be analysed in the context of a number of lesser duties which are based on the principles derived from *Trojan* and *Cleveland*. The first of these duties is that the executive has to be transparent around its determinations of the content of these criteria; such information must be made fully available and accessible to all stakeholders, including citizens, contractors and members of the legislature, so that everyone is aware of exactly how these individuals are to be held accountable for the use of public money. The second of these duties is specificity on the part of the executive around the criteria of accountability because, currently, each has many supporting theories and methods. The duty of specificity would involve the executive choosing which one of these theories is to be applied, so that – as *Trojan* established – there is a standardised interpretation for the contracting officers.

It has to be noted that to a limited extent, this provision of standards to contracting officers takes place through the Federal Acquisition Regulations (FAR). The FAR is a government regulation, which became effective in 1984[264] and is issued under the joint authorities of the Administrator of General Services, the Secretary of Defense, and the Administrator for the National Aeronautics and Space Administration, under the broad guidelines of the Administrator of the Office of Federal Procurement Policy of the OMB. The FAR is 'established for the codification and publication of uniform policies and procedures for acquisition by all executive agencies'.[265] As the rationale of the document suggests it focuses on policies and procedures, rather than establishing uniform standards on the criteria. However, in some cases, to which we will refer, it does, however, provide a substantial level of discretion to agencies.

A good illustration of this point relates to the criterion of the 'reasonableness' of the price. The FAR in its section 31.201–3 provides that 'a cost is reasonable if, in its nature and amount, it does not exceed that which would be incurred by a prudent person in the conduct of competitive business'.[266] However, earlier on, in 31.100, it clarifies that deviation from these specific rules is possible if the head of the agency consents. In a similar way, in 42.15,[267] the FAR provides different standards for measuring contractor's performance, in the form of tables, and it distinguishes performance evaluation into 'exceptional, very good, satisfactory, marginal, unsatisfactory'. Such standards are provided in a very broad, non-technical way, and they include factors such as the use of small business in the provision of services as sub-contractors, the meeting of the contract requirements and others. At the same time, in spite of these broad standards, the FAR clarifies in 42.1503 that 'the ultimate conclusion on the performance evaluation is a decision of the contracting agency'.[268]

The FAR, thus already provides – in a limited number of cases – standards to the contracting officers. These standards can be very broad, while they provide the agency with significant discretion on their implementation. For this reason, it is indeed doubtful how far they are genuine standards which comply with requirements of certainty and regularity which are parts of the due process doctrine.

The third duty must be that of consistency in the executive's application of the criteria of accountability; the need for consistency derives from the principle of certainty and regularity which are the foundation of the doctrine of due process. With consistent interpretations of the criteria by the executive, there will be certainty and regularity over the pathways that the executive will use in holding and in being held accountable. These duties, including those of

---

264 Geert Dewulf, Anneloes Blanken and Mirjam Bult-Spiering, *Strategic Issues in Public-Private Partnerships* (2nd edn, Wiley-Blackwell 2012) 67.
265 48 C.F.R. § 1.101 (2015).
266 48 C.F.R. § 31.201–3.
267 48 C.F.R. § 42.15.
268 48 C.F.R. § 42.1503.

transparency, specificity and consistency, should be considered as exemplifications of the broader duty of the executive to systematise the criteria of accountability. They should also serve to promote the constitutional prohibition of vagueness in the promotion of PPPs in the Economic Constitution.

It is worth drawing our attention to the notion that the way that we construe the specific duties of the executive in terms of due process might be based on case law originating from due process, but that they exceed the general construction of the doctrine in terms of their strictness. This general construction provides for an element of regularity in the conduct of governance. The reason why we construed a more intense version of due process with respect to PPPs is that the duty of the executive to systematise is not solely based on the requirement of due process. As we have analysed, in addition to the due process basis, there is also the basis of the executive to uphold the Constitution. In this way, the duties of the executive – which we have exemplified – have to be seen as promoting both the respect of the doctrine of due process, and also the needs of effective accountability rooted in the Constitution.

In cases where the criteria of accountability for PPPs are linked to the imposition of criminal sanctions, the need for certainty and the prohibition of vagueness is even more intense. The principle, established in *Rayco*, as applied in the criteria of accountability for PPPs, contains a strong focus on the legislation itself, rather than any possible guidance on behalf of the executive. It is legislation which should provide the exact criteria, to a level of specificity which should enable those individuals involved to calculate as accurately as possible, and to avoid criminal charges. The focus of the principle on the legislation itself suggests to us that the systematisation of these criteria of evaluation should be achieved through the enactment of legislation. In this case, therefore, the duty to systematise the criteria of evaluation is towards the legislature, rather than towards the executive, because the executive cannot enact legislation. There are two constitutional foundations of this duty of the legislature, which largely mirror the two bases on the duty to systematise carried by the executive. The first foundation is the general constitutional duty of the members of the Congress to 'support the Constitution', established in Art. VI of the US Constitution. Based on this, first, foundation, if the vague criteria of accountability hinder the oversight of the legislature over the executive which is required by the Constitution, then the legislature has a duty to correct this problem in order to 'support the Constitution'. The second foundation is the constitutional prohibition of vagueness of laws, as has been established by *Rayco*. It is a due process duty of the legislature, given that the constitutional prohibition of vagueness is a prohibition which is rooted in, and is a part of, the due process doctrine.[269] It would also be useful to note that the Congress, as the federal legislature, has the constitutional power to issue laws systematising criteria of

---

269 Erwin Chemerinsky, *Constitutional Law* (4th edn, Wolters Kluwer 2013) 1236.

accountability provided by state legislation, when these are unconstitutionally vague. This power is provided by the XIVth Amendment which, as we saw earlier, establishes due process at the state level and which provides the Congress with the power to enforce its provisions 'by appropriate legislation'.[270]

The fact that this duty of due process is directed towards the legislature, however, does not necessarily mean that the initiative of the enactment of this legislation should solely originate from the legislature. The President, exercising his own duty to systematise, which is rooted in due process and in the duty to uphold the Constitution, has the duty to propose this systematising legislation, if Congress does not do so on its own. He can propose the necessary systematisation in a two-stage process: firstly, the President sets out his legislative proposals in the annual 'State of the Union' address, and, secondly, the proposed legislation which materialises these proposals can be introduced in Congress by a member of the President's political party.[271]

This legislation should provide an accurate description of how each one of the criteria should be perceived and interpreted, and it should not leave ambiguous margins from which the interpretation of the criteria would depend on the discretion of the executive and evaluation teams. Alternatively, the *Rayco* principles provide an additional direction which the systematisation can follow: this is that the criteria should be able to be defined by themselves. This approach offers another route with which to achieve the duty to systematise the criteria of accountability. It could work by adopting legislation which does not systematise the existing criteria, but which provides criteria which are able to define themselves. In this way, for instance, one criterion which would be able to define itself, and which is rarely used, is that of the prescription of selecting the lowest offer. When a contracting officer is prescribed by law to select the lowest offer, this prescription is able to define itself, in other words, it is self-evident. The said officer knows that he will be held accountable based on whether he has selected the offer which has a mathematical value which is lower than any others. When, however, as is frequently the case, the prescription is that the contracting officer has to choose the offer which is most advantageous for the government, this criterion is not able to be defined by itself, and there is an obvious need for systematising legislation. In this way, the duty of systematisation is incumbent upon the executive and the legislature in cases where criteria of accountability for PPPs are linked with the imposition of criminal sanctions and this is exemplified by a duty of promotion of legislation.

---

270 U.S. Const. amend. XIV. See also Sedler 42.
271 Sedler 55. Additional details on how the president suggests legislation can be found in Andrew Rudalvige, 'The Executive Branch and the Legislative Process' in Joel D. Aberbach and Mark A. Peterson (eds), *The Executive Branch* (Oxford University Press 2005) 420–43.

As part of our exploration of the issue of the various means that the executive and the legislature can use in order to implement the systematisation process, we need to extend our enquiry around the level of specificity which we need them to achieve. This question is linked to the distinction between the promotion of efficiency and public accountability, which we last met when we examined the way to apply the Concordat in the UK. This distinction is particularly relevant when we consider the question of what level of specificity we propose for the government – the executive and the legislature – to achieve in its systematisation of the criteria of accountability. With the government systematising the criteria of accountability to the highest possible level of specificity, the result will be a very effective system of public overview and accountability. The Congress will thereby know precisely where it is exercising its scrutiny to the government, and precisely what the government needs to scrutinise in order to hold the bureaucracy accountable. This will enhance the constitutional and democratic conception of accountability, because Congress will be better able to hold the government and the bureaucracy to account. Similarly, at state level, if the state governments systematise the criteria of accountability provided for by state legislation for PPPs, the state legislatures will be better able to exercise oversight and accountability. However, the maximum specificity of the criteria will necessarily lead to a decrease in the bureaucratic effectiveness of PPPs. This is because flexibility will be minimised. If the administration is bound by specific notions in its contracting activity, then it will be much less flexible in the exercise of the said contracting activity towards the private sector. It would be useful to illustrate this point with an example, here.

A fictitious example will suffice to best illustrate our point. Let us suppose that an existing piece of federal PPP legislation provides that the contracting officer for water projects has to perform contracts based on the principle of 'best value'. At the same time, there is a second piece of legislation which deals with federal assistance in such PPPs, and which defines that this assistance will be given when it is determined that the projects satisfy the 'public interest'. In addition to this, there is a third piece of legislation, which provides that, for federal tax exemption for these projects, the projects have to be 'efficient' and 'economic'. As may be apparent by now, all three contributions to these criteria are ambiguous and, consequently, they do not create certainty with respect to the accountability process. Now, if we imagine that the government issues a federal regulation, in its exercise of its duty to systematise, and that this regulation provides common, exact and precise formulae over which these criteria will be measured. This will render the criteria absolutely stable, specific and in harmony with each other and the legislature in its exercise of oversight will be able to know precisely over what each of the individuals involved at every step is held accountable. This democratic and constitutional benefit however, means that the administration will have much less flexibility in determining the concepts themselves, because it will have less chance of taking into account changes in circumstances. In this way, we find ourselves facing the same exact dilemma which we faced in the case of the Concordat in the UK, namely, the dilemma between democratic and constitutional accountability and bureaucratic effectiveness.

This dilemma will have a relatively straightforward solution in the case of criteria of accountability for PPPs which are provided in connection with criminal charges. It is clear that in these cases, where the most fundamental rights of the individuals involved are at stake, the need for bureaucratic effectiveness has necessarily to become a second priority. In these cases, the need for specificity, which will safeguard a sound accountability process, will prevail. The legislation which should be adopted, following the principles at *Rayco*, should reflect the principles that this case enshrined: the criteria of accountability will have to be specific to the highest level of detail.

With respect to the other non-criminally related contexts, the legislation providing for PPPs aims predominantly at economic regulation, so the dilemma between the promotion of economic effectiveness and broader goals of account-ability is more intense, and thus more difficult to resolve. We will now outline two possible strategies which would permit a proper balancing between these two values at the level of specificity involved.

A first strategy could be the conversion of as many non-technical criteria as possible to technical ones. As we saw earlier, the introduction of techniques has the effect of limiting problematic subjectivity to a certain extent. By adopting techniques, the criteria can acquire a greater level of certainty without the total compromise of the factors which provide the administration with flexibility. In this way, the executive, exercising its due process duty to systematise the criteria of accountability, could be required to set techniques for the criteria which are not technical. Providing techniques for as many criteria of accountability as possible will increase the certainty and the predictability of the application of these criteria, and will limit their exposure to subjectivity. In order for this step to be compliant with the duty of the executive to systematise, the executive needs to follow the principles which we distinguished earlier, when exemplifying the duty to supervise. First, the techniques which will be set have to be trans-parent, and widely available for the information of citizens, bureaucrats, contrac-tors and members of the legislature. In this way, the members of the various accountability chains will be able to source the knowledge, and, therefore know, how they are supposed to be held accountable for PPPs. Furthermore, the techniques which will be set, following the principle from *Trojan*, should provide standards which should be followed by the contracting officers in the ways that they are construed. This element of specificity is important for the predictability of the applicability of the techniques by the evaluation teams. Finally, the setting of techniques has to satisfy the principle of consistency; the need for consistency of techniques derives from the principles of certainty and regularity of government action, which are fundamental values in the due process. These values would benefit from the setting of techniques which are consistent and they are not exposed to changes which are too frequent and diverse.

A further strategy which could be useful in the proper balancing between the values of economic effectiveness and accountability in the exercise of the due process duty of the government to systematise the criteria of accountability, refers to the creation of a central co-ordinating agency. We saw in the earlier part of this chapter that there are many voices in the critical literature which have stressed the important place that an agency of this kind would have. The pattern which could be followed could be the one exemplified by PUK, or the Treasury. This body would consist of civil servants and practitioners and its basic duty would be to systematise the criteria of accountability. According to the principle established in *Trojan*, the importance of guidance in the construction of vagueness is fundamental, while according to the principle established by *Cleveland*, commercial practice has to be taken into account when constructing vagueness. A body equipped by practitioners and civil servants could serve as a forum which would be informed in matters of commercial practice of PPPs, as the principle of *Cleveland* has suggested, and it could also provide guidance for the evaluation teams on how to construe the criteria of accountability. A further advantage of this body would also be that it would be able to develop and stabilise its own practice and criteria, in similar ways to those that the PAC has been undertaking with respect to VfM. This will facilitate the creation of a level of consistency, which is one of the values of the doctrine of due process. In turn, this will lead to greater benefits, in particular, a more stable and accurate understanding of the notions on which accountability is based, benefitting the oversight of the legislature over the executive. Furthermore, due to its composition of both practitioners and civil servants, it will be able to produce systematisations which will not deprive both of these groups of the necessary level of flexibility which an effective promotion of PPPs would require. In this sense, the Economic Constitution for PPPs seems to suggest not only clarity of the rules of accountability, but also effectiveness of the institutional organisation.

5. Conclusions

In terms of the present chapter, we have examined the interaction between the criteria of accountability and the Economic Constitution in the USA. We began our research from the premise that the Economic Constitution provides at the federal level, that Congress should oversee and supervise the executive in terms of its expenditures, and that it holds important instruments of regulation for these economic activities. This characteristic of the Economic Constitution leads to a legal culture – which exists at both state and federal levels – and which demands legislation as a base for the PPP activities of the government. In this way, the importance that the legislature has in the promotion of PPPs in the USA is characteristic, and this appears at both federal and state levels.

This power of the legislature has led to the existence of a large corpus of legislation with respect to PPPs. This legislation provides a variety of criteria of accountability and evaluation, and a large number of accountability mechanisms. The problem is that all this involvement of the legislature through the enactment of legislation has been carried out with limited focus on the co-ordination of all the co-existing criteria and mechanisms. The result of this situation is that there is limited consistency in the meanings of the criteria of accountability, and increased complexity of the mechanisms of accountability.

We examined the most prevalent of the criteria of evaluation and noticed that there are numerous theories which have been supported for the definition of each criterion, and that each criterion is significantly exposed to a considerable degree of subjectivity. This situation has a negative impact on the legislature's ability to supervise the executive, as well as on the operation of accountability in general inside the bureaucracy, because it is not clear which determinations of the criteria of accountability matter in relation to these. The solution which we proposed was that there should be a recognised constitutional duty of the executive (to the large degree) and the legislature (to a lesser degree) to systematise the criteria and mechanisms of accountability that legislation provides.

A first basis for this duty is to be found in the provisions of the Constitution which provide for the Constitutional duties of the holders of these offices. The President is required to uphold the Constitution, while the members of the Congress are required to support it. The exposure of the criteria of evaluation to subjectivity hinders the oversight of the Congress over the executive when it uses PPPs, as this oversight is established by the Constitution. Therefore, the President and the Congress have a duty to correct this problem, so that the provisions of the Constitution, which provide for the oversight, work effectively. A second basis for the respective duties of the executive and the legislature originate from the constitutional prohibition of vagueness of laws which is rooted in the institution of due process. In constructing this duty, we have completed the theories of Metzger and Verkuil, which have constructed a due process duty of the government to oversee and to keep certain activities public, by providing a third duty: the duty to systematise the criteria of accountability for PPPs.

Case law on due process which we examined indicated an important distinction. This distinction exists between criteria which govern accountability for PPPs without being connected with criminal sanctions, and criteria which can lead to the criminal prosecution of people involved. For the first case, we supported that the duty of systematisation is to be exercised by the executive, while for the second case, we argued that this same duty rests on the shoulders of the legislature, which will need to adopt systematising legislation.

The Congress will have to provide systematising legislation detailing the application of these criteria and determining, in fine detail, and following the principles of *Rayco*, how the respective criteria are to be interpreted. For other cases in which the criteria of accountability are not connected with criminal sanctions, the executive has to systematise them whilst maintaining a balance between the values of economic effectiveness and constitutional accountability.

A very intense systematisation process, which would involve the stabilisation of each of the criteria into very concrete notions, would have benefits for the accountability process, because it would be more certain how and over which notions the process is to operate. It would, however, experience significant problems in the field of economic effectiveness. This is because government authorities would lose their wide discretion to interpret the criteria as they see fit in every individual case, thereby losing flexibility. The opposite action would also involve problems. A minimal exercise of the systematisation process would mean that the criteria maintain their flexibility and the economic effectiveness of administrative action, but that constitutional accountability would suffer. The reason for this is that it would be less clear over which notions this accountability and overview should take place.

Two additional possible means for overcoming these difficulties in cases of criteria which are not connected with criminal sanctions are the following: the first is that as many criteria as possible are converted to technical, with the introduction of techniques for their establishment through executive guidelines. The introduction of techniques would potentially limit their ambiguity to some extent, without eliminating it completely, leaving an element of discretion with the public authorities. The second means which we suggested for the exercise of the duty of the executive to systematise is based on the creation of a central co-ordinating authority, following the pattern of PUK. Such an authority, composed of civil servants and practitioners, would be assigned with the discharge of the duty to systematise the criteria. Benefiting from the backgrounds of its members, it would be able to produce systematisations which would lend an element of stability without jeopardising or losing the flexibility appropriate for their effective use in PPP settings.

Conclusions

1. Introduction

In terms of the present book we have focused on the examination of the mechanisms through which the government is held accountable over its decisions on PPPs in the UK and the USA. The perspective from which we approached this examination was that of the constitutional principles and institutional arrangements which direct these mechanisms and on which they base their existence and operation.

The framework which we used in order to process this question is that of the Economic Constitution. The sense of the Economic Constitution which we used is predominantly the first of the four which are determined by Tony Prosser, and according to which the Economic Constitution focuses to 'the key constitutional principles and institutional arrangements which may be relevant to the management of the economy'.[1] In approaching our research question, we focused on the Economic Constitutions of the UK and of the USA, and upon the constitutional principles and institutional arrangements through which public accountability for PPPs operate.

Our work has a descriptive and a normative dimension. In terms of the descriptive dimension, we delineated, and distinguished between, the mechanisms of holding the executive to account over the use of PPPs, and the constitutional principles which direct them. In terms of the normative dimension, we suggested which improvements would be desirable for these mechanisms and which respective constitutional principles should be instituted so that the government is held accountable over the promotion of PPPs in a more effective way.

With respect to the UK, in the descriptive dimension we distinguished that the basic constitutional position for the promotion of PPPs by the government is that this promotion can be carried out by virtue of the inherent, non-prerogative powers of the Crown. Currently, this constitutional position does not explicitly recognise that there is a constitutional need for legislation which would provide the foundation of this promotion and would create systems of

1 Prosser 8.

accountability specifically designed for PPPs. The predominant structure of constitutional accountability is based on the system developed between the NAO and the PAC, and it is the default structure, which has been in use since the nineteenth century and covering all financial matters.

In the normative dimension of the UK, we distinguished that the constitutional position should, instead, provide that legislation is required for the promotion of PPPs by the government and also for establishing accountability arrangements for this promotion. As a matter of principle of the Economic Constitution for PPPs, there should be specific legislation enacted for every PPP sector; this legislation should provide for a mechanism of accountability which will be based on the affirmative resolution procedure for every new PPP project in each sector. The foundation of this normative proposition is the Concordat of 1932, which has to be recognised as a constitutional convention applicable to PPPs.

In summary, the existing position of the Economic Constitution for the UK is that legislation is not constitutionally required for the promotion of PPPs and for the setting of accountability arrangements over this promotion. In the normative dimension of our work we argue that the Economic Constitution of the UK should recognise that this legislation is necessary by virtue of the Concordat of 1932 properly applied to PPPs.

Similarly, in the USA, in the descriptive dimension of our work we distinguish that the existing constitutional position for PPPs is that legislation is required for the promotion of PPPs and for the setting of accountability arrangements for this promotion. This legislation provides for various aspects of PPPs: it provides for the authorisation of the executive to embark on PPP programmes and projects, for mechanisms and criteria of accountability, and for the maximum term and value of the projects, to name but three. The criteria which this legislation provides are exposed to a significant degree of subjectivity and complexity. The existing constitutional principle does not provide for the need for these criteria of accountability to be co-ordinated in such a way that they work with each other and are systematised by some kind of central authority, such as those that exist in the UK.

In the normative dimension of our work describing practice in the USA, we distinguished that the constitutional principle should instead provide for a positive duty of the executive and the legislature to systematise and co-ordinate the criteria of accountability that the various pieces of legislation provide. The first basis of this duty lies in the constitutional requirement that the President upholds the Constitution and that the members of the Congress support it. The second basis is the institution of due process which prohibits, as unconstitutional, the vagueness of laws. The duty of systematisation should be carried out with the enactment of legislation by the legislature, in cases where the criteria are linked to criminal charges, and with the adoption of guidelines by the executive in other cases. Two useful means for the latter case could be the introduction of techniques in as many criteria as possible and the creation of a central authority in the pattern of PUK.

In other words, the existing position of the Economic Constitution for the USA is that legislation is required for the promotion of PPPs and for the setting of accountability criteria, but co-ordination and systematisation of these criteria is not considered constitutionally necessary. In the normative dimension of our work we argue that the Economic Constitution for PPPs in the USA should recognise that the executive and the legislature have a positive duty to proceed into this co-ordination and systematisation of the criteria.

Having provided the skeletal summary of our argument, we will now proceed towards providing the detailed steps which we followed to reach our conclusions. Afterwards, we will discuss whether any of the conclusions which we reached could be useful – beyond the realm of PPPs – for broader discussions associated with the Economic Constitution.

2. The Economic Constitution for PPPs in the UK

One of the characteristics of the integration of PPPs to the Economic Constitution in the UK refers to the limited use of legislation. The government has promoted the PFI predominantly via its inherent non-prerogative powers to contract, instead of seeking to establish the authority to contract in specific legislation. Although legislation which authorises the PFI involvement exists in certain cases, these cases are not the norm, and they serve to re-affirm, rather than establish, the inherent contractual capacity of the Crown. In this way, legislation cannot fairly be said to have been the foundation of the promotion of the PFI in the UK.

This focus on economic effectiveness, and the extensive use of the inherent powers of the Crown to contract in tandem with the associated limited use of legislation has a number of outcomes which are relatively negative from the perspective of public accountability. The first of these outcomes is the role of the NAO and the PAC. These two bodies are envisioned by the constituent documents to be organs of audit examination, with powers which safeguard the quality of the exercise of this role. However, apart from this role of audit examination, they also exercise a role which is normative and which is not provided by their constituent documents. The rules which they produce in terms of the exercise of their normative function are very substantial for PPPs, yet these two organs have not been expressly invested with authority to establish these norms. Arguably, one of the reasons why they are comfortable in establishing norms for the system of PPPs, without having a direct mandate to do so, is the fact that the norms which the system needs to operate are not provided by means of primary legislation.

The second negative outcome of the focus on economic effectiveness and the extensive use of the inherent powers of the Crown to contract is that aspects of PPPs which are broadly political and unrelated to economic effectiveness receive limited attention. Aspects of this kind are those associated with the environmental aspects of the promotion of PPPs, for instance, the suitability of activities which are to be outsourced for that very outsourcing, and establishing the level of integration of the private sector to the exercise of government function which is desirable, among others. All these aspects have one characteristic in common: they are aspects of the PPP activities of the government which are not directly related to concerns of economic effectiveness. Due to the orientation of the system to economic effectiveness, there is a gap of political accountability over these aspects. This means that the government decides on them with limited input from the side of the legislature, an input which would be desirable and which should be much more involved and available, in case more legislation on PPPs was deemed necessary.

As part of a solution towards filling this gap of political accountability over the promotion of PPPs, and simultaneously, a solution for the problems which we highlighted, we proposed that legislation should be used more for PPPs. This can be effectuated with the explicit recognition of the Concordat of 1932 as a constitutional convention which is applicable for PPPs. Pursuant to this solution, there should be primary legislation for every sector which uses PPPs, in which the government will have the chance to discuss, with the gravitas and close attention due to the enactment of legislation, all the aspects of PPP involvement in this sector. These aspects will be related to economic effectiveness but they will also include subjects which are not directly related to economic effectiveness, such as environmental concerns, and the suitability of an activity for outsourcing, and others. This legislation will also include provisions which will provide for the need for statutory instruments for every PPP project of the respective sector. In order to satisfy the requirements that we set for the revised form of the 1932 Concordat, this statutory instrument will have to follow a version of the affirmative resolution procedure. The statutory instrument will be in force immediately after its making, but it will be invalidated in cases where the Parliament will not affirm it within a given period of 28–40 days after it has been established.

The reasons why we selected this particular one from all the available procedures related to statutory instruments relates to the proper balance between the values of constitutional accountability and those of bureaucratic effectiveness. A strong involvement of Parliament, at every point in the PPP process, on a project-by-project basis, would have benefits of constitutional accountability but it would negatively impact on the bureaucratic effectiveness of these transactions. On the other hand, a minimal symbolic involvement of the Parliament, and the award of all the powers of the promotion of PPPs to the executive could perhaps lead to more bureaucratic effectiveness and speed, but it would negatively impact upon constitutional accountability. The solution which we propose attempts to strike an optimal, healthy balance between these two values: the need for affirmation by the Parliament in 28–40 days safeguards the involvement of the Parliament before every new PPP project without having such a profound and heavy impact on the productivity of the promotion of PPPs. The average PPP project involves public expenditure in the form of unitary and usage charges which extends for decades. A requirement for a mere extra 28–40 days in the context of these lengthy time frames does not seem an unreasonable request if accountability for these projects will correspondingly increase.

Underlying this proposal is a normative request for the Economic Constitution of the UK with respect to PPPs: as the Economic Constitution of PPPs currently operates, we recognise as a norm that legislation is not required for the promotion of PPPs. The government can promote PPPs with the use of its inherent powers to contract, and important rules for the system are established by the NAO and the PAC. We argue that the position of the Economic Constitution should be different: the Economic Constitution should require that legislation is required on a sector-by-sector basis, by virtue of the Concordat, and that it will be this legislation setting the important norms of the system. Furthermore, the Economic Constitution should require that this legislation should provide for an affirmative resolution procedure for every new PPP project.

Having illustrated the basic steps and outcomes of our examination of the UK Economic Constitution on PPPs, we may now follow the same process with respect to the USA Economic Constitution for these transactions.

3. The Economic Constitution for PPPs in the USA

An important characteristic of the integration of PPPs to the Economic Constitution in the USA, is that, typically, behind every PPP there is legislation. While in the UK, the basic position of the Economic Constitution towards PPPs is that the executive is recognised as having the power to promote them by virtue of its inherent non-prerogative powers, in the USA the rule is different. This is because the Economic Constitution requires that there is legislation behind every PPP project. This legislation provides numerous aspects of PPPs: it authorises them, it defines maximum terms and amounts which can be used, and, most importantly, it provides mechanisms and criteria of accountability. Given that this pattern appears in both federal and state PPP activity, we may refer to this rule of the Economic Constitution as a rule of national recognition by the American polity.

The wide use of legislation which creates patterns and mechanisms of accountability for PPPs, however, creates problems of accountability which are very different to the ones which we examined in the UK. In the UK, the underlying problem was that, with the limited use of legislation, and with the focus on economic effectiveness, the burden of establishing rules for PPPs falls – to a significant degree – on the shoulders of the PAC and the NAO. In the USA, the problem of accountability is different: it is that there is wide use of legislation, and a limited focus on the co-ordination of this legislation. There are many pieces of legislation, each one of them providing for its own criteria of accountability, and there is no body with the task or the real function of co-ordinating and systematising them. Similarly, there is no PAC equivalent, which, by serving as a common umpire of accountability, would be able to provide some common understandings of the criteria of accountability, as the PAC does for VfM in the UK.

This situation has important effects on accountability. The absence of a co-ordinating mechanism leads – to a large extent – to the different criteria of accountability which the different pieces of legislation provide to be fairly exposed to subjectivity. This exposure to subjectivity hinders the accountability of PPPs and the overview of Congress; the reason for this is that it is not clear to the different organs which participate to the accountability mechanisms or to Congress over what notions the accountability will take place. The exemplification of the criteria that the law provides falls to the different evaluation teams across the executive, something which limits consistency and regularity over the promotion of PPPs.

The solution which we proposed was based on the recognition of a positive duty of the government to systematise the criteria and the mechanisms of accountability that all the different pieces of legislation provide. This duty is to be exercised by the executive in cases of criteria which are not linked with criminal sanctions, and by the legislature in cases of criteria which can lead to criminal prosecution. The foundation for the duty of these bodies is dual. The first basis is the duty of the President and the members of the Congress to uphold and support the constitution, respectively. The second basis is the constitutional institution of due process.

We also examined how the due process duty is to be discharged by the executive and the legislature. The solution which we found is based, again, on a delicate balance between the two values of economic effectiveness and accountability. The wide powers of the evaluation teams to exemplify the criteria as they see fit in every particular case is potentially positive for the economic effectiveness of PPPs, because it provides plenty of flexibility. It is, however, also potentially detrimental to the accountability of PPPs, because it hinders the scrutiny of Congress over them. For this reason, the means that the government will use to systematise the criteria of accountability should strike a balance between the two extremes, which are those of a very flexible, effective, but less accountable promotion of PPPs as opposed to a very accountable promotion, but one which is largely inflexible and ineffective.

In this context, we provide an analytical framework for the beneficial exercise of the duty of the executive and the legislature to systematise. According to this framework, for cases in which the vague criteria of accountability can result in criminal liability, their systematisation should be achieved through the enactment of additional legislation by the legislature. Following the principles established through *Rayco*, this legislation should be highly detailed and specific, in order to enable everyone involved to avoid criminal charges. In this case the value of effectiveness is to receive second priority over the value of accountability, given the possible criminal liability of all of the individuals involved. In other cases, where the ambiguity of the criteria of accountability is not linked to criminal incrimination, the executive should provide systematisation using means which balance the pursuance of accountability and effectiveness. We distinguish two means which could be used in the process. The first is that techniques are introduced to as many criteria as possible. The use of techniques is a factor which, to a certain degree, mitigates the ambiguity, giving a level of certainty over the accountability process, without rendering the use of criteria inflexible and ineffective. The second solution is that a central authority, similar to the PUK, is created at federal level. This authority should aim to co-ordinate the various criteria and mechanisms of accountability. Ideally, it would be composed of both civil servants and practitioners, and, due to this composition, it would be adequately equipped to proceed to the systematisation process without the resulting methods of systematisation being inflexible or leading to economic or administrative ineffectiveness.

As was the case for the UK, underlying this proposal is a normative request on the Economic Constitution of the USA with respect to PPPs. The Economic Constitution of PPPs operates in the USA in such a way as to provide – typically, at both federal and state level – that the promotion of PPPs should take place by virtue of enabling legislation, which provides for criteria of accountability. The Economic Constitution of PPPs in the USA in its current operation does not provide for a constitutional duty to systematise all of these criteria of accountability. We argue that the position of the Economic Constitution for PPPs in the USA should be different. It should provide for a positive duty of the executive and the legislature to systematise the mechanisms and criteria to accountability. This duty should be exercised with the enactment of legislation in cases of criteria of accountability connected with criminal sanctions and with systematising guidelines in non-criminal settings. In the last cases, two appropriate means for the discharge of this duty are the integration of techniques to as many criteria as possible and the creation of a central co-ordinating authority.

Having provided the basic analysis and conclusions of each one of the constitutional systems which we explored, we will now move on to an evaluative discussion of the points which have been gained from the comparison of the UK and the USA.

4. The benefits of comparing the UK and the USA

4.1. *The benefits of comparing the UK and the USA, on the specific subject of PPPs*

Both the UK and the USA governments are using PPPs, and they rely on them for the provision of their infrastructure and the offer of public services to citizens. They are both interested in achieving economic effectiveness while using PPPs. Further to that, they are both constitutional models which accept the principle of constitutional accountability of the executive when it uses PPPs and when it commits public money to them. The choices which they make, however, in pursuing the goals of economic effectiveness of PPPs and constitutional accountability are different.

As we have demonstrated, the basic point of focus for the UK has been on the promotion of bureaucratic and economic effectiveness in PPPs. Government has pursued the organisation of a solid system of bureaucratic relationships aiming at effectiveness, being less keen on designing mechanisms of constitutional accountability specifically for PPPs, which would safeguard an active input from the legislature. On the other side, the USA has provided its point of focus in involving the legislature to a significant degree on PPPs. In doing so, it did not simultaneously aim to provide a centralised system which would potentially be able to provide the government with a strong role of co-ordinating the promotion of PPPs. In this way, the UK and the USA represent two potential archetypes with respect to the choices that the Economic Constitution for PPPs can make between the focus on the achievement of economic effectiveness for PPPs and the pursuance of structures of constitutional accountability within them.

The basic lesson which the UK can take from the USA relates to the role of the legislature. The promotion of PPPs in the USA represents a working model, delivering results and being used extensively. For this reason, if the UK adopts a more active role of the legislature in PPPs, imitating the USA in this respect, as we suggest, it does not risk losing a great deal on the promotion of economic effectiveness which is its basic point of focus. At the same time, the use of more legislation will increase accountability so that this accountability covers additional aspects of PPPs, which are unrelated to economic performance. In this framework, the solution which we suggested with respect to the affirmative resolution procedure puts a very small burden, equal to a couple of weeks, upon the productivity and the speed of PPPs.

The basic lesson which the USA can take from the UK is exactly the opposite, and it relates to the role of the executive in the promotion of PPPs. The UK model, which is based on strong co-ordination of the executive is one which achieves a level of accountability which is not completely satisfactory, but which is very strong with respect to the principally economic aspects of PPPs. For this reason, the USA could learn from the UK that a stronger role of the executive can deliver results with respect to PPPs, achieving a good level of accountability for economic matters. If the solution which we proposed for the USA is adopted with respect to the means through which this stronger role is to be exercised, this will have a minimal negative impact, barely disturbing the focus of the USA on the enactment of legislation.

A further point which we need to highlight here refers to the role of auditors. In the UK chapter, we distinguished a number of voices in the auditing literature which suggest that the wide discretion of auditors is a matter of democratic necessity. We disagreed with this view, and we revealed that the wide discretion of the C&AG leads him to exercise powers which are not provided for him in the relevant legislation. The example of the USA, however, revealed a Comptroller General who has much less power than the UK equivalent with respect to PPPs, being limited to his descriptive role, and abstaining from normative prescriptions. The reason for that is that the normative needs of the system in the USA are directly established by the PPP specific legislation. The USA model thus serves as an exemplification of our position towards the said literature, that a weaker auditor does not necessarily mean that a democratic principle is sacrificed. This is because the enactment of legislation and the wide role of the legislature coincide with the promotion of democratic goals, without requiring an auditor with wide powers to advance these values.

4.2. *The benefits of comparing the UK and the USA, on broader conclusions for the Economic Constitution*

The question which arises towards the end of this work is whether there are any of the outcomes of our research on PPPs which might be relevant or useful in the broader debate over the Economic Constitution outside the area of PPPs.

One plausible useful outcome could be the recognition of the value of bureaucratic and economic effectiveness as a normative principle of the Economic Constitution. One of the most persistent interplays which we have encountered in terms of the present book is one between the pursuit of economic effectiveness and constitutional accountability. Our analysis of PPPs seems to suggest that the two values of economic effectiveness and constitutional accountability are values which require some effort and shaping in order to be able to sit comfortably with each other.

In this way, with respect to the UK, if we were to push the pursuit of constitutional accountability to its most extreme limit, the Concordat would have to be interpreted as requiring primary legislation for every single PPP project. This would result in an increase in constitutional accountability, because the Parliament would have a powerful instrument – the enactment of legislation – with which to hold the government accountable. It would, however, significantly detract from the economic effectiveness of the promotion of PPPs, because the enactment of legislation is a lengthy process and following it too frequently would make the promotion of PPPs too slow for the modern economic reality. Similarly, if we were to push the pursuance of economic effectiveness to its most extreme form, the Concordat would have to be construed as requiring minimal involvement of the Parliament, possibly through a negative resolution procedure. This would benefit the bureaucratic and economic effectiveness of PPPs, given that the speed of its promotion would increase, but it would come at the cost of constitutional accountability.

We also encounter this UK-related dilemma between effectiveness and constitutional accountability in the USA. If, theoretically-speaking, constitutional accountability was pushed to its extreme, the due process duty of the government to systematise would suggest a duty to define the criteria of accountability in a very high level of detail. This would have benefits for constitutional accountability, because there would be near-absolute, or absolute, clarity over the construction of each criterion of accountability. However, it would come at the cost of bureaucratic and economic effectiveness, because the administration would have very narrow limits to exemplify the criteria in the specificities in the case of each particular PPP project. On the contrary, if we were to select to push the value of bureaucratic effectiveness to its extreme, the due process duty of the government to systematise would have to be construed as requiring that the government would provide very few standards of common understandings of the criteria. This would have benefits for economic effectiveness, because the administration would have considerable discretion to adapt the interpretation of the criteria as it saw fit, on a case-by-case basis, having optimum flexibility in the promotion of PPPs. However, this would come at the cost of constitutional accountability because, with little systematisation accountability, very little would be known about how to navigate the parameters and points of reference for the process of accountability.

In approaching both of these two jurisdictions – the UK and the USA – we tried to coin our solutions based on the interplay between the values of effectiveness and accountability, which were not found to fit squarely with each other. This interplay, and this conflicting relationship between the two values, could be useful in the broader theory of Economic Constitution, when evaluating patterns of institutional and bureaucratic design and when seeking for means of promoting and balancing these values within them.

We would be highly unlikely to meet with any disagreement that one of the values of the Economic Constitution is the promotion of constitutional accountability. It is a truth universally acknowledged that the government has to be accountable for its actions in the economic sphere. However, the extreme prioritisation of this value over discretion can lead to the loss of one key advantage that discretion carries, and which is inherent to its nature, irrespective of whether it is private or public. This is the advantage of economic effectiveness. Bureaucracies contain specialised and trained personnel who depend on flexibility and speed in order to promote the economic wellbeing of the citizens. Prioritising the value of constitutional accountability within the Economic Constitution in an extreme way can lead to the loss of this advantage, since the bureaucracy will have to be submitted to, potentially at the cost of the intense mechanisms of constitutional accountability of the legislature. As a consequence, the solutions which have to be sought in order to promote the constitutional values over governmental discretion have to take into account the value of economic effectiveness when they acquire their shape. To clarify, our research has shown that economic effectiveness is a value of the Economic Constitution which has to be protected when we seek solutions for promoting the classical constitutional values, such as that of constitutional accountability.

The value of economic effectiveness, however, is not a value which has to be promoted over constitutional accountability at all costs. We have seen that one of the outcomes of this prioritisation can be the exercise of broad normative powers by the auditors. In the case of the promotion of PPPs in the UK, the pursuance of economic effectiveness has been a matter of main priority. Since the 1992 initiation of the PFI, there has been considerable focus on the creation of bodies which aim to pursue economic effectiveness and less focus on the creation of constitutional accountability mechanisms specifically for PPPs. This is coupled with the fact that the NAO is found to exercise wide normative functions. The reason for this is that, if our point of focus is the promotion of effectiveness through specialised bureaucracies which have extended powers to advance the said effectiveness, then we need other experts with equally wide powers to control them and to hold them accountable. These experts are the auditors, and indeed, there are many voices in the relevant critical literature which advocate that the central auditing agencies – such as the NAO – must have, 'by matter of democratic necessity', wide discretion over all aspects of their work. This, however, can lead them to exercise powers which are remote from their role of examination, and these are normative. In summary, this means they may exercise powers which are better suited for a legislature which has the democratic and constitutional mandate to establish rules for the system.

In this way, our research has shown that the over-prioritisation of effectiveness over constitutional accountability in the Economic Constitution can lead to outcomes which are not always desirable, and that these outcomes can affect the role of the central auditing units. To clarify, our societies are perhaps ready to recognise the wide discretion of the auditors to establish norms over some aspects of economic activity. However, when our societies are preparing to be bound through contracts for projects that can last for generations, as happens with PPPs, an element of constitutional accountability in the establishing of norms is both desirable and necessary, and it would not be appropriate to jeopardise or even sacrifice this in favour of the pursuance of economic effectiveness.

The third contribution which we extrapolate from our work, and could offer to the broader debate – unrelated to PPPs – on the Economic Constitution, relates to the fabric from which the Economic Constitution is composed. The theory of Economic Constitution is a framework of constitutional analysis which addresses many of the concerns of modern society, which – in the wake of the worldwide economic depression of 2008 – is anxious about controlling the ways that governments manage economies. From this context, a question arises relating to the values and the constitutional principles which the new theory is going to embrace. In our work we processed solutions around the Economic Constitution of PPPs, which are novel but based on the revisiting of very old and well-used constitutional doctrines. For the UK, the traditional constitutional doctrine used was that of Concordat, agreed in 1932. Consequently, the convention established between the PAC and the NAO is not applied directly, in its original form, to PPPs, but required adaptation to fit the needs of the Economic Constitution for these transactions. Similarly, in the USA, we explored the un-plumbed potential of the ancient doctrine of the prohibition of vagueness of laws, established with the Fourteenth Amendment in the late nineteenth century, and rooted in the truly ancient doctrine of due process. These doctrines have not been applied directly to the modern Economic Constitution for PPPs, but we have reflected other scholars in the field who have attempted to apply them in a way which they called 'reformed'. In both of these cases, we followed the same pattern: we took an old doctrine and modified it in order to apply it to the modern needs of the Economic Constitution for PPPs.

This shows that the Economic Constitution can evolve in ways which are not only through constructing novel constitutional principles, as may theoretically be the case in the future, but can also encompass older, tried-and-tested theories in Constitutional Law, and adapt their application to modern settings. Some of the key instruments which we used when we tried to do this, with precision, with respect to the Concordat in PPPs in the UK and the prohibition of vagueness of laws in PPPs in the USA, were the following: focus on the intention of the parties which originally agreed the principles (in the case of the Concordat, these were the PAC and the NAO), focus on the jurisprudence (in the case of the prohibition of vagueness of laws) and focus on the needs of effectiveness which have to be taken into account (in both cases). These points of focus could be useful springboards for future research on the Economic Constitution, as the new constitutional framework tries to find its normative co-ordinates within the landscape of the long history of Constitutional Law.

Bibliography

Primary sources – official publications

United Kingdom

Allen G, *The Private Finance Initiative (PFI)* (House of Commons Research Paper 01/117, 2001)

Allen G, *The Private Finance Initiative (PFI)* (House of Commons Research Paper 03/79, 2003)

Baber M, *Criminal Injuries Compensation* (House of Commons Research Paper 95/64, 1995)

Booth L and Starodubtseva V, *PFI: Costs and Benefits* (House of Commons Research Paper 6007, 2005)

Collins A, *Prison Conditions in the United Kingdom* (Human Rights Watch 1992)

Committee of Public Accounts, *Assurance for Major Projects* (HC 2012–13, 384)

——, *Contracting out Public Services to the Private Sector* (HC 2013–14, 777)

——, *The Department for Environment, Food and Rural Affairs: Oversight of three PFI Waste Projects* (HC 2014–15, 106)

——, *Equity Investment in Privately Financed Projects* (HC 2010–12, 1846)

——, *Financing PFI Projects in the Credit Crisis and the Treasury's Response* (HC 2010–11, 553)

——, *Lessons from PFI and other Projects* (HC 2010–12, 1201)

——, *M25 Private Finance Contract* (HC 2010–11, 651)

——, *Major Projects Authority* (HC 2014–15, 147)

——, *Managing the Relationship to Secure a Successful Partnership in PFI Projects* (HC 2001–02, 460)

——, *PFI Construction Performance* (HC 2002–03, 567)

——, *PFI in Housing and Hospitals* (HC 2010–11, 631)

Committee on Economic Affairs, *Private Finance Projects and off-Balance Sheet Debt: Volume 1* (HL 2009–10, 63-I)

Committee on the Constitution, *The Pre-Emption of Parliament* (HL 2012–13, 165, 2013)

Defence Committee, *Defence Acquisition* (HC 2012–13, 9)

——, *Defence Equipment 2009* (HC 2008–09, 107)

——, *Defence Equipment 2010* (HC 2009–10, 99)

——, *Defence Procurement* (HC 2002–03, 694)

——, *Major Procurement Projects* (HC 2001–02, 779)

——, *Major Procurement Projects* (HC 2000–01, 463)

——, *Strategic Lift* (HC 2006–07, 462)

Department of Health, *Liberating the NHS: Report of the Arm's Length Bodies Review* (2010)

Gay O, *Comptroller and Auditor General* (House of Commons Briefing paper SN/PC/4595, 2008)

HC Deb 11 July 1932, vol 268, cols 1019–20

HC Deb 10 July 1933, vol 280, col 895

HC Deb 10 July 1933, vol 280, col 897

HC Deb 18 February 1988, vol 127, cols 1132–3

HC Deb 21 July 1988, vol 137, col 1281

HC Deb 12 November 1992, vol 213, col 998

HC Deb 21 July 1994, vol 247, col 426W

HC Deb 29 November 1994, vol 250, cols 1084–5

HC Deb 24 January 1995, vol 253, col 168W

HC Deb 31 October 1995, vol 265, col 141W

HC Deb 1 November 1995, vol 265, col 260W

HC Deb 28 November 1995, vol 267, cols 606–7W

HC Deb 14 May 1996, vol 277, col 416W

HC Deb 10 June 1996, vol 279, col 17

HC Deb 26 November 1996, vol 286, col 156W

Health Committee, *2012 Accountability Hearing with Monitor* (HC 2012–13, 652)

——, *Annual Accountability Hearing with Monitor* (HC 2010–12, 1431)

——, *Commissioning – Volume II* (HC 2010–11, 513-II)

——, *Public Expenditure on Health and Care Services – Volume I* (HC 2012–13, 651)

——, *Social Care – Volume II* (HC 2010–12, 1583-II)

Hillyard M and Twigger R, *The Government Resources and Accounts Bill: Bill 3 of 1999–2000* (House of Commons Research Paper 99/97, 1999)

HL Deb 3 May 1989, vol 507, cols 141–4

HL Deb 3 March 2003, vol 645, col 607

HM Treasury, *The Green Book: Appraisal and Evaluation in Central Government* (2003)

——, *Major Project Approval and Assurance Guidance* (2011)

——, *Managing Public Money* (2013)

——, *A New Approach to Public-Private Partnerships* (HMSO, 2012)

——, *Paymaster General Announces Kick-start to PFI (Public/Private partnerships) – Review of Private Finance Machinery – End of Universal Testing* (News release 41/97, 8 May 1997)

——, *PFI: Meeting the Investment Challenge* (HMSO, 2003)

——, *Private Finance Initiative Projects: 2014 Summary Data* (2014)

——, *Reform of the Private Finance Initiative* (HMSO, 2011)

——, *Value for Money Assessment Guidance* (November 2006)

——, *Whole of Government Accounts: Year ended 31 March 2010* (HC 1601, 2011)

HM Treasury Committee, *Private Finance 2: Volume 1* (HC 2012–13, 97)

——, *The Private Finance Initiative* (HC 1999–2000, 147)

——, *The Private Finance Initiative: Volume I* (HC 2010–12, 1146)

House of Commons – Scrutiny Unit, *Private Finance Initative – its Rationale and Accounting Treatment* (2008)

Lord Sharman of Redlynch, *Holding to Account: The Review of Audit and Accountability of Central Government* (2001)

National Audit Office, *Annual Report 2012* (2012)

——, 'Assessing Value for Money' <https://www.nao.org.uk/successful-commissioning/general-principles/value-for-money/assessing-value-for-money/> accessed 10 September 2017

——, *Cabinet Office – Managing Early Departures in Central Government* (HC 2010–12, 1795)

——, *Department for Environment, Food and Rural Affairs – Managing the Waste PFI Programme* (HC 2008–09, 66)

——, *Equity Investment in Privately Financed Projects* (HC 2010–12, 1792)

——, *Financing PFI Projects in the Credit Crisis and the Treasury Response* (HC 2010–11, 287)

——, *A Framework for Evaluating the Implementation of Private Finance Initiative Projects: Volume 1* (May 2006)

——, *A Framework for Evaluating the Implementation of Private Finance Initiative Projects: Volume 2* (May 2006)

——, *Highways Agency – Procurement of the M25 Private Finance Contract* (HC 2010–11, 566)

——, *Lessons from PFI and other Projects* (HC 2010–12, 920)

——, *Major Projects Authority Annual Report 2012–13 and Government Project Assurance* (HC 2013–14, 1047)

——, *Managing the Relationship to Secure a Successful Partnership in PFI Projects* (HC 2001–02, 375)

——, *Ministry of Defence – Delivering Multi-Role Tanker Aircraft Capability* (HC 2009–10, 433)

——, *The Performance and Management of Hospital PFI Contracts* (HC 2010–11, 68)

——, *PFI in Housing* (HC 2010–11, 71)

——, *Review of the VFM Assessment Process for PFI* (2013)

——, *Savings from Operational PFI Contracts* (2013)

United States of America

'About OGC' <http://webarchive.nationalarchives.gov.uk/20100503135839/http://www.ogc.gov.uk/about_ogc_who_we_are.asp> accessed 10 September 2017

'AFB Solicitation No. F41689–96-R0025' (2000) <http://www.afcee.brooks.af.mil/dc/dch/hpdata/hpdata.asp> accessed 8 November 2015

'Military Housing Privatization Initiative: Hearings Before the Subcommittee on Military Installations and Facilities of the House Committee on Armed Services, 106th Congress (statement of Randall A. Yim, Deputy Under Secretary of Defence, Installations' (2000) <http://www.defenselink.mil/acq/installation/hrso> accessed 8 November 2015

Administration DoT-FH, 'Excellence in Highway Design: Category 8-Public/Private Participation' (2003) <http://www.fhwa.dot.gov/eihd/91exp.cfm> accessed 10 September 2017

——, 'Glossary' <http://www.fhwa.dot.gov/ipd/glossary/> accessed 4 July 2016

Agency UEP, 'Learn About the Water Infrastructure Finance and Innovation Act Program' (2003) <https://www.epa.gov/wifia/learn-about-water-infrastructure-finance-and-innovation-act-program> accessed 10 September 2017

Committee on Health, Education, Labor, and Pensions of the United States Senate, *Hearing on Reducing Childhood Obesity: Public-Private Partnerships to Improve Nutrition and Increase Physical Activity in Children* (108th Congress, 2004)

Jefferson T, *Report to the House of Representatives: Plan for Establishing Uniformity in the Coinage, Weights, and Measures of the United States* (1st Congress, 1790)

Panel on Public-Private Partnerships of the Committee on Transportation and Infrastructure of the House of Representatives, *Overview of Public-Private Partnerships in Highway and Transit Projects* (113th Congress, 2014)

Partnerships TNCoP-P, 'Glossary of Terms' <http://www.ncppp.org/ppp-basics/glossary-of-terms/> accessed 10 September 2017

Subcommittee on Economic Development, Public Buildings, and Energy Management of the Committee on Transportation and Infrastructure of the House of Representatives, *Hearing on Federal Triangle South: Redeveloping Underutilized Federal Property through Public-Private Partnerships* (113th Congress, 2013)

Subcommittee on Highways and Transit of the Committee on Transportation and Infrastructure of the House of Representatives, *Hearing on Public-Private Partnerships: Innovative Financing and Protecting the Public Interest* (110th Congress, 2007)

——, *Hearing on Public-Private Partnerships: State and User Perspectives* (110th Congress, 2007)

Subcommittee on Infrastructure and Border Security, and Subcommittee on Cybersecurity, Science and Research and Development of the Select Committee on Homeland Security of the House of Representatives, *Hearing on the DHS Infrastructure Protection Division; Public-Private Partnerships to Secure Critical Infrastructures* (108th Congress, 2014)

Subcommittee on Technology and Procurement Policy of the Committee on Government Reform of the House of Representatives, *Hearing on the Use of Public-Private Partnerships as a Management Tool for Federal Real Property* (107th Congress, 2001)

Trask RR, United States General Accounting Office: History Program: GAO History 1921–1991 (OP-3-HP, 1991)

Treasury Inspector General for Tax Administration, *Future Tax Revenues are at Risk because certain Tax-Exempt Bonds may exceed Annual Dollar Limits without Detection* (2009-10-097)

U.S. Department of Transportation – Federal Highway Administration, *Case Studies of Transportation Public-Private Partnerships in the United States* (Final Report – Work Order 05-002, 2007)

U.S. Department of the Treasury – Office of Economic Policy, *Expanding our Nation's Infrastructure through Innovative Financing* (2014)

United States General Accountability Office, *Public Transportation – Federal Project Approval Process Remains a Barrier to Greater Private Sector Role and DOT Could Enhance Efforts to Assist Project Sponsors* (Report to Congressional Committees, GAO-10-19, 2009)

United States General Accounting Office, *GAO's Congressional Protocols* (GAO/OCG-00-2, 2000)

——, *Public-Private Partnerships: Key Elements of Federal Building and Facility Partnerships* (Report to the Hon Stephen Horn Committee on Government Reform House of Representatives GAO/GGD-99-23, 1999)

——, *Public-Private Partnerships: Pilot Program Needed to Demonstrate the Actual Benefits of Using Partnerships* (Report to Congressional Requests, GAO-01-906, 2001)

——, *Public-Private Partnerships – Terms Related to Building and Facility Partnerships* (Glossary, GAO/GGD-99-71, 1999)

United States Government Accountability Office, *About GAO* (2014)

——, *DCAA Audits: Widespread Problems with Audit Quality Require Significant Reform* (Report to the Committee on Homeland Security and Governmental Affairs of the US Senate, GAO-09-468, 2009)

——, *Depot Maintenance: Persistent Deficiencies Limit Accuracy and Usefulness of DOD's Funding Allocation Data Reported to Congress* (Report to Congressional Committees, GAO-06-88, 2005)

——, *Depot Maintenance: Status of the Public-Private Partnerships for Repair of the Dual-Mode Transmitter in the F-16 Fire-Control Radar* (Briefing to the Senate Armed Services Committee, GAO-15-249R, 2015)

——, *Federal Highways: Increased Reliance on Contractors can Pose Oversight Challenges for Federal and State Officials* (Report to the Chairman, Committee on Transportation and Infrastructure, House of Representatives, GAO-08-198, 2008)

——, *Highway Public-Private Partnerships: More Rigorous Up-front Analysis Could Better Secure Potential Benefits and Protect the Public Interest* (Report to Congressional Requests, GAO-08-44, 2008)

Secondary sources

Akintoye A and others, 'Achieving Best Value in Private Finance Initiative Project Procurement' (2003) 21 Construction Management and Economics 461

Bar Cendón A, 'Accountability and Public Administration: Concepts, Dimensions, Developments' (Openness and Transparency in Governance: Challenges and Opportunities, Maastricht, October 1999)

Behn RD, 'Why Measure Performance? Different Purposes Require Different Measures' (2003) 63 Public Administration Review 586

Bloxham E, *Economic Value Management: Applications and Techniques* (Wiley 2003)

Boardman AE and Vining AR, 'P3s in North America: Renting the Money (in Canada), Selling the Roads (in the USA)' in Hodge GA, Greve C and Boardman AE (eds), *International Handbook on Public-Private Partnerships* (Edward Elgar Publishing 2010)

Boers I and others, 'Public-Private Partnerships: International Audit Findings' in De Vries P and Yehoue EB (eds), *The Routledge Companion to Public-Private Partnerships* (Routledge 2013)

Bovens M, 'Analysing and Assessing Accountability: A Conceptual Framework' (2007) 13 European Law Journal 447

——, 'The Integrity of the Managerial State' (1996) 4 Journal of Contingencies and Crisis Management 125

Bovens M, Schillemans T and Hart PT, 'Does Public Accountability Work? An Assessment Tool' (2008) 86 Public Administration 225

Brazier R, *Ministers of the Crown* (The Clarendon Press 1997)

Brereton M and Temple M, 'The New Public Service Ethos: An Ethical Environment for Governance' (1999) 77 Public Administration 455

Broadbent J and Laughlin R, 'Control and Legitimation in Government Accountability Processes: The Private Finance Initiative in the UK' (2003) 14 Critical Perspectives on Accounting 23

——, 'The Role of PFI in the UK Government's Modernisation Agenda' (2005) 21 Financial Accountability & Management 75

Broadbent J, Gill J and Laughlin R, 'Evaluating the Private Finance Initiative in the National Health Service in the UK' (2003) 16 Accounting, Auditing & Accountability Journal 422

——, *The Private Finance Initiative in the National Health Service: Nature Emergence and the Role of Management Accounting in Decision Making and Post-Decision Project Evaluation* (Chartered Institute of Management Accountants 2004)

Chemerinsky E, *Constitutional Law* (4th edn, Wolters Kluwer 2013)

Cohn M, 'Medieval Chains, Invisible Inks: On Non-Statutory Powers of the Executive' (2005) 25 Oxford Journal of Legal Studies 97

Craig P, *Administrative Law* (7th edn, Sweet & Maxwell 2012)

Daintith T, 'Regulation by Contract: The New Prerogative' 32 Current Legal Problems 41

——, 'The Techniques of Government' in Jowell J and Oliver D (eds), *The Changing Constitution* (3rd edn, Oxford University Press 1994)

Davies ACL, *The Public Law of Government Contracts* (Oxford University Press 2008)

Demirag I and Khadaroo I, 'Accountability and Value for Money: A Theoretical Framework for the Relationship in Public-Private Partnerships' (2011) 15 Journal of Management & Governance 271

Dewulf G, Blanken A and Bult-Spiering M, *Strategic Issues in Public-Private Partnerships* (2nd edn, Wiley-Blackwell 2012)

Donahue JD, *Making Washington Work: Tales of Innovation in the Federal Government* (Brookings Institution Press 1999)

——, 'The Transformation of Government Work – Causes, Consequences and Distortions' in Minow M and Freeman J (eds), *Government by Contract: Outsourcing and American Democracy* (Harvard University Press 2009)

Donnelly C, *Delegation of Governmental Power to Private Parties: A Comparative Perspective* (Oxford University Press 2007)

Easterbook F, 'Substance and Due Process' (1982) Supreme Court Review 85

Elsenaar M, 'Law, Accountability and the Private Finance Initiative in the National Health Service' (1999) Public Law 35

Feldman D, 'The Limits of Law: Can Laws Regulate Public Administration?' in Peters BG and Pierre J (eds), *The SAGE Handbook of Public Administration* (SAGE Publications 2012)

Freedland MR, 'Government by Contract and Public Law' (1994) Public Law 86

——, 'Public Law and Private Finance – Placing the Private Finance Initiative in Public Frame' (1998) Public Law 288

Freeman RJ and others, *Governmental and Nonprofit Accounting: Theory and Practice* (International edn, Pearson Prentice Hall 2009)

Furubo J-E, 'Performance Auditing: Audit or Misnomer?' in Lonsdale J, Wilkins P and Ling T (eds), *Performance Auditing – Contributing to Accountability in Democratic Government* (Edward Elgar Publishing 2011)

Gaffney D and others, 'PFI in the NHS – Is there an Economic Case?' (1999) 319 British Medical Journal 116

Glendinning R, 'The Concept of Value for Money' (1988) 1 International Journal of Public Sector Management 42

Grimsey D and Lewis MK, 'Are Public Private Partnerships Value for Money? Evaluating Alternative Approaches and Comparing Academic and Practitioner Views' (2005) 29 Accounting Forum 345

Grout P, 'The Economics of the Private Finance Initiative' (1997) 13 Oxford Review of Economic Policy 53

Hall D, *Criminal Law and Procedure* (6th edn, Delmar 2012)

Harden I, 'Value for Money and Administrative Law' (1996) Public Law 661

Hollingsworth K, White F and Harden I, 'Audit, Accountability and Independence: The Role of the Audit Commission' (1998) 18 Legal Studies 78

Hood C, 'A Public Management for all Seasons?' (1991) 69 Public Administration 3

James SC, 'The Evolution of Presidency: Between the Promise and the Fear' in Aberbach JD and Peterson MA (eds), *The Executive Branch* (Oxford University Press 2005)

Jennings SI, *The Law and the Constitution* (5th edn, University of London Press 1959)

Jones R and Pendlebury MW, *Public Sector Accounting* (4th edn, Pitman Publishing 1996)

Kraakman R and others, *The Anatomy of Corporate Law: a Comparative and Functional Approach* (2nd edn, Oxford University Press 2009)

Lane J-E, 'Will Public Management Drive out Public Administration?' (1994) 16 Asian Journal of Public Administration 139

Lewis CW and Bayard LC, 'Professional Standards and Ethics' in Perry JL (ed.), *Handbook of Public Administration* (2nd edn, Jossey-Bass 1996)

Maitland FW, 'The Crown as a Corporation' in Hazeltine HD, Lapsley G and Winfield PHS (eds), *Maitland Selected Essays* (Cambridge University Press 1936)

Mansfield HC, *The Comptroller General: A Study of the Law and Practice of Financial Administration* (Yale University Press 1939)

Marshall G, *Constitutional Conventions: The Rules and Forms of Political Accountability* (Oxford University Press 1984)

McGarvey N, 'Accountability in Public Administration: A Multi-Perspective Framework of Analysis' (2001) 16 Public Policy and Administration 17

McLean JM, 'The Crown in Contract and Administrative Law' (2004) 24 Oxford Journal of Legal Studies 129

Merna T and Njiru C, *Financing Infrastructure Projects* (Thomas Telford 2002)

Metzger G, 'Private Delegations, Due Process, and the Duty to Supervise' in Minow M and Freeman J (eds), *Government by Contract: Outsourcing and American Democracy* (Harvard University Press 2009)

Morgan TD, 'The General Accounting Office: One Hope for Congress to Regain Parity of Power with the President' (1972–1973) 51 North Carolina Law Review 1279

Mosher FC, *The GAO: The Quest for Accountability in American Government* (Westview Press 1979)

Mulgan R, '"Accountability": An Ever-Expanding Concept?' (2000) 78 Public Administration 555

Newcomer KE, 'Evaluating Public Programs' in Perry JL (ed.), *Handbook of Public Administration* (2nd edn, Jossey-Bass 1996)

Oehmke JF, 'Anomalies in Net Present Value Calculations' (2000) 67 Economics Letters 349

Overly SD, 'Government Contractors, Beware: Civil and Criminal Penalties Abound for Defective Pricing' (1987) 20 Loyola of Los Angeles Law Review 597

Peel E and Treitel GH, *The Law of Contract* (12th edn, Sweet & Maxwell 2007)

Perry JL, 'Effective Enterprises, Effective Administrators' in Perry JL (ed.), *Handbook of Public Administration* (2nd edn, Jossey-Bass 1996)

Peters BG, '"With a little help from our friends": Public-Private Partnerships as Institutions and Instruments' in Pierre J (ed.), *Partnerships in Urban Governance: European and American Experience* (St Martin's Press 1998)

Pettet BG, *Company Law* (2nd edn, Pearson Longman 2005)

Pois J, *Watchdog on the Potomac: A Study of the Comptroller General of the United States* (University Press of America 1979)

Pollock AM and Price D, 'Has the NAO Audited Risk Transfer in Operational Private Finance Initiative Schemes?' (2008) 28 Public Money & Management 173

Pollock AM, Price D and Player S, 'An Examination of the UK Treasury's Evidence Base for Cost and Time Overrun Data in UK Value-for-Money Policy and Appraisal' (2007) 27 Public Money & Management 127

Pollock AM, Shaoul J and Vickers N, 'Private Finance and "Value for Money" in NHS hospitals: A Policy in Search of a Rationale?' (2002) 324 British Medical Journal 1205

Prosser T, *The Economic Constitution* (Oxford University Press 2014)

Pula K, *Public-Private Partnerships for Transportation – Categorisation and Analysis of State Statutes* (National Conference of State Legislatures, January 2016)

Put V and Turksema R, 'Selection of Topics' in Lonsdale J, Wilkins P and Ling T (eds), *Performance Auditing – Contributing to Accountability in Democratic Government* (Edward Elgar Publishing 2011)

Quiggin J, 'Risk, PPPs and the Public Sector Comparator' (2004) 14 Australian Accounting Review 51

Rhodes RAW, 'The New Governance: Governing without Government' (1996) 44 Political Studies 652

Roe P and Craig A, *Reforming the Private Finance Initiative* (Centre for Policy Studies 2004)

Rose R, 'Elections and Electoral Systems: Choices and Alternatives' in Bogdanor V and Butler D (eds), *Democracy and Elections: Electoral Systems and their Political Consequences* (1983)

Rosen HS, *Public Finance* (3rd edn, Irwin 1992)

Rudalvige A, 'The Executive Branch and the Legislative Process' in Aberbach JD and Peterson MA (eds), *The Executive Branch* (Oxford University Press 2005)

Sawyer M, 'The Private Finance Initiative: The UK Experience' (2005) 15 Research in Transportation Economics 231

Sedler RA, *Constitutional Law in the United States* (2nd edn, Kluwer Law International 2014)

Seifter M, 'Rent-a-Regulator – Design and Innovation in Environmental Decision Making' in Minow M and Freeman J (eds), *Government by Contract: Outsourcing and American Democracy* (Harvard University Press 2009)

Smith AL, 'PPP Financing in the USA' in Akintoye A and Beck M (eds), *Policy, Finance and Management for Public-Private Partnerships* (Wiley-Blackwell 2009)

Smith DH, *The General Accounting Office: Its History, Activities, and Organization* (Johns Hopkins University Press 1927)

Solomon DF, 'Fundamental Fairness, Judicial Efficiency and Uniformity: Revisiting the Administrative Procedure Act' (2013) 33 Journal of the National Association of Administrative Law Judiciary 52

Turpin C and Tomkins A, *British Government and the Constitution: Text and Materials* (6th edn, Cambridge University Press 2007)

Turpin CC, *Government Contracts* (Penguin 1972)

——, *Government Procurement and Contracts* (Longman 1989)

Van Wart M, *Changing Public Sector Values* (Garland 1998)

Verkuil P, 'Outsourcing and the Duty to Govern' in Minow M and Freeman J (eds), *Government by Contract: Outsourcing and American Democracy* (Harvard University Press 2009)

Wall A, *Public-Private Partnerships in the USA: Lessons to be learned for the United Kingdom* (Routledge 2012)

Weait M and Lester A, 'The Use of Ministerial Powers without Parliamentary Authority: The Ram Doctrine' (2003) Public Law 415

Weber M, 'Bureaucracy' in Gunther R and Wittich C (eds), *Economy and Society: An Outline of Interpretive Sociology* (University of California Press 1979)

Wise C, 'Understanding your Liability as Public Administrator' in Perry JL (ed.), *Handbook of Public Administration* (2nd edn, Jossey-Bass 1996)

Yehoue EB, 'Financial and Sovereign Debt Crises and PPP Market Structure' in De Vries P and Yehoue EB (eds), *The Routledge Companion to Public-Private Partnerships* (Routledge 2013)

Yescombe ER, *Public-Private Partnerships: Principles of Policy and Finance* (Elsevier 2007)

Zajac EJ and Olsen CP, 'From Transaction Cost to Transactional Value Analysis: Implications for the Study of Interorganisational Strategies' (1993) 30 Journal of Management Studies 131

Index

For Product Safety Concerns and Information please contact our EU
representative GPSR@taylorandfrancis.com
Taylor & Francis Verlag GmbH, Kaufingerstraße 24, 80331 München, Germany

www.ingramcontent.com/pod-product-compliance
Ingram Content Group UK Ltd.
Pitfield, Milton Keynes, MK11 3LW, UK
UKHW020958180425
457613UK00019B/734